UNDERSTANDING
FRED CHAPPELL

Understanding Contemporary American Literature
Matthew J. Bruccoli, Series Editor

Volumes on

Edward Albee • Nicholson Baker • John Barth • Donald Barthelme
The Beats • Barbara Bennett • The Black Mountain Poets
Robert Bly • Raymond Carver • Fred Chappell • Chicano Literature
Contemporary American Drama
Contemporary American Horror Fiction
Contemporary American Literary Theory
Contemporary American Science Fiction • James Dickey
E. L. Doctorow • John Gardner • George Garrett • John Hawkes
Joseph Heller • Lillian Hellman • John Irving • Randall Jarrell
William Kennedy • Jack Kerouac • Ursula K. Le Guin
Denise Levertov • Bernard Malamud • Jill McCorkle
Carson McCullers • W. S. Merwin • Arthur Miller
Toni Morrison's Fiction • Vladimir Nabokov • Gloria Naylor
Joyce Carol Oates • Tim O'Brien • Flannery O'Connor
Cynthia Ozick • Walker Percy • Katherine Anne Porter
Reynolds Price • Thomas Pynchon • Theodore Roethke
Philip Roth • Hubert Selby, Jr. • Mary Lee Settle
Isaac Bashevis Singer • Jane Smiley • Gary Snyder
William Stafford • Anne Tyler • Kurt Vonnegut • James Welch
Eudora Welty • Tennessee Williams • August Wilson

UNDERSTANDING
FRED
CHAPPELL

John Lang

University of South Carolina Press

Published in Columbia, South Carolina, by the
University of South Carolina Press

Manufactured in the United States of America

04   03   02   01   00   5   4   3   2   1

Library of Congress Cataloging-in-Publication Data

Lang, John, 1947–
    Understanding Fred Chappell / John Lang.
        p.   cm. — (Understanding contemporary American literature)
    Includes bibliographical references and index.
    ISBN 1-57003-377-3 (alk. paper)
    1. Chappell, Fred, 1936– —Criticism and interpretation.
    2. North Carolina—In literature.   I. Title.   II. Series.
    PS3553.H298 Z75   2000
    818'.5409—dc21   00-010794

Grateful acknowledgment is made to Fred Chappell for permission to quote from *Dagon* (Harcourt, Brace & World, © 1968), *The Gaudy Place* (Harcourt, Brace & World, © 1973), *The Inkling* (Harcourt, Brace & World, © 1965), *It Is Time, Lord* (Atheneum, © 1963), and *Moments of Light* (New South Press, © 1980); to Louisiana State University Press for permission to quote from *C* (© 1993), *Caste Tzingal* (© 1984), *First and Last Words* (© 1989), *I Am One of You Forever* (© 1985), *Midquest* (© 1981), *Source* (© 1985), *Spring Garden* (© 1995), and *The World between the Eyes* (© 1971); and to St. Martin's Press, LLC, for permission to quote from *Brighten the Corner Where You Are* (© 1989), *Farewell, I'm Bound to Leave You* (© 1996), *Look Back All the Green Valley* (© 1999), and *More Shapes Than One* (© 1991). All copyright © by Fred Chappell.

Grateful acknowledgment is also made to the following publications for permission to reprint all or part of two articles by John Lang, in slightly different form: *North Carolina Literary Review,* "Intimations of Order: Fred Chappell's *More Shapes Than One,*" which appeared in the special section on Chappell in the 1998 volume; and *South Central Review* (Winter 1986), "Illuminating the Stricken World: Fred Chappell's *Moments of Light.*"

For Jerry Thorson and Al Gelpi

CONTENTS

CONTENTS

EDITOR'S PREFACE

The volumes of *Understanding Contemporary American Literature* have been planned as guides or companions for students as well as good nonacademic readers. The editor and publisher perceive a need for these volumes because much of the influential contemporary literature makes special demands. Uninitiated readers encounter difficulty in approaching works that depart from the traditional forms and techniques of prose and poetry. Literature relies on conventions, but the conventions keep evolving; new writers form their own conventions—which in time may become familiar. Put simply, *UCAL* provides instruction in how to read certain contemporary writers—identifying and explicating their material, themes, use of language, point of view, structures, symbolism, and responses to experience.

The word *understanding* in the titles was deliberately chosen. Many willing readers lack an adequate understanding of how contemporary literature works; that is, what the author is attempting to express and the means by which it is conveyed. Although the criticism and analysis in the series have been aimed at a level of general accessibility, these introductory volumes are meant to be applied in conjunction with the works they cover. They do not provide a substitute for the works and authors they introduce, but rather prepare the reader for more profitable literary experiences.

M. J. B.

ACKNOWLEDGMENTS

Much of this book was completed during a year-long sabbatical funded jointly by Emory & Henry College and the Appalachian College Association, which is supported by the Andrew W. Mellon Foundation Trust. I thank all three for their generosity. Thanks also to the staff of the North Carolina Collection at the University of North Carolina and the staff of the Special Collections Library at Duke University for their assistance with my research. The interlibrary loan librarians at Emory & Henry College were equally helpful in tracking down additional material by and about Chappell.

I am deeply grateful to Fred Hobson of the University of North Carolina, who read the chapters of this book as I completed them and offered many helpful suggestions. For thirty years now, the love and encouragement of my wife, Esther, have likewise helped to sustain my scholarly work and my career in academe.

Finally, I would like to thank Fred Chappell, who writes of his famed storyteller Uncle Zeno, "He only told stories, he didn't answer questions." Chappell himself, in contrast, throughout the preparation of this book, always responded to my questions promptly and completely, providing information about the sources and inspiration of various poems and stories that would otherwise have been unavailable to me. His careful reading of my manuscript, like Fred Hobson's, markedly improved it. Any remaining errors of fact and judgment are mine.

UNDERSTANDING
FRED CHAPPELL

CHAPTER ONE

Understanding Fred Chappell

"I learned to write," Fred Chappell has said, "more or less in the same manner that I learned to type: by doing it so dreadfully wrong that now and then I would hit upon something acceptable by merest accident. . . . An eon of trial was followed by an infinitude of error."[1] The modesty and comic hyperbole of that statement are characteristic of the author. Chappell was born on May 28, 1936, in Canton, North Carolina, a small industrial town, home of the Champion paper mill that appears in many of his works. Canton is located in the mountains of North Carolina about twenty miles west of Asheville. The author's parents, James Taylor (J. T.) and Anne Davis Chappell, lived three miles outside of town on his grandparents' one-hundred-acre farm. "I grew up in two houses," Chappell has said: his grandparents' hilltop brick home and his parents' white frame house, both built by his grandfather.[2] The former house plays a prominent role in his fiction, especially in his first novel, *It Is Time, Lord,* in *Dagon,* and in the tetralogy that began with *I Am One of You Forever.* To supplement the family's income from farming, Chappell's parents taught school, as had his grandmother. For a time his father worked in a factory, and he also ran a retail furniture store. But it was an agrarian lifestyle that shaped the author's childhood, for with his parents away much of the day, he was raised on the farm by his grandmother, who supervised his chores there. The rural setting of much of Chappell's fiction and poetry stems from his experiences during these formative years, as does his sensitivity to the natural world. Yet the presence of the Champion paper mill, as Fred Hobson has pointed out, taught Chappell "the perils of an industrial [lifestyle]" even while he was learning "the virtues of an agrarian life."[3] In his writing Chappell names that mill *Challenger,* not Champion, and associates it with William Blake's Satanic mill.

By age twelve or thirteen Chappell was writing poems and had already decided that he wanted to become a writer. That decision, which his parents actively discouraged in favor of some more practical vocation, had been shaped by avid reading of the classics on his parents' bookshelves—Shakespeare, Poe, Twain, Robert Louis Stevenson—and by his growing interest in science fiction—"about the only *modern* literature . . . that I could get my hands on" (Chappell's italics).[4] His aspirations were also fired, he admits, by his ill-founded impression "that what a writer did was live on a million dollars a year in some Fifth Avenue penthouse and date movie stars."[5] During his high school years he discovered Thomas Mann's *Doctor Faustus,* the fiction of Leo Tolstoy, and the poetry of Arthur Rimbaud, among others, and continued to write regularly, often producing two or three short stories a month, mainly works of science fiction or tales of terror inspired by those in such pulp magazines as *Weird Tales.*[6] While in high school he published several of those stories under a pseudonym that he has steadfastly refused to divulge. That fiction appeared in Robert Silverberg's *Spaceship* and Harlan Ellison's *Dimensions,* among other magazines.

But Chappell dates his "writing seriously" from 1954, the year he enrolled at Duke University. He chose Duke so that he could study with the widely respected William Blackburn, whose pupils had already included William Styron, Mac Hyman, and Reynolds Price and were to include novelist Anne Tyler and poet James Applewhite, along with Chappell himself. "By the time I could have taken one of his classes," Chappell reports, "we were personal friends, he'd read some of my stuff, and he said, 'Man, just stay home and write. Don't come to class.'"[7] As Chappell's essay, "Welcome to High Culture," makes clear, Reynolds Price was an even more important influence during these years than Blackburn. Price meticulously critiqued the writing Chappell brought to him, and Price also directed an informal writing workshop in which Chappell and Tyler and Applewhite participated.

After what Chappell has called a typical college-boy scandal ("Got drunk and sassed a cop, got throwed in jail") led to his suspension from Duke at the beginning of his junior year,[8] he returned home to Canton. There he remained for three years, working in a supply store and a furniture company while helping with the family farm. Near the end of those three years, in August of 1959, he married Susan Nicholls, also of Canton. The importance of this enduring relationship is evident to any reader of *Midquest* and is further highlighted by Chappell's decision to begin his essay in the *Contemporary Authors Autobiography Series* not with his birth or with a childhood experience but with his marriage.

Returning to Duke in the fall of 1959, Chappell found Price teaching in the English Department. Their friendship deepened as Chappell continued to share work-in-progress with Price. During his senior year Chappell became editor of *The Archive,* Duke's literary magazine, which published both his fiction and his poetry during his years there. Completing his B.A. degree in

1961, Chappell remained at Duke as an M.A. candidate. His master's thesis was an eleven-hundred-page concordance to the English poetry of Samuel Johnson, painstakingly compiled in the precomputer era. By the time he had earned his M.A. in 1964, Chappell had already published his first novel, *It Is Time, Lord* (1963), and been offered a teaching position at the University of North Carolina at Greensboro, where he has continued to teach throughout his career.

It would be difficult to overestimate the significance of Chappell's years at Duke on his literary sensibility. The two most powerful influences on his writing remain his childhood experiences on a mountain farm and his vast erudition. Chappell employs the folk materials of the agrarian world and the wide-ranging allusions of the scholarly world with equal facility. The catholicity of his literary interests—his willingness to embrace such popular genres as science fiction and the horror tale as well as the folktale and fantasy—combines with his mastery of traditional poetic forms to produce a truly distinctive body of work.

While at Duke, Chappell viewed himself as principally a poet, and he has continued to voice his primary allegiance to poetry. Yet four of his first five books were novels. *It Is Time, Lord* grew out of a piece titled "January" first published in *The Archive,* a story that editor Hiram Haydn of Atheneum read during a visit to the Duke campus. Haydn invited Chappell to submit a novel to Atheneum, an invitation the young author at first declined. But finding himself in need of financial support during his first summer of graduate school, Chappell obtained an advance from Haydn and completed the novel in six weeks. Though reviewers found flaws in the book, *It Is Time, Lord* also earned high praise. Granville Hicks of the *Saturday Review* declared the writing "fresh and vigorous" and noted that "Chappell has a sharp eye for telling details, and his imagery is powerful."[9] Denis Donoghue stated, "*It Is Time, Lord* is beautifully written, page on page; written, composed, balanced from word to word. . . . It is a remarkable first novel."[10] In the book's exploration of childhood memories, its focus on family relationships, its introduction of the country storekeeper Virgil Campbell, and its moral and philosophical concerns, *It Is Time, Lord* anticipates the major work Chappell was later to do in *Midquest* and in the corresponding cycle of novels that occupied his imagination for over twenty-five years.

Chappell completed the draft of his second novel, *The Inkling,* during the summer of 1964. Shortly after his arrival in Greensboro that fall to join an English Department that included Randall Jarrell and Peter Taylor, Jarrell's untimely death thrust Chappell into a larger role in the university's highly respected creative writing program. Teaching has always been a major part of Chappell's professional life, and he speaks with great satisfaction about the achievements of his former students. For his work in the classroom, Chappell has received the University of North Carolina's highest award for teaching, the O. Max Gardner Award.

With the exception of one year (1967–68) spent in Florence on a Rockefeller Foundation grant, Chappell has lived in North Carolina all his life, teaching in Greensboro for over thirty-five years. The stability of his public life contrasts, however, with the apparent emotional turmoil reflected in his excessive drinking over a twenty-year period. This is a problem that he has addressed in assorted essays and interviews.[11] Whatever the underlying cause or causes of that drinking, it surfaces repeatedly in the characters of his fiction and poetry, from James Christopher of *It Is Time, Lord* and Peter Leland of *Dagon* to Virgil Campbell in *Midquest* and Uncle Luden in *I Am One of You Forever.* One critic has even identified alcohol as the "fifth element" (along with water, fire, air, and earth) in *Midquest.*[12] Chappell's difficulties with alcohol, especially in his early years as a writer, no doubt contribute to the recurrent conflict between will and appetite in his first three novels and to the mental anguish he reports having experienced while composing *Dagon* (1968).[13]

What Chappell has called "this awful, horrifying, scary, sickening novel [*Dagon*]" won France's prestigious *Prix de Meilleur des Livres Étrangers* for the best foreign novel when it was translated into French in 1971 by Maurice-Edgar Coindreau.[14] From the psychic hell portrayed in that novel, Chappell turned toward greater use of comedy and toward the composition of poetry. Having drafted his fourth novel, *The Gaudy Place,* on the back of the galleys of *Dagon* during his year in Florence (that novel wasn't published until 1973), Chappell returned to his first love, the writing of poetry (a return prompted by a request for a manuscript from Louisiana State University Press). That press published *The World between the Eyes* in 1971 and has continued to publish Chappell's poetry throughout his career. During the 1970s Chappell devoted himself primarily to the writing of poetry, in 1975 publishing *River,* the first of the four volumes that comprise his epic, semiautobiographical poem *Midquest.* Yet he also revised and published *The Gaudy Place* and produced many short stories. His first collection of short fiction, *Moments of Light,* appeared in 1980. But it is *Midquest* (1981) that represents Chappell's highest literary achievement in the 1970s, the book for which he won the 1985 Bollingen Prize, an award he shared that year with John Ashbery.

During the past two decades Chappell has continued to win major literary prizes (most notably, the T. S. Eliot Award in 1993) and larger audiences while demonstrating his astonishing range as a writer. Since *Midquest* he has published five additional volumes of poetry, four more novels, a second collection of short stories, and two books of essays. *The Fred Chappell Reader* (1987) helped to expand Chappell's readership, which has grown throughout the 1990s with the appearance of each new novel in the Kirkman tetralogy and with the publication of the poems of *C* (1993) and *Spring Garden* (1995).

Asked which of his many gifted students was the most talented, William Blackburn is said to have responded, "Fred Chappell, without any question. . . . Of course, whether he will ever manage to *do* anything with all that talent, and whether he will ever be *recognized,* remain to be seen."[15] That Chappell has indeed done something with his enormous talent now seems obvious. *Midquest* alone is a truly remarkable achievement. Yet between 1963 and 1981 only one critical article on Chappell's work appeared in a scholarly journal.[16] The publication of *Midquest* prompted several lengthy review-essays, most notably those of Kelly Cherry, Rodney Jones, and Robert Morgan. That book also inspired special Chappell issues of *Abatis One, Mississippi Quarterly,* and *The Iron Mountain Review.*[17] Despite the quantity and variety and quality of Chappell's publications, despite the Bollingen Prize and the T. S. Eliot Award, during the ten-year period between 1985, when *I Am One of You Forever* was published, and 1995, scarcely one critical essay a year appeared in books and scholarly periodicals other than standard reference works.

One major cause of this critical opacity is the perception that Chappell is "merely" a *regional* writer—an impression fostered by many of the reviews of his first three novels, reviews that linked those books to the Southern Gothic tradition. Not only is Chappell a lifelong resident of North Carolina and hence readily classified as a Southern writer, but he is also a member of that subset of Southern authors whose roots are in the Appalachian mountains. The less said of Appalachia, it would seem, in many parts of even the Southern literary establishment, the better.

Despite the apparent disadvantages of identifying oneself with the Appalachian region, Chappell has increasingly done so, as his comments in interviews and the title of his 1985 novel, *I Am One of You Forever,* suggest. From *Midquest* on, moreover, his work has drawn heavily on folk materials, including the tall tale tradition. Yet his writing, though grounded in the regional, is in no sense provincial. *Midquest* draws its larger metaphoric structure and some of its most telling details from Dante's *Divine Comedy.* In both *Midquest* and *I Am One of You Forever,* the rural raconteur rubs elbows with the university-trained scholar; folktales are juxtaposed with the paradoxes of the pre-Socratic philosopher Zeno, and Chappell plays with metafictional strategies. The allusiveness of Chappell's writing, his profound erudition, and the kinds of philosophical issues he addresses enlarge the scope of his work well beyond its immediate locale, which is often (though hardly exclusively) the mountains of western North Carolina.

A second reason for Chappell's relative neglect by critics may be the protean variety of his literary achievement. Not content to be primarily a poet or primarily a novelist, he is a writer at home in both genres as well as in the short story. Moreover, each of his books of poems, including *Midquest,* has been strikingly different in structure. Chappell's first four novels demonstrate a comparable distinctiveness in relation to one another, as do the short stories within each collection, several of which focus on historical figures. Such stories make special demands on their readers, as do Chappell's early novels. Though vividly detailed, those books often build upon a symbolic or allegorical structure that is not readily apparent. Chappell himself has judged his early novels to be less "humane" than his later work.[18]

The humor Chappell utilizes so successfully in *Midquest* and the tetralogy launched by *I Am One of You Forever* may provide another explanation for many critics' apparent disregard for his work. It is in part the playfulness of Chappell's imagination that leads him to adopt such popular culture genres as the horror story, science fiction, and fantasy. *Dagon,* for example, draws on the horror fiction of H. P. Lovecraft and that author's Cthulhu mythos. *More Shapes Than One,* Chappell's most recent collection of short stories, includes the Lovecraftian "Weird Tales" and "The Adder" as well as a science fiction tale like "The Somewhere Doors" and such fables as "Alma" and "After Revelation." In his historical fictions, too, Chappell tends to dissolve the distinction between the factual and the imagined. Here again, his playfulness and his use of the forms of popular culture may prevent some critics from appreciating the depth of implication and the thematic complexity these works involve.

One final factor that has contributed to Chappell's relative obscurity among contemporary American writers is, as George Garrett has indicated, the author's natural modesty.[19] Chappell's literary reputation is not something he appears to attend to—except to deprecate it. Popularity is not Chappell's aim.

Chappell's fiction and poetry often exhibit traits commonly associated with Southern literature: profound identification with place, strong family ties and a commitment to community, vivid narrative voices that draw on the oral tradition, a powerful sense of history and the ongoing effects of the past, and a preoccupation with religious issues. He has often cited Graham Greene's remark that "childhood is a writer's capital," observing that he himself must already have spent that capital two or three times.[20] The mountains and farmland around Canton provide his principal setting, and much of his writing is markedly autobiographical, though without being confessional. Chappell uses his life to explore fundamental human concerns such as time and mortality; the struggle between will and appetite; the quests for truth and order; the nature and function of storytelling; the possibilities of rebirth or renewal; and the longing for religious insight, for transcendence. Chappell's concern with the past is one he shares with many other American writers, and not just those of the South. It is a theme, after all, central to Nathaniel Hawthorne's fiction, and Chappell shares as well Hawthorne's interest in moral allegory and symbolism. The various short stories Chappell has written about historical figures also underscore his sense of the past's continuing relevance to the present and of the resources for self-understanding that the past, whether personal or communal, provides. Underlying this thematic focus is Chappell's recognition of the archetypal structure that defines the nature of the past in the Judeo-Christian tradition, a pattern repeated in classical myths of the Golden Age and in the events of Southern history: "*Once upon a time things were the way they were supposed to be. Then something happened. Since that point, things have never been the same. . . .* We inhabit," he concludes, "a fallen world."[21] This recognition is crucial to the plight of James Christopher in *It Is Time, Lord,* to many of the characters in the stories in *Moments of Light,* to the protagonist of *Midquest,* and to many other of Chappell's protagonists.

Amidst such a fallen world, Chappell's characters undertake a quest for order, a search for truth. That quest takes many forms. Chappell's interest in the sense of order to be derived from the natural sciences is apparent in his portraits of Herschel and Linnaeus and Feuerbach as well as in his use of a natural philosopher like Lucretius. The logical order of philosophical thought is also invoked in *Midquest*'s many allusions to other philosophers and theologians and in Chappell's attraction to the eighteenth-century rationalism represented by Samuel Johnson. But the essential order for which his characters yearn ultimately depends on something more than the material structures of the physical sciences or the concepts of human reason. That yearning is, in essence, spiritual, and it seeks fulfillment in the spheres of art and religion, expressions of the human imagination.

For Chappell, one crucial embodiment of that artistic imagination occurs in music. As an artistic form that is invisible yet sensuous, music offers an apt metaphor for the mysterious, ineluctable bond between the physical and the spiritual. In its creation of beauty and its evocation of the timeless, music testifies to an order both human and transhuman.

Literary artists too aspire to such a transcendent order. The carefully designed structure Chappell creates for a novel like *The Gaudy Place,* a book of poems like *Midquest,* or a volume of stories like *More Shapes Than One* attests to the author's desire to order experience, to arrange it in meaningful patterns. That impulse to order is fundamental to the artistic imagination—and, Chappell implies, to human consciousness generally.

That sense of order ultimately arises from Chappell's religious sensibility. Though uninterested in organized religion, Chappell does think of himself as a religious person.[22] His recognition that humanity inhabits a fallen world is balanced by his belief in the individual's potential for rebirth. The Dantean substructure of *Midquest* is perhaps the clearest example of this conviction, but it appears as well in the closing pages of *It Is Time, Lord,* in the portrait of Stovebolt Johnson in "Blue Dive," and in the various myths of origin and the creation stories that pervade his work. Chappell rebelled against the otherworldly Protestantism he encountered as a child in Canton's First Methodist Church and the judgmental pietism that afflicts Virgil Campbell in the person of Canary in "The Change of Heart." Chappell's theology, in contrast, is profoundly incarnational. Its central trope is the garden, which grounds human beings in the physical world while suggesting both the lost innocence of Eden and the still-to-be-established Earthly Paradise of Dante's *Purgatorio.* Chappell celebrates the union of body and soul while also acknowledging the tension between them, the potential for conflict their union creates.

This consciousness of duality suffuses Chappell's writing, lending it much of its tension and drama. For all its use of the tall tale tradition, of elements of fantasy and horror, Chappell's work is deeply philosophical in its underlying themes. Chappell is also a moralist. In one of his essays he refers to "moral reality" as "the only reality an artist is interested in" and contends that "the same urgent moral necessities are always with us."[23] The didacticism to which the gravity of such a moral vision might lead is counterbalanced, however, by his extensive use of humor and by the often whimsical forms his imagination creates.

Given the great diversity of his publications, it is not surprising that Chappell's style, like his literary forms, varies widely from work to work. There is nothing as distinctive about Chappell's style as there is about Faulkner's or Hemingway's or A. R. Ammons's. In fact Chappell has demonstrated a stylistic range that confirms his virtuosity both in prose and poetry. Yet certain recognizable qualities do predominate. Among them, in addition to humor, are clarity and concreteness of diction; apt figurative language; skilled re-creation of the speaking voice, whether in dialogue, first-person narratives, or poetic monologues; vivid imagery and symbols that tend to assume allegorical significance; and wide-ranging allusiveness, in prose as well as poetry.

That allusiveness should remind readers that, though grounded in the landscape of Appalachia, Chappell's imagination remains unbounded by place or time. *Midquest* is as dependent on Dante for its meaning as it is on the oral tradition and tall-tale humor of the mountain South. Writers have good reason for growing impatient with all of the labels that critics attempt to impose upon them and their work. Fred Chappell is an Appalachian writer, a Southern writer, a profoundly American writer, but he is also simply a poet and fiction writer, an author whose work intersects powerfully with the western literary and philosophical and religious traditions while achieving an excellence uniquely its own.

CHAPTER TWO

Fables of Will and Appetite
The Early Novels

Chappell's early reputation as a writer was based on his fiction, not his poetry. Four of the five books he published between 1963 and 1973 were novels, each of them under two hundred pages in length. At that time he stated, "my ideal is to keep a novel short enough to be read in one sitting."[1] These early novels—*It Is Time, Lord* (1963), *The Inkling* (1965), *Dagon* (1968), and *The Gaudy Place* (1973), particularly the first three—pose special difficulties of interpretation due to their subject matter and literary techniques. The protagonists in these books are often rather unappealing characters from whom many readers are likely to want to distance themselves. The philosophical themes that underlie the texts add to the books' complexity. The nature of time, the burden and promise of the past, freedom vs. bondage of the will, and the conflict between will and appetite are all important themes in Chappell's early novels. Preeminent among them, especially in the first three novels, is the conflict between will and appetite.[2]

Chappell has acknowledged the real-life sources of *It Is Time, Lord* and *The Inkling,* calling them "close autobiographical projections."[3] Given the author's struggle with alcohol over many years, a problem that intensified during the composition of *Dagon,* it seems reasonable to assume that Chappell's third novel also exhibits strong autobiographical elements in its exploration of its protagonist's excessive drinking, marked passivity, and lack of will. This assumption does not intend to attribute the complex meaning and artistry of these novels to a single cause, only to suggest one significant impetus for the intense, persistent, often scarifying investigation of the ineffectual or paralyzed will in Chappell's first three novels.

Much of the power of these texts originates in the author's vivid, precise language, which moves fluidly from the literal to the figurative. As David Paul Ragan has observed, Chappell's first four novels "exhibit the sort of condensation and economy of language associated with poetry, along with much of the poet's symbolic method."[4] That symbolic method accounts for part of the difficulty these books pose. Equally challenging is Chappell's use of what might be called submerged thematic structures. In his essay "A Pact with Faustus" Chappell describes his method of composing these early novels. "I decided that the intellectual structure of a novel, its larger themes and purposes, could be drawn up outside the literal narrative, could be determined in the preliminary working stages and then abandoned except as a large system of reference. No need to talk directly about theme; since it was the motive force for the story, the Ur-impulse, it would necessarily *seep through.*" Noting that this approach produced *The Inkling* and *Dagon,* he adds, "I did not foresee some of the unfortunate consequences of this method: that I would be producing works which . . . might seem unmercifully brief, puzzling, hermetic, unpleasantly singleminded, humorless, and inhumane."[5] Though Chappell's self-criticism is excessive, his methods did propel these two novels toward allegory, just as the three dreams that dominate the closing chapters of *It Is Time, Lord* offer a resolution more dependent on symbolism than on literal event.

FABLES OF WILL AND APPETITE

Henry Taylor aptly sums up the impression conveyed by these first three novels when he says, "They are brilliant, brief, allusive, densely textured, and difficult."[6]

It Is Time, Lord

The experimental nature of Chappell's early novels is nowhere more evident than in the structure of *It Is Time, Lord.* The book's title and the image of the clock in the opening paragraph announce one of the book's major themes—the nature of time. The first-person narrator, thirty-year-old James Christopher, struggles throughout the book to recover a sense of purpose and identity. In portraying that struggle, Chappell alternates between chapters devoted to Christopher's memories of his childhood in the mountains of western North Carolina and chapters that describe his present life in Winton (read Durham), where he lives with his wife, Sylvia, and their two children. Chapters 1 through 3 focus on Christopher's past, though occasionally he refers to his adult self. Not until chapter 4 does the reader encounter Christopher in time present (June 1962)—and then only to learn that chapters 1 through 3 are part of a manuscript Christopher is composing, a document in which he describes himself as a minister, though he is, in fact, unemployed, having quit his job at the Winton College Press three months earlier.

This narrative structure forces the reader to reconsider the truthfulness of Christopher's account of his childhood and the accuracy of his memories. The recurrence of certain memories—the burning of his grandparents' home, for example—in strikingly different versions leads to a similar skepticism, as does

Chappell's blurring of the distinction between memory and dream.[7] Throughout the first twelve chapters Chappell shifts back and forth from past to present, devoting clusters of three chapters to each time frame. (Chapter 10, unparagraphed, is a transitional chapter that blends the two.) Chapter 13 returns to the past, while the final two chapters are set in the present. In its overall design the book thus moves Christopher from the past into the present, placing him in a position to affirm the potential of his present life. That affirmation does not arise from a rejection of the past but rather from a new understanding of it and a new recognition of the resources for the future that it contains. In this sense *It Is Time, Lord* anticipates, in muted fashion, the affirmation of rootedness celebrated more fully in *I Am One of You Forever.*

Two specific memories haunt James Christopher. One (also retold as "January" in *Moments of Light*) involves his father's false assumption that James has been cruel to his sister when, in fact, James has been trying unsuccessfully to persuade his sister to seek refuge from the harsh weather. This experience is first recounted in chapter 1 (pp. 6–8), then reappears in chapter 13 (pp. 131, 146–48), where James's sister Julia indicates that her brother may have been molested by the escaped convicts the children discover in a barn. The second memory focuses on the burning of James's grandparents' home when the boy was nine. This event is first described at the close of chapter 1, though there the person responsible is not identified with certainty; again in chapter 8, where James's father explains what he assumes was *James's* action; and once more in chapter 13, when the reader learns that it was indeed James who set the fire. Even though his father believes James caused the fire, he does not punish his son; he simply establishes a new work regimen for the boy.

Initially these childhood memories may seem to account for the adult Christopher's malaise, his profound sense of alienation. But Chappell was less interested in writing yet another Southern novel detailing the burden of the past than in showing how present perceptions and emotions color memories, and thereby affect people's understanding of the past. It is "the effect of present time upon the past," says Chappell, that is one of the novel's major themes,[8] what he calls in the book itself "memory's impure Doppler effect" (35). For much of the book, however, Christopher sees his past rather than his present mode of life as the central threat to his identity. "I can face hell," he writes in his manuscript, "with more composure than I could face any single day of my past come back to accost me" (34). Yet just before he launches into his first version of "January," he refers to "the counterfeiting of memory" and acknowledges that "certain reminiscences gain especial value by the significance of subsequent events, . . . nor can we discover ourselves by the single remembrances that fasten to us" (6).

James Christopher is so obsessed with his past that he fails to exercise his will in the present, and that very lack of resolution reinforces his bleaker memories of childhood. Rejecting the love and understanding of his wife and ignoring his children, he falls under the influence of Preacher, a heavy-drinking, unemployed womanizer who has been separated from his wife for two years. Preacher—whose given name, like the protagonist's, is James—is Christopher's alter ego, one version of his future possibilities. Preacher introduces Christopher to Judy, with whom Christopher begins a brief, unimpassioned affair, a relationship that ends when Judy's husband beats Preacher so severely that Preacher is hospitalized and later dies. Judy accuses James of causing Preacher's death, but James and Sylvia agree (correctly, Chappell implies) that James is not culpable. Instead, James experiences a sense of release: "I feel happy, . . . like I had chains taken off me. I feel like I just burned down a house with all the bad things in it" (171).

These images of liberation result from Christopher's admission of his affair with Judy, whom he refers to as "appetite personified" (101), and from his recognition that he can move beyond the identity posited for him by Preacher. Throughout this novel Chappell emphasizes the duality of human nature, a duality sometimes evident in temporal and structural terms by way of the interrelationship between past and present, childhood and adulthood; sometimes evident thematically in the tension between will and appetite; and sometimes evident stylistically. As Chappell has remarked about the book, "It's a novel in two distinctly different styles because of the double time-scheme. The present time-present tense is a much faster kind of story than the more deliberate past-time story."[9]

It is in the book's portrait of the narrator that this dualism is most pronounced. Christopher notes that he was "born in Gemini, which is the sign of the arms and denotes balance" (3). Gemini is also, he adds, "an air sign" and thus has "the disadvantage of inconstancy, as of the winds, but air is the temple of space, of infinity" (4). Initially, at least, James Christopher is anything but balanced. Yet the image of duality implicit in Gemini, together with Chappell's reference to infinity, suggests an as yet unrealized potential in James Christopher. He is clearly an embattled character, one appropriately lodged at "the sign of the arms." Later in the novel he states, "I keep two bloody red apes chained to myself. Named Will and Appetite, these beasts tear and bite me" (103). Images of war and conflict pervade the novel, from allusions to Tolstoy's *War and Peace* and H. G. Wells's *War of the Worlds* through the defeats James suffers as a child at the hands of Hurl, the son of the tenant farmer on his grandparents' homestead, to the apocalyptic violence James envisions in his childhood epic poem about the Ironbird (chapter 9). Even his recurring memories of playing chess with his grandfather reflect ritualized or sublimated conflict.

At three key points in the novel Chappell stresses this issue of conflict in relation to his theme of the will's quest for freedom. In each of these episodes Christopher ponders the military Code of Conduct, especially its second, third, and fourth principles, which read: "*I will never surrender of my own free will*"; "*If I am captured I will continue to resist by all means available*"; and "*If I become a prisoner of war, I will keep faith with my fellow prisoners*" (52; Chappell's italics). Clearly, Chappell uses these principles to raise the philosophical issue of freedom of the will, a freedom he does not assume to be absolute. At first the adult Christopher thinks of himself as a person deprived of free will. "It's clear to me that I have been completely usurped" (50). Yet later he recognizes, "The trouble has been that I did surrender of my own free will. . . . The real true trouble," he adds, "is that I have been thinking of my will as an enemy, something inimical to my self. . . . To begin again, and to go straight forward and never to surrender: isn't this the purpose of the self?" (115).

Chappell's use of the military Code of Conduct implies, however, that the will cannot, in fact, always avoid surrender, that its responsibility, in defeat, becomes *resistance* and the establishment of a sense of community with other prisoners. Following defeat, one is obliged to begin again, to seek renewal.

At the precise center of this first novel, Chappell places an exchange between James Christopher and his father that revolves around the issue of choice: the father's decision to quit his teaching job because of the parents' and principal's reaction to a science experiment he has conducted. Through this episode, which anticipates events in *Brighten the Corner Where You Are* (1989), Chappell highlights the capacity to make choices that alter one's life. James's father rejects the identity he would have been compelled to accept had he retained his job; yet he knows the difficulties his decision will produce. "Well, anyway," he tells his son rather diffidently, "you've seen me make a choice" (92). Although the boy did indeed *see* his father make that decision, the James Christopher the reader encounters throughout much of the novel is characterized as *blind*.

Several key events help enlarge and clarify Christopher's vision. One is his return to the mountains to visit his parents, whom he hasn't seen, written, or called in five years. This journey is one he makes in the novel's penultimate chapter. Unfortunately, Chappell doesn't provide his character with any precise motive for this sudden visit. Instead, Christopher's departure from Winton seems prompted less by his conscious desires than by the author's need to have Christopher out of town when Judy's husband comes seeking his wife's lover. In any case the visit is hardly a success. Nevertheless, while home, James realizes, "I don't think I want to live any longer in the way I do; my present way of living has made this crazy hash out of my past life" (160). Somewhat heavy-handedly, Chappell signals this nascent transformation by having James carry with him on this visit a copy of Wells's novel *When the Sleeper Wakes.*

A second factor in Christopher's altered outlook is the violence that transpires in his absence. The assault on Preacher heightens James's sense of mortality and prompts him to greater appreciation of Sylvia's love and of the consequences of human action or inaction. The subsequent death of his alter ego, Preacher, forces him to reconsider his own identity and the choices that shape it.

The most important device by which Chappell reveals the change in James's outlook is the description of James's three recurring dreams in the novel's final chapter. By using dreams to resolve the conflicts the novel has established, Chappell transcends the antagonism between past and present that so oppresses James, for dreams exist in a realm beyond temporal specificity. Like the novel itself, these dreams involve rapid shifts in time and place and character and incident, and thus resist simple summary. But each dream does emphasize key events or people.

James insists that these visions are *dreams,* not nightmares, and he is struck by "their brightness and moral insistence" and by their having "the same comforting force as those hymns which I have known since my childhood" (182). The reference to religion here helps reinforce the theological implications of James's earlier plight. As R. H. W. Dillard was the first to point out, the title of this novel is taken from the opening line of

Rilke's brief poem "*Herbsttag*" ("Autumn Day"), which reads, "*Herr es ist Zeit. Der Sommer war sehr gross*" ("Lord, it is time. The summer was too long").[10] Fall is indeed James Christopher's season, emotionally and theologically. He is a fallen creature who has allowed his consciousness of guilt to blot out his aware- ness of the ongoing availability of forgiveness, of grace. Yet as his surname suggests, he continues to bear, albeit subcon- sciously, the image or memory of redemption. Chappell takes pains to mute these specifically Christian motifs, content simply to point James in the direction of emotional and spiritual rebirth.

That rebirth occurs in the context of Christopher's family, as James lies in bed with Sylvia waiting for the household to awake. Rilke's poem speaks of autumn as a time when he "who has no house now will not build him one. / Who is alone now will be long alone."[11] But James Christopher is not homeless, nor is he alone. He has a house, a wife, and children. Turning to embrace Sylvia, James anticipates the gesture Ole Fred makes repeatedly in *Midquest* in his relationship with Susan. The morning setting and the dew dripping on the roof underscore James's capacity for rebirth.

In other ways too *It Is Time, Lord* foreshadows Chappell's later writing: in its focus, for example, on an agrarian lifestyle; in its concern for the roles played by grandparents and parents in shaping a child's identity; and in its use, as in *Dagon* and the Kirkman tetralogy, of the grandparents' home as a principal set- ting. In addition *It Is Time, Lord* first introduces the character of Virgil Campbell, the country storekeeper who figures so promi- nently in *Midquest* and who reappears in *I Am One of You For- ever* and the novels that follow it. *It Is Time, Lord* is, as Ragan has said, "a remarkable achievement for a first novel."[12] Original in conception, complex in structure, elegantly and powerfully written, it earned Chappell the well-deserved respect of reviewers and mined imaginative resources that would come to fuller flowering in his subsequent poetry and fiction.

The Inkling

In many respects Chappell's second novel is far more accessible than his first. Its story line is clearer; its structure more straightforwardly chronological. The cast of characters is smaller, and the action focuses more tightly on a single household, without the alternation of scenes from two distinct time periods that is so fundamental to Chappell's design of his first book. Yet the characters and events portrayed in *The Inkling* are more grotesque, more extreme, than those in *It Is Time, Lord,* thus leading some reviewers to find the book disturbing and repellent, however brilliantly written. Chappell himself has referred to the novel as "short and savage and serious, a book that took no prisoners."[13] Its conclusion contains none of the hopefulness of the final chapter of *It Is Time, Lord.* Moreover, adding to the interpretive difficulties a reader faces are the author's allegorical intentions and the fact that one of the two principal characters is the protagonist's retarded—and later insane—sister. With incest also among the novel's motifs, it is not surprising that some reviews identified the book as yet another instance of the Southern Gothic popularized by Faulkner, McCullers, and O'Connor.[14]

While *The Inkling* clearly shares certain features of such writing, Chappell's aim was to produce "an allegorical novel of

Desire and Will, distantly based upon the unhappy story of the French symbolist poets, Rimbaud and Verlaine."[15] The tumultuous, tortured relationship between the two poets culminated in Paul Verlaine's firing shots at Arthur Rimbaud and spending a year and a half in prison for attempted manslaughter. Chappell has stated that "Rimbaud always seemed to me a figure of pure will—just sheer willpower transforming the world in so far as possible to its own ends, absolutely shaping the world," and Chappell seems to have seen Verlaine as an emblem of more passive appetite.[16] In "A Pact with Faustus" Chappell describes *The Inkling* as "a story about a boy who represents pure Will and his sister who is Appetite. . . . At that time I felt that I saw the largest conflicts of our western societies as determined by the antagonistic forces of will and appetite."[17]

The brother and sister thus conceived are Jan and Timmie Anderson, whose lives Chappell traces over a ten-year period from the early 1940s to the early 1950s. The children live on a six-acre farm just outside a small town in western North Carolina, a town which, like Chappell's Canton, has a paper mill as its dominant industry. Jan and Timmie live with their mother and their mother's brother, Uncle Hake—their father having been killed at Pearl Harbor. Over the course of the novel, Timmie goes mad, and Uncle Hake marries Lora, a young woman more than thirty years his junior who has entered the household as a maid. The mother, Jenny, dies of cancer, and on the day of her funeral Lora seduces Jan. Upon discovering Jan's relationship with Lora, Hake unsuccessfully attempts to kill Jan and is in turn shot to death by Jan, who uses his uncle's pistol to commit that act.

So bald a plot summary of the novel's highly episodic structure omits, of course, all the carefully detailed experiences, thoughts, and emotions that shape the characters' lives. Though allegorical in thematic conception, *The Inkling* is vividly realized on the literal level, as almost any page of the novel will demonstrate. The book opens with the following paragraph: "A young man, sixteen years old, was sitting hunkered on his heels in a stretch of tall yellow sagegrass. His hair was yellow like the sagegrass and the slight down sprinkled on his jaws and down his neck was yellow. . . .The wind moved in the sage and worried it over, and the young man did not move except now and then to tip back his head when he drank from the dark bottle. The liquor was yellow and flamed in his throat. The fellow was hunkered in the field, fiercely self-willed; he was like a belligerent voice."[18]

Approached by Timmie and Jan, the young man inexplicably cries out, "You goddam kids! . . . What if you was to die? What if you was to die one day?" (6). Later in the opening chapter the children receive a second warning or hint—inkling—about their mortality. Thus Chappell introduces one of the major themes *The Inkling* shares with his first novel, time and mortality. But whereas time in the first book was the necessary locus of human action, providing opportunities for self-transformation and rebirth, time in *The Inkling* is presented more as an opponent to be conquered through fierce self-will or self-aggrandizing appetite.

In contrast to the first-person point of view in *It Is Time, Lord,* in *The Inkling* Chappell uses third-person narration. He allows the reader to enter most fully, however, only the minds of Jan and Timmie, enforcing a greater degree of detachment from Jenny and Hake and Lora. Yet Chappell skillfully intersperses chapters that focus on these secondary characters among those that focus on Jan and Timmie, both to provide variety and to avoid what might have been an all but claustrophobic intensity had he relentlessly pursued his central characters' consciousness. Uncle Hake, in fact, with his practiced indolence and lechery, often provides moments of comic relief. Yet it is the silent, sensitive, intelligent Jan who from the first commands the reader's attention, this boy "who spent all his time training his will" (12). Jan thus stands in sharp contrast to James Christopher. James's failure is *lack* of will, while Jan's is his inability to make the world conform to his will. As the novel progresses, Jan finds his will baffled not only by others but also by profound self-betrayals, especially those that arise with the onset of adolescence and the awakening of sexual desire.

Two episodes early in the novel indicate Jan's initial success in imposing his will on the world. Both episodes also reveal Chappell's indebtedness to Poe rather than to twentieth-century examples of the Southern Gothic tradition. The first occurs in chapter 3, when Jan tests his will by staring down the family cat, Buddha, and then killing the animal. The second episode involves the revenge he takes on a schoolmate.

Such triumphs are short lived, however, for Jan finds his powers of will increasingly negated both by Timmie and by his own developing sexuality. Chappell's portrait of Timmie produces some of the novel's most experimental—and most complicated—passages.[19] Though initially dependent on Jan, Timmie's powers of self-assertion intensify as she grows older. She becomes increasingly manipulative and appears, ironically, to develop greater self-consciousness *after* she goes mad at age fifteen, halfway through the book's twenty chapters. "The tighter [Jan's] will got," Chappell writes, "the more easily she was able to evade its grasp. The closer his surveillance of her became, the more he felt, though obscurely, that she was watching back" (85).

Chappell's portrait of the mad Timmie's thought processes and feelings relies heavily both on her dreams or fantasies and on symbolism. The way in which Chappell links chapters 12 and 16, both narrated from Timmie's point of view, brilliantly reflects her virtual independence from time as the other characters experience it. The opening sentence of chapter 16 picks up where the closing sentence of chapter 12 ends—as if all the intervening events, including Hake's marriage to Lora—had failed to impinge on Timmie's consciousness or to have any impact on her. As Chappell says of Timmie's outlook, "Timmie felt no responsibility, none. Her mode of understanding was desire; she wasn't burdened with (or mastered by) will" (116–17). It is Timmie more than Jan who seems to embody the qualities evoked in the novel's epigraph: *Monstru horrendu, informe, ingens, cui lumen ademptum* (a terrible monster, misshapen, huge, with his eye put out). These words from book 3 of the *Aeneid* are Virgil's portrait of the cyclops Polyphemos, words that Chappell also cites in *Midquest,* though there they describe "the will made totally single" (85).

In *The Inkling* Chappell effectively depicts the need for balance, for an acceptance of what Hawthorne in "The Birthmark" calls "the limits of natural possibility."[20] As the novel unfolds, Jan is forced to recognize that his will is not absolute. His mother's illness and death in chapter 17 attest to the body's ultimate independence of the will, as do his adolescent sexual desires. After nineteen-year-old Lora Bowen becomes the family's maid, fifteen-year-old Jan becomes aware of his own sexual impulses as he watches Uncle Hake flirt with Lora. "Everything was evading the grasp of his mind and coming under the control of his body," Chappell writes, "that wearying machine he comprehended only dimly" (105). Jan yearns to be disincarnate; yet he also longs to have sex with Lora, a longing that Chappell has Jan voice in the concluding sentence of chapter 14 only to announce Lora's marriage to Hake in the opening paragraph of chapter 15. Such an ironic juxtaposition contributes to the reader's view of Lora as a person who not only serves her own appetites but also knows how to exploit the appetites of others.

Lora seems to seduce Jan out of boredom, or perhaps simply to test her power. But as the relationship continues, it becomes apparent even to Jan that Lora receives little sexual pleasure from their lovemaking, for she fosters in him "the impression of his excruciating inadequacy" (142). During one of Jan's sexual encounters with Lora in her bedroom, Timmie bursts in and stabs him, thereby disclosing the affair to Hake. But Chappell informs the reader in the final chapter's opening sentence that Lora had *intended* for the affair to be discovered, though not in this specific manner. Why should Lora want her relationship with Jan to be discovered? Presumably to complete her takeover of the Anderson home, an act of dispossession that began with her marriage to Hake and Jenny's surrender of her room to the newlyweds, that was consolidated by Jenny's death, and that would have culminated with Jan's (and no doubt Timmie's) expulsion from the household by an enraged Hake. Timmie's unforeseen action sabotages Lora's intention, whatever its precise nature, and thus points to another factor that limits the free operation of the individual will. That factor might be defined as chance in this case, but more broadly it is the willing of others as those individual wills and impulses resist or negate one's own. The human situation as Chappell presents it is invariably intersubjective. It is a world where actions have surprising, often unanticipated consequences. In the final chapter of *The Inkling* Hake's unsuccessful attempt to kill Jan eventuates instead in his own death.

Chappell does not conclude the novel with this act of violence, however; instead he follows the fleeing Jan outside the house into the same field where the book began. Jan himself is the sixteen-year-old young man with the bandaged hand who had demanded of the children in the opening scene, "What if you was to die?" The mirroring effect Chappell achieves here, like the reader's discovery that the first three chapters of *It Is Time, Lord* are part of a manuscript written by that novel's protagonist, is disorienting. This looping of time back upon itself is certainly the most experimental, most original element of the book's design, more original than Chappell's efforts to reflect Timmie's thought processes.

Chappell uses this structure for several reasons. First of all, it suggests the ongoing nature of the struggle between will and appetite, the eternal tensions within the self. The Jan the reader meets in *The Inkling* has no conception of the genial "Uncle Body" whom Chappell celebrates in *Midquest*. Second, this structure allows the author to stress the memento mori in his text. The young man in the closing chapter repeats the questions asked as the book opens: "You goddam kids! What if you was to die? What if you was to die one day?" (152). These questions have a new resonance in light of Jenny's death and Uncle Hake's murder as well as the reader's knowledge of the children's father's death. The novel's concluding sentences also echo this theme, as Chappell describes Jan's departure from his home: "He began walking. Beneath his confused feet the earth ebbed and swayed, as it might ebb and sway below the feet of a man who has been hanged" (153). Less allusive and more tightly structured than *It Is Time, Lord, The Inkling* remains a gripping portrait of the self *in extremis,* a dark meditation on the trammeled human will.

Dagon

An even darker vision presides over Chappell's third novel, *Dagon* (1968). Unlike *The Inkling,* which has generated little critical commentary, *Dagon* has received more extended treatment, both in interviews with its author and in essays by and about him, than any of his other first four novels. The most widely known of the books discussed in this chapter, it is also the bleakest in its themes and characterization.

One of the interpretive problems facing readers of this book is the question of its genre. Chappell has said that "*Dagon* was designed as a horror story, tenuously and ironically connected to that tradition of horror fiction initiated by H. P. Lovecraft, the Cthulhu mythos."[21] But Chappell has also said, "My purpose in *Dagon* was not simply to scare people or to thrill them. You can do that just by making a loud noise. I wanted to disturb them in a different way. . . . The horror story is only the surface. There's a great deal of literary intention below that."[22] Part of that intention, as the author has remarked, involves "a parody of books written about Puritanism," specifically *The Scarlet Letter* and *Moby-Dick*.[23] Like such literary antecedents, *Dagon* tends toward allegory, and like them as well, it is in part a meditation on the legacy of Puritanism in American culture. In his essay "Fantasia on the Theme of Theme and Fantasy" Chappell critiques *Dagon* for being "theme-ridden." "I had erected too many ambitions for the story to fulfill; it was to be a thesis about American fecklessness and wastefulness; it was to be an exposé of a hidden American religion; it was to tell the Biblical story of Samson in modern terms; it was to employ the artificial mythology of the H. P. Lovecraft circle of writers, the Cthulhu mythos, in a sarcastic pop-art fashion."[24] Not all these themes are of equal significance to the book's plot, nor are they all fully realized. Moreover, other themes, especially Chappell's analysis of the recurring conflict between will and appetite, assume greater prominence than those the author cites.

On one level, of course, *Dagon* is indeed a horror story, a searing vision of human degradation. Although one reviewer dismissed the book as "another horse from the dilapidated stable of the Southern gothic novel,"[25] *Dagon* owes more to Poe and Hawthorne and Lovecraft than to Faulkner and McCullers. Lovecraft himself had published a story titled "Dagon," and Chappell's debt to Lovecraft is apparent in the novel's epigraph, which reads, in the language Lovecraft invented for his Cthulhu mythos, *Ph'nglui mglw'nafh Cthulhu R'lyeh wgah'nagl fhtagn* ("In his house at R'lyeh dead Cthulhu lies sleeping").[26] That indebtedness is also evident in the scattered references throughout the book to Yogg Sothoth, Nephreu, and Nyarlath, figures from Lovecraft's mythology. Yet as Amy Tipton Gray has shown, whereas Lovecraft finds the source of horror in humanity's helplessness in relation to *external* powers, Chappell identifies the sources of horror as *internal,* for they are founded on the divisions within the individual psyche.[27] Gray suggests that *Dagon,* along with Chappell's first two novels, might best be read as examples of the "romance" as Richard Chase defines that term in *The American Novel and Its Tradition.* According to Chase, the romance is willing to forgo the plausibility of motive and event characteristic of the novel and "will more freely veer toward mythic, allegorical, and symbolistic forms."[28] Equally pertinent to *Dagon,* however, is Chase's assessment of "the Manichaean sensibility" in American Puritanism and hence in American literature: "The American imagination, like the New England Puritan mind itself, seems less interested in redemption than in the melodrama of the eternal struggle of good and evil, less interested in incarnation and reconciliation than in alienation and disorder."[29]

It is precisely such alienation and disorder that characterize Peter Leland, the protagonist of *Dagon.* A thirty-two-year-old minister, Peter has recently inherited his grandparents' home on a four-hundred-acre farm in western North Carolina. He and his wife, Sheila, have moved to the farm so that Peter can write a book titled *Remnant Pagan Forces in American Puritanism,* a book that centers not on Lovecraft's Cthulhu mythos but on the Old Testament pagan deity of the novel's title. Dagon also appears in William Bradford's *Of Plymouth Plantation,* where the god is linked to the hedonism of Thomas Morton's Merry

Mount. "I invented the myth," says Chappell, "that there was a secret cult that still worshiped [Dagon] that went on all through American history."[30] The existence of this cult is central to the novel's plot.

Chapter 1 describes Peter's scrutiny of "two rooms (really, one room divided)" on the main floor of his grandparents' home. This image of duality is reinforced by the two pillows Peter observes on a sofa, "companion pillows, shouldered so closely together that they looked like the Decalogue tablets."[31] Like the home of Poe's Usher or the ancestral home in Hawthorne's *The House of the Seven Gables,* this house is haunted. Of the room in which he stands, Peter says, "It was a room truly made for secondary presences, for reverberations" (4). With its "eyed" windows, it seems to observe him as much as he does it. Everywhere he looks, Peter finds layers of dust, suggestive both of the detritus of the past and of mortality. The book's opening paragraph concludes, significantly, with Peter examining his own reflection in the glass doors that subdivide this west-facing sun parlor. "In the left door," Chappell writes, "his image stood, hand still over his face, and he was all cut into pieces in the panes" (4). This image indicates the fragmentation of Peter's personality and foreshadows his fate at novel's end. Elsewhere in this initial chapter, the third-person narrator says of Peter, "He had never before felt his will to be so ringed about, so much at bay" (12).

Given the use of an agrarian landscape in a horror story, *Dagon* can be read, in part, as an antipastoral book, one that undermines the conventional association of the countryside with innocence, as does Flannery O'Connor's "Good Country People." Chappell's juxtaposition of events in chapters 1 and 2, the latter describing Peter's picnic with Sheila on the same day, initially offers a contrast not only in setting and mood but also in mode of presentation, with its extensive reliance on dialogue. But the couple's idyll beside a brook is interrupted by Ed Morgan, the grandparents' tenant farmer, whose family has occupied the land for generations. At Morgan's invitation Peter accompanies him to his squalid cabin and there first encounters Morgan's teenaged daughter Mina, the priestess of Dagon, the Delilah to Chappell's weak-willed Samson. Chapter 2 thus concludes with Peter once again closed up indoors. And the Morgan cabin is even more stifling than the old home of chapter 1. "At first [Peter] couldn't breathe. The air was hot and viscous; . . . he had the quick impression of dark vegetation of immense luxuriance blooming up and momentarily rotting away; it was the smell of rank incredibly rich semen" (27–28). As for Mina herself, she is, like Judy in *It Is Time, Lord* or Lora in *The Inkling,* an emblem of appetite personified. Her name seems meant to suggest menace or threat (from the term "minatory"), and she is compared both to a fish (a creature linked to the god Dagon) and to a snake (29). "[Peter] couldn't unthink her image," chapter 2 ends (30), as Peter stands poised to begin his descent into utter impotence and degradation.

With the exception of chapter 3, in which Chappell uses a flashback to recount a sermon that Peter had delivered on the subject of Dagon, the remainder of the novel traces that process of dissolution. The pivotal episode occurs in chapter 4 in the attic of the grandparents' home. There, amid "tons of dust" (46), Peter discovers a network of chains attached to iron bands. After locking his right wrist in one of the bands, he finds that he cannot free himself. Hours pass before Sheila comes to the attic searching for her husband, hours during which he is haunted both by visions of Mina and by memories of his long-dead father similarly chained in the attic. This episode seems to parallel the famous scaffold scene in *The Scarlet Letter.* Unlike Dimmesdale, however, who has particular sins to repent, Peter has only a free-floating but pervasive sense of guilt. Such guilt, Chappell implies, is one of the most destructive legacies of Puritanism, for it vitiates productive action and undermines a sense of joy. Asked in an interview, "What do you owe your puritanism?" Chappell responded, "A boatload of useless guilt, I expect. The absolute conviction that the past is going to catch up with you."[32] Both these responses are pertinent to Chappell's portrait of Peter Leland.

Like Jan Anderson of *The Inkling,* as Ragan points out, Peter "is victimized by circumstances he can neither control nor understand."[33] Unlike Jan, however, who at least initially is notable for his strength of will, Peter is singularly torpid, straining credibility in his extreme passivity, as Chappell himself has acknowledged.[34] Moreover, unlike Jan, Peter is not a child or an adolescent and thus lacks the youthfulness to gain the reader's sympathy—particularly not after his murder of Sheila, an event that is inadequately motivated in terms of Peter's psychology though necessitated by the demands of Chappell's plot. The author recognized this problem, remarking in an interview, "The difficult thing was in getting the reader to accept a sudden violent event, the murder of the wife. . . . I didn't know how to work it out. Finally, I had to do it twice, once as a dream and once as reality."[35] This solution is unlikely to satisfy most readers.

Part 1 of *Dagon,* which consists of six chapters, culminates with Peter's murder of Sheila and his arrival at the Morgan cabin, where he is greeted by Mina. Part 2, also six chapters in length, depicts Mina's domination of Peter through sex and alcohol until he is reduced to such a state that he welcomes her use of him as a sacrifice to Dagon. This process of disintegration occurs over approximately ten weeks, from late June or early July into September. During this time the landscape outside the cabin bears the lineaments of T. S. Eliot's waste land, as Chappell creates a setting that mirrors Peter's spiritual desolation. As in the farmhouse in chapter 1, dust covers everything. On one of the few occasions when a thunderstorm arises, Peter imagines that he hears God speaking to him in the storm, but Mina promptly drowns his memory of that voice in the whiskey she thrusts upon him (89–91).

One of the principal symbols Chappell uses in part 2 is the iron pump handle Peter finds under the Morgan cabin. Driven there during a fight with Coke Rymer, a young man Mina has found to drive Peter's car and to service her sexually after Peter becomes impotent, Peter seizes upon the pump handle as a defense against Rymer's knife. But the handle is more than a weapon; Peter clings to it through most of part 2 as a symbol of his masculinity. Moreover, the pump handle, totally detached from any source of water, becomes another emblem of the sterility of the world Peter inhabits. Yet in its association with water rather than the whiskey Mina provides, the pump handle reminds the reader of physical and spiritual resources from which Peter has been cut off.

Whereas for James Christopher of *It Is Time, Lord* a journey to the mountains provides an important turning point in his life, Peter Leland is transported away from the mountains in the third chapter of part 2 of *Dagon*. Mina and Coke carry Peter to Gordon, a coastal town, on a journey that has temporal as well as geographical significance. Since the word *dagan* "derive[s] from a Semitic root meaning 'fish,'" according to Peter's earlier sermon (35), the town is an appropriate setting for Mina's sacrificial offering to the god. But the movement to the coast also retraces in reverse the pattern of North Carolina's settlement, thus emphasizing the historical continuity of the Dagon cult.

Once he arrives in Gordon, Peter's disintegration accelerates. The reader finds him in chains as chapter 4 opens, chains that are reminiscent of his experience in his grandparents' attic in the fourth chapter of part 1 but that also seem intended to recall the Puritan doctrine of the bondage of the will. This concept originates in the writings of Saint Paul and occupies a central place in Christian accounts of human sinfulness. But in Jonathan Edwards's theology this concept, in combination with the idea of God's absolute sovereignty, leads to a denial of freedom of the will. Chappell refers to Edwards's "gloominess" in introducing Peter's sermon in part 1 and may have had Edwards, among others, in mind when conceiving of *Dagon* as an exploration of Puritanism. Dillard points to another connection with the Puritan sensibility when he describes Peter as "Young Goodman Brown in the modern world."[36] Brown is certainly among the most pessimistic of Hawthorne's characters, the one who, like Peter, overwhelmed by guilt, seems to despair of humanity's potential for goodness.

One of the episodes in *Dagon* that bears directly on this

theme of the human will and its status occurs during the trip to Gordon. In this scene Peter finds himself alone in the restroom of a service station. Peter "looked out the window before him, a narrow slot in the white concrete block wall, and thought absurdly of escape. But there was nothing to escape from. He was not a prisoner, not held by force. He was simply bound to Mina wholly; he was his own prisoner, he could escape by dying, by no other way" (129). This passage echoes Coke Rymer's earlier advice to Peter to flee while he has the chance, since there is nothing compelling him to stay at the Morgan cabin (110). Yet shortly after Peter leaves the restroom, as the group continues their drive eastward, he has a dream in which he is a daddy long legs scouring the fields, "searching out water with an unerring hunger. . . . But in the heated fields his six-legged unstable body was painful. . . . He moved crookedly; he did not want to move. . . . The six-legged machine was its own volition, and he a prisoner trapped. It came to him that this at last was the true image of his sickness" (131).

The debate on freedom of the will that these passages articulate is crucial to Chappell's first three novels. One need only recall James Christopher's repeated references to the military Code of Conduct or Jan Anderson's failed efforts to retain his independence of will. In this last passage, however, Peter views the daddy longlegs's *body* as the source of his imprisonment. Here Chappell reveals another of the bases for his argument with the Puritan tradition—specifically, its Gnostic impulse. Although Christianity is in essence a religion of *incarnation,* historically it has often tended to emphasize the salvation of the soul while denigrating the body and the physical world. This emphasis has certainly been prominent in the otherworldliness of the Calvinist tradition that shaped religious attitudes in Protestant Appalachia. Many twentieth-century writers from the mountain South have expressed the desire for what Robert Morgan calls a "coming out from under Calvinism,"[37] an impulse evident in various ways in much of Chappell's work. That impulse may also account for Chappell's reference to *Dagon* as "a gnostic horror story,"[38] that is, a fiction in which the spirit or soul is overwhelmed by its incarceration in the physical world represented by the body. For Peter, in his lethargy and despair, the only escape from such imprisonment is death. For Chappell, however, the true nature of Peter's sickness is not his sense of imprisonment but his capitulation to the image of his impotence.

Peter's death is preceded by the painful tattooing of his body. While initially this activity gives him "the feeling of being new-made" (157), Peter eventually realizes that the effect of the tattoo's elaborate designs is to annul his identity, specifically his physical being. Staring at his reflection in a mirror, he notes, "His legs were still naked, untouched by the needle, but they were no longer his, no longer even supported his body. They looked irrelevant and alien, detachable. The remainder of his body was obliterated; it had been absorbed entirely into another manner of existence, a lurid placeless universe. . . . His body now was a river, was flowing away" (170). Peter's tattoos, Chappell has said, were meant to recall those of Queequeg in chapter 110 of *Moby-Dick* and the designs Queequeg carves on his coffin in imitation of his tattoos.[39] For Melville, those indecipherable hieroglyphics speak to the mystery of human existence; Ahab refers to them as the "devilish tantalization of the gods."[40] Seemingly fraught with import, Queequeg's tattoos and his carving invite interpretation—and baffle interpreters. Peter's tattoos, in contrast, are emblems not of elusive meaning but rather of annihilation of the self and of meaning; they testify to the void Peter confronts. "In the center of the world," thinks Peter, "was a fast deep iciness, pure recalcitrant cold, which could absorb the whole heat of the sun and every point of light; yearned after it" (160). In Dantean terms, what Peter envisions here is Cocytus and Satan, but whereas Dante locks Satan in that icy lake, subjecting him to the will of God, Peter unleashes Satan, surrendering to Mina, baring his throat to the knife she yields.

What Peter has lost is Puritanism's capacity to interpret the world and its events typologically. In the opening chapter of part 2 he tells Mina that in the past "every event that happened to me was a moral event. I could interpret it. And now I can't. It seems to me that a morality just won't attach any more; . . . no one thing seems to produce another. Things are what they are themselves, and that's all they are" (99). In such a passage Chappell sharply differentiates his protagonist's outlook not only from the Puritan sensibility but also from that of such nineteenth-century writers as Hawthorne and Emerson and Melville, among others, authors for whom moral issues and symbolic structures are integral to their work. Chappell's own views are closer to those of Hawthorne than to Peter Leland's. Just as Hawthorne and Melville expressed deep ambivalence about the Puritan legacy in the United States, so Chappell sees both strengths and weaknesses. In Peter Leland he creates a character who embraces only the grimmer features of Puritanism, including a version of its notion of Predestination. Reflecting, for instance, on his suffering at Mina's hands, Peter considers the possibility that it stems from retribution. "The idea of punishment formed in his mind, but the idea of the crime for which he was being punished would not come. It was not murder . . . no, not murder, but something more terrifying, something previous to anything he could ever remember, previous, he sometimes thought, maybe to his whole life" (127–28).

Fatalistic and passive as Peter becomes, he nevertheless retains a spark of humanity. Chappell seems unable—or unwilling—to deny Peter's capacity for moral judgment and compassion even when Peter is willing to jettison both. Amid his own debilitation, Peter is able to recognize the inadequacies of Coke Rymer and is even able to feel sympathy for Coke. At one point, too, Peter corrects his thought, "before the death of Sheila," to "before he had murdered her," thus showing his ability to make accurate self-assessments, however fleeting (158). Peter somehow manages to cling to "a last thin shard of integrity" (159) that he believes perplexes Mina. That vestige of integrity helps sustain him during his final confrontation with Dagon himself. Yet Peter has no will to live, no allegiance to life, and thus his self-assertion in the presence of Dagon seems a pyrrhic victory.

But Chappell's novel does not end with Peter's death. Instead the author includes a brief closing chapter, just four paragraphs long, in which Peter reviews his earthly life from "a new mode of existence." The effectiveness of this device—borrowed, Chappell says, from Chaucer's *Troilus and Criseyde*[41]—has been much debated. Peter Taylor, one of those to whom the book is dedicated, recommended that it be omitted, but Chappell chose to retain it: "I didn't have it in me to just leave [*Dagon*] in such a black, horrible shape as it was left at first," he once told an interviewer.[42] In the same interview Chappell described the painful three-year process of composition that *Dagon* required: "Halfway through the novel I had to stop to write the last chapter because I knew what I was getting into and I wanted to extend [the story line] somehow."[43] To allow Mina and her pagan deity the last word would have contradicted Chappell's most fundamental beliefs, for as he states about *Dagon* in another interview, "I don't finally believe in the triumph of evil in that way in the world."[44]

The final chapter of *Dagon* provides Peter with an afterlife in which he can comprehend, with utter if benevolent detachment, his earthly existence and the purpose of human suffering. "In an almost totally insentient cosmos only human feeling is interesting or relevant to what the soul searches for. . . . Suffering is the most expensive of human feelings, but it is the most intense and most precious of them, because suffering most efficiently humanizes the unfeeling universe" (175–76). In the novel's visionary closing paragraph Peter assumes the shape of Leviathan, sporting "upon the rich darkness that flows between the stars" (177). Such a visionary conclusion is ill suited, unfortunately, to the brutal naturalism of Peter's earlier moral disintegration. The final chapter fails to convince. Nor does it resolve the conflict between will and appetite that produces in Peter a sense of diseased or paralyzed volition.

Dagon, however, is a book not just about the decay of individual powers of will but also about the broader decay of cultural and religious values. Dagon is, after all, a pagan deity. The novel's title suggests not just the secularization of the modern world, the displacement of spiritual values by American materialism; it suggests the deification of those values, the substitution of one object of worship for another. Dagon's association with the fish may thus be meant to evoke, by contrast, Christianity's use of the fish as a symbol of Christ. In *Dagon* the reader finds Christianity's incarnational theology distorted in either one of two ways: by an immersion in physical appetites, in the sheer carnality represented by Mina (and by the sexual revolution of the era of the novel's composition), or by the Gnostic impulse that Chappell sees as a prominent part of America's Puritan legacy (along with Puritanism's "enervating sense of guilt" [40]). Only in the final chapter does Peter manage to transcend these two extremes. By then he is dead.

The Gaudy Place

In *Dagon* Chappell concedes, "I had taken the downer about as far as I could have taken it." But, he adds, *Dagon* was "one of those books you have to write whether you want to or not. I didn't want to, but having got past that novel my writing lightened up a lot."[45] Whatever the specific causes of this change in outlook, it produced *The Gaudy Place* (1973), a novel strikingly different in tone and structure. Like its predecessors, however, Chappell's fourth novel continued to explore time and causality and the relationship between will and appetite as well as between will and luck.

Set in Braceboro, North Carolina, a fictionalized version of Asheville as Chappell had experienced it in the 1950s, *The Gaudy Place* has an urban setting rather than the rural settings of *The Inkling* and *Dagon* and the portions of *It Is Time, Lord* set in the past. Its time frame is far more concentrated, for the book covers a period of just two days in early May. Four of the novel's five unnumbered sections are named for one of the five main characters (Arkie, Clemmie, Oxie, Andrew Harper), and Chappell has chosen those characters to provide a cross section of Asheville's social classes. The novel's central section, titled "Ignominy of a Skylark," focuses on Linn Harper, Andrew's seventeen-year-old son. A sixth major character, Andrew's wife's Uncle Zeb, appears in the final chapter. Thus in *The Gaudy Place* Chappell enlarges the scope of his fictional world, moving beyond a single extended family like James Christopher's or Jan Anderson's and beyond the claustrophobic psychological intensity of a novel like *Dagon,* narrated exclusively from Peter Leland's point of view. As Chappell comments, "This was the first and last time I tried to write what I considered a more or less conventional novel with a gallery of recognizable characters and in the mode of ordinary American romantic realism."[46]

The key terms in this remark are "more or less conventional" and "romantic realism." Chappell's shifts in point of view and in time, his ironic juxtaposition of two or more perspectives on the same character or event, and his flamboyant use of coincidence—all energize this novel, lending it an air of playfulness, freshness, and originality. Unlike *The Inkling* and *Dagon,* which originated, Chappell says, "from intellectual constructs first, and then I tried to choose elements of story . . . to fit those ideas,"[47] *The Gaudy Place* seems to have characterization and event at its center, with the novel's themes arising from the interplay of these two elements of fiction. The book reflects "romantic realism" insofar as it focuses on the dreams and aspirations of individuals who struggle to shape their lives in a clearly defined social milieu.

Readers inclined to distance themselves from the overwrought sensibility of Peter Leland or Jan Anderson are invited in the opening sentences of *The Gaudy Place* to engage with the life of the first of Chappell's five central characters. "Consider Arkie," the novel begins. "(But it breaks your heart.) Teacher used to tell him he didn't exist."[48] Chappell's direct address to the reader, his use of "your," and the cruelty and philosophical import of Teacher's remark immediately draw the reader into the novel. Arkie is a fourteen-year-old child of the streets, of Gimlet Street (Asheville's Lexington Avenue) specifically, an area of about fourteen blocks. Quick-witted, resourceful, energetic, Arkie supports himself by odd jobs and gambling, mainly the latter. Like Mark Twain's Jim Smiley, "Arkie would bet you." Arkie has mastered the pinball machines and other gaming devices on Gimlet Street, but he also sings and dances, composing impromptu poems and the lyrics to songs about escaping to Arkansas that have earned him his nickname. The book's opening chapter traces Arkie's activities throughout one Friday as he moves from bar to bar, pool hall to hole-in-the-wall café, scoring dimes, quarters, and occasionally dollars from the mules (farmers), gunghoes (soldiers), and other marks that frequent Gimlet Street. Chappell is extraordinarily successful in rendering Arkie's linguistic environment, the slang that shapes his experience of the world: "stab" (cigarette), "pieraker" (politician), "dump" (money), "mauds" (prostitutes).

Though Arkie is not planning to leave Gimlet Street, he is ambitious and longs for some "action" that will make him more

secure financially. In hopes of obtaining information about such
an opportunity, he asks Clemmie, one of the neighborhood's
whores, to inquire of her pimp, Oxie. Arkie is in love with Clemmie and believes that the upwardly mobile Oxie will soon abandon her to pursue his new, more legitimate position as a bail
bondsman. Arkie thus proposes that he become her pimp should
Oxie step aside, a proposal that outrages Clemmie; she prefers to
think of her "johns" as dates.

The plot of *The Gaudy Place* grows more complicated—
intentionally and comically so—with each shift in narrative point
of view. When Chappell turns to Clemmie in the novel's second
section, he again invites the reader to "Consider Clemmie. (Poor
speck of flotsam)" (31). The time is now Saturday, and Oxie has
come looking for Clemmie to collect his money. That noon when
Oxie finds Linn Harper in the Braceboro jail, Oxie's hope of
ingratiating himself with the well-to-do Harpers provides him
with the incentive to sever his ties with Clemmie. Unwilling to
let Arkie know that she has been cut free by Oxie, Clemmie fab-
ricates a story about a new pimp Oxie has arranged for her, an
older man with a reputation for beating women. Arkie immediately decides to borrow Clemmie's gun and seek out this new
pimp. There being no such person, it is Uncle Zeb whom Arkie
shoots when Uncle Zeb and Linn's father arrive to secure Linn's
release.

Much of the artistry and interest of this novel derives from
Chappell's skillful use of ironic comparisons and contrasts
among the book's five sections. The first two, devoted to Arkie
and Clemmie, are the shortest, and their brevity in relation to the
others suggests the more narrowly circumscribed lives that these

two characters lead. Neither character's past experiences are described in any detail, and of this pair only Arkie appears to give serious thought to the future. Arkie attempts to plan ahead, seeking a more lucrative scam, a larger piece of the action— though, as Chappell notes, "Vain hopes were what Arkie fed upon" (7). Arkie's illusions, however, seem utterly believable when compared to Clemmie's. At nineteen, Clemmie has been a prostitute for three years. Oxie describes her as "thin as a rifle barrel, "hatchet-faced," with hair "like long broomstraw, beaten and battered and frazzled" (114). Yet as Clemmie observes herself in her mirror, she thinks of herself as having "a model's figure, a model's face. Several times she's been thinking she might go into that. . . . She was young, after all, and she had her whole future before her. She was a live one" (32). The last statement runs in her mind like a leitmotif throughout section 2.

Oxie, the third character linked most directly to Gimlet Street, is in many respects an older, more successful version of Arkie. Unlike the Clemmie and Arkie sections, "Oxie" does not open with the word "Consider" as an imperative addressed to the reader but instead with the declarative sentence, "In the fond glass Oxie *considers* himself" (101; italics added). Oxie is thus set apart not only from Arkie and Clemmie but also from Linn Harper in section 3. The reader is not invited to feel the same degree of sympathy for or engagement with Oxie. Yet like Clemmie, Oxie appears before his mirror, gravely concerned with the image he conveys, convinced—as society daily confirms, implies Chappell—that appearance often counts more than substance. Chappell does provide a sketch of Oxie's past, for Oxie, unlike Arkie and Clemmie, has moved up the social ladder and now lives outside—literally above—the Gimlet Street neighborhood. But Oxie is haunted by a sense of insecurity, of vulnerability. He yearns to continue his ascent, insulating himself against what he thinks of as "the icy abysses" of past and future. His aim is to obliterate his past: "He would turn his back on this feverish gaudy place for good. He would have no connection, nothing there would ever touch his life again" (134).

The longing Oxie expresses reflects an all but archetypal impulse in American literature and in the American psyche—to turn one's back on the Old World and begin anew. When Oxie attempts to ingratiate himself with Andrew Harper, however, the bail bondsman's grammatical lapses reveal his lack of education. And when he gives Mr. Harper his telephone number, the two men discover that Oxie has written it on the back of a baseball tip sheet. Andrew has already identified Oxie as "a gambler" (140) and later refers to him as "our riverboat gambler" (148) in speaking to Mrs. Harper. Yet the novel's final scene—Arkie's shooting of Uncle Zeb—is the most obvious and delightfully ironic example of Oxie's inability simply to discard his past. Although Arkie and Oxie have never met, both know one another on sight, and Arkie identifies Uncle Zeb as Clemmie's new pimp only because Zeb is standing with Oxie—the first occasion on which Oxie and Zeb meet as well. Adding to these ironies is the fact that Arkie shoots Zeb with a gun *Oxie* has given to Clemmie.

Were Oxie's and Uncle Zeb's motives the only ones operating in *The Gaudy Place,* the novel might justify Dillard's assumption that it has "at its heart the deepest darkness of . . . all" of Chappell's early novels.[49] But at the center of this book Chappell

places seventeen-year-old Linn Harper. Unlike Arkie and Clemmie, Linn is a child of privilege. Arkie's and Clemmie's lives
stand in painful contrast to his. Chappell begins section 3 with the
directive, "Consider the Skylark Society," and then asks, "In a
flint-tough pragmatic world is there even a tiny niche where idealism may survive?" (61). The Skylark Society, the reader
quickly learns, had been organized by Linn three years earlier—
the same number of years, significantly, that Clemmie has been a
prostitute. Named for a spaceship, the Skylark Society had originally brought together nine boys with an interest in science fiction. The local newspaper had done a Sunday feature on the group
under the headline, "YOUNG SKYLARKS LOOK TO
FUTURE" (68). Such a headline reinforces the reader's sense of
the vistas of opportunity that await these privileged members of
society in contrast to Arkie and Clemmie and Oxie. Clemmie, in
fact, flatly rejects "that future stuff." "Anything can happen, but I
don't believe in it," she adds (36). The original membership of the
Skylark Society had dwindled as Linn encouraged the group to
read more widely, first in scientific writing and then in modern literature. By the Friday of time present, the day on which Arkie's
section also begins, the society has just three members. As Chappell notes, not wholly ironically, "Our modern age is one of wan-
ing faith, nervous apostasy, and it is filled with distracting
enticements toward the unreflective life" (61).

The diction and syntax of such a sentence clearly differentiate it from the sections devoted to Arkie and Clemmie. The same
is true of the reading and the analysis of ideas that draw Linn and
his friends together, as well as of the boys' sense of a mutually
supportive social and economic environment. But Chappell con-

nects Linn to Arkie and Clemmie and Oxie and Uncle Zeb by having the three remaining members of the Skylark Society, at what becomes their final meeting, debate the implications of Camus's *The Stranger*. As a result of this debate, fueled in Linn's case alone by eight beers, Linn offers to perform a "gratuitous act," like Camus's Mersault, by stealing a twenty-five-pound bag of chicken feed from a warehouse. During the attempt, he is arrested and jailed, but he refuses to divulge his name. Thus he is still locked up on Saturday noon when Oxie appears at the jail. Recognizing Linn from the photograph that accompanied the newspaper story about the Skylark Society, Oxie believes his fortune made.

While the events and logic that lead to Linn's arrest are absurd, enhancing the novel's comedy, the boy's experiences in jail force him to recognize that his imagination has failed him. The fights and the brawl he witnesses there are a microcosm of the social struggle prevailing outside the jail. But Linn, unlike Oxie or Uncle Zeb, is motivated less by appetite or will than by a "loyalty to ideas" (165), as his father puts it. Such loyalty may be a luxury the residents of Gimlet Street can ill afford, but Chappell shows, through Linn and his father, its continuing claims on the human imagination. Andrew Harper senses a "kinship" with his son in their "abstract double allegiance to an idea of justice" (139) that largely accounts for Andrew's reluctance to ask Zeb to assist with Linn's release.

Although Chappell suffuses his portrait of Linn with irony, especially when the boy envisions spending the rest of his life as a criminal, in and out of jail, and thinks of that prospect as "something exhilarating, . . . a new idea of freedom" (97), Chap-

pell also uses Linn to satirize the existentialist notion of a gratuitous act, insisting instead on the ethical implications of human
conduct. The epigraph to *The Gaudy Place* is used ironically to
raise just this issue. That epigraph, taken from Yeats's play *Purgatory,* reads: "What's right and wrong? My grand-dad got the
girl and the money." As a result of the experiences Linn has, he
seems poised to seek the deeply consequential in human action.
Despite his youth and folly, the world Linn inhabits is larger than
that of any of the other characters. In contrast to Oxie, who sees
Gimlet Street as a "feverish gaudy place" he longs to escape,
Linn uses his powers of imagination to envision a world of
immense possibility. For Linn, it is "the universe" itself that is "a
gaudy place in which to live" (64).

The final section of the novel, narrated by Linn's father, also
contributes to the reader's sense that *The Gaudy Place* is more
than an ironic portrait of what one critic has called "Six Characters in Search of an Illusion."[50] Whereas the preceding section
opens with Oxie considering his image in a mirror, Andrew's
begins with questions about parenthood and thus about human
relationships that necessitate a sense of responsibility. "Is there
anyone who honestly considers himself a good parent? Is there
anyone who has a viable notion of what that phrase *good parent*
means?" (139). The capacity for moral self-examination implicit
in such questions contrasts with Oxie's attention to his physical
appearance. Andrew's actions in the final section, unlike Uncle
Zeb's, are prompted by love and respect for Linn. Zeb is motivated more by the desire to flex his political muscle—and to curb
Oxie's. In this respect, it should be noted, Andrew's motives
resemble those of Arkie in the novel's closing scene. Just before

Andrew describes the shooting, he informs the reader, "I cannot know the causes and mechanics of the event" (176). Thanks, however, to Chappell's careful structuring of this novel, the reader can. It is not just a privileged character like Linn who is capable of acting selflessly. Despite Arkie's constricted economic circumstances, it is love, not greed or lust, that causes him to act on Clemmie's behalf. The consequences of his action are likely to be grim, foreclosing his immediate future on Gimlet Street, but he manages to transcend the polarities of will and appetite that beset Jan Anderson and Peter Leland as well as the material values represented by Oxie and Uncle Zeb. While ironies abound in *The Gaudy Place,* including the fact that Clemmie never recognizes Arkie's love for her, the novel diverges from the nearly nihilistic vision of *Dagon* and moves toward the comic celebration of love and life in *Midquest.*

Yet *The Gaudy Place* also reflects Chappell's awareness of the ways that chance and circumstance affect individual freedom. The Arkie who is lucky on Friday has the course of his life dramatically altered for the worse by his shooting of Zeb on Saturday; the Clemmie who imagines that she has everything going precisely as it should and who believes, "You can trust Oxie" (42), has her life overturned by what Oxie perceives as his own stroke of good fortune; and that good fortune, in turn, literally explodes in Oxie's face as his Gimlet Street past returns to haunt him when Arkie shoots Zeb, an act based on Clemmie's lie and on Arkie's mistaken assumption that Zeb is a pimp. Like *The Inkling, The Gaudy Place* shows that the human will is often subject to influences beyond its control. Yet in the latter novel those influences do not originate in the destructive appetites represented by Lora's sexual power over Jan, Mina's lust, or Peter's thirst for whiskey. They arise, at least in part, from Arkie's love for Clemmie and the parental affection that leads Andrew to bring Zeb and Oxie together in the jail's parking lot. Hopes and intentions go awry, but not in irreversible ways. Uncle Zeb is only wounded, not dead. For Arkie and Oxie the repercussions of this event will be more profound, but that differential impact is a measure of the structures of class advantage that *The Gaudy Place* explores. The portrait of Arkie, the novel's most vivid character, enlists the reader's sympathy and reflects Chappell's conception of the moral powers of literature. Similarly, Linn and Andrew Harper, whose surname links them to the Homeric bard or minstrel, embody powers of imagination capable of fostering such sympathy.

The novel's design encourages the reader to develop a more comprehensive outlook on society. The book's five-part structure, Chappell has said, is meant "to show that all the [social] classes are intertwined, that they affect one another's destinies."[51] (The arrangement of the first four sections—with their alternating focus on Friday, Saturday, Friday, and Saturday—also indicates the interpenetration of past, present, and future.) Chappell's shifts in point of view heighten the reader's consciousness of the need to examine the world from multiple perspectives. Those shifts, likewise, reveal how often people misinterpret the thoughts and feelings and motives of others, as Zeb mistakes Linn's motive for his attempted crime. *The Gaudy Place* humanizes Gimlet Street and its residents. No one who has read carefully the first two sections can share the detachment from the neighborhood that Andrew expresses in the novel's final section, especially not when Andrew observes a nameless (to him), drunken prostitute whom the reader recognizes as Clemmie. The book thus cultivates the reader's social conscience, in part by reminding readers of the role good fortune plays in human affairs. Americans may prefer to think of the United States as a meritocracy, where hard work earns people rewards, but *The Gaudy Place* demonstrates that individuals enter society differentially advantaged not only by heredity but also by social class, race, and gender, in fact by the status of the very family into which each happens to be born. It is surely no accident that the only character whose section bears a surname as well as a given name is Andrew's. Arkie, Clemmie, and Oxie, in effect, have no family on whose resources they can depend. Andrew, in contrast, does—and, consequently, so does Linn, whose section need not even bear his name, just as Linn need not reveal his name at the jail and yet is still recognized by the police as coming "from a good family" (88).

It is not always adherence to the principles of the work ethic that assures one's social position or economic success, as Chappell knows well from the arduous labor for little pay that attends farming. Arkie is uneducated but hard working, as is Oxie. Yet neither advances significantly on the social ladder. Unlike them, Linn can afford to play—to skylark—because of his family's economic position. Nor is his attempted robbery likely to have any lasting effect on his life, in contrast to Arkie's shooting of Zeb. The good fortune of social position is among the forms of luck this novel depicts, and it bears little resemblance to the luck that Arkie woos in his section of the book.

FABLES OF WILL AND APPETITE

The Gaudy Place marks a pivotal moment in Chappell's career. In the novel's comic tone, its carefully wrought design, its variety of characters, and its larger social scope, the book anticipates the poetic universe of *Midquest.* If, as Dabney Stuart has said, Chappell's first three novels reflect "a descent into the maelstrom it appears now to have been necessary [for the novelist] to hazard and survive,"[52] *The Gaudy Place* traces its author's ascent toward an artistic vision grounded in comedy and in a profound sense of community. "My first three novels," Chappell has said, "have hard, tough, private things, and I wanted to get away from that."[53] In *The Gaudy Place* and the poetry and fiction he wrote during the 1970s and subsequent decades, Chappell accomplished that goal.

CHAPTER THREE

Shaping the Self in Poetry
The World between the Eyes and Midquest

By the time Chappell's first book of poems, *The World between the Eyes,* appeared in 1971, the author had already published three novels and had completed a draft of his fourth. Yet despite the variety of fictional forms in which he has worked, Chappell's first allegiance has always been to poetry, which he calls a "nobler sort of art" than fiction.[1] "It's enormously more fun writing poetry than fiction and nonfiction," he told an interviewer, "because of the concentration on themes and on language, particularly language. . . . It's also more difficult."[2] That challenge is one he has successfully embraced in ten book-length collections of poems as well as three chapbooks.[3]

Chappell's poetics derives from the organicism first espoused in American literature by Ralph Waldo Emerson, for whom the poem originates in "a thought so passionate and alive that, like the spirit of a plant or an animal, it has an architecture of its own, and adorns nature with a new thing."[4] As Chappell puts it, "Every work of art . . . creates its own separate aesthetic laws, the way in which it's to be understood. I think that really means that it must have created its own special way to be written if it's a genuine work of art."[5] Chappell has repeatedly avowed his commitment to the Horatian aims of literature, to entertain and to instruct, and has said that "the only important considerations" in assessing a poem or a book of poems "[are] that it be beautiful, honest, and interesting—that is, that it intrigue the mind or affect the feelings."[6] These aesthetic principles help to account for the range of forms that readers encounter in Chappell's poetry as well as the varied styles he uses. Chappell has often written in free verse, not just in traditional forms, while the range of such forms, especially in *Midquest,* demonstrates his mastery of poetic craft and technique. As for the absence of a distinctive poetic style in his work, Chappell has commented: "I'm not interested in creating a fixed poetic style for myself, but [in] matching each separate poem to the subject matter. I deliberately try to be as fluid as possible."[7]

Yet another important aesthetic principle governing Chappell's collections of poetry is his assumption that a book of poems should form a whole and not be simply a gathering of discrete individual poems. The four books that compose *Midquest,* each of them organized around one of the four classical elements, exhibit such unity, as does the text as a whole, which is subtitled *A Poem. Castle Tzingal* (1984) certainly has such unity, as do, in varying degrees, each of his subsequent volumes, whether the book's impression of wholeness results from similarity of themes and motifs, as in *Source* (1985); similarity of subject matter and approach, as in *First and Last Words* (1989); or similarity of poetic form, as in the epigrams of *C* (1993). Chappell's most important precursor in this regard is Charles Baudelaire's *Fleurs du mal.* "Baudelaire said," Chappell told an interviewer, "if you have twenty-four poems, the order of the poems makes up the twenty-fifth poem; that is, the design of the whole book is a poem itself."[8]

The World between the Eyes

It is for the absence of such design, among other flaws, that Chappell has criticized *The World between the Eyes,* calling it "weak in conception and execution."[9] Yet while it is true that the thirty-seven poems collected in this initial volume lack the structural unity and the refinement of Chappell's later poetic compositions, the book contains a number of poems, as Kathryn Stripling Byer has noted, "which are [among] the most intense in contemporary poetry, almost overwhelming in their obsessive imagery and unrelenting rhythms."[10] These qualities are especially notable in the eight longer narrative poems that fill nearly half of the book's pages. In fact those eight poems—"February," "The World between the Eyes," "The Farm," "The Father," "The Mother," "Tin Roof Blues," "Sunday," and "The Dying"— though often separated from one another by shorter lyric poems, can usefully be read as a sequence. Taken together, they provide an insightful portrait of the artist as child and young man, and they thus anticipate both the narrative structure of many of *Midquest*'s poems and some of that later volume's major subjects, themes, images, and stances.

The World between the Eyes opens with "February," a poem that vividly describes, in a syntax often disjointed and a free verse that frequently employs an iambic base, a hog killing. This subject matter situates poet and reader squarely in the rural environment so typical of Chappell's work. The poem's events are presented from the perspective of "the boy," a semiautobiographical point of view to which Chappell returns not only in much of *Midquest* but also in *I Am One of You Forever* and the other Kirkman novels. The child's ambivalence toward the hog killing is captured in such phrases as "dismayed / With delight" and "elated-drunk / With the horror."[11] The communal dimension of this activity is one of its most important features, for Chappell seeks to locate the reader not only in proximity to the natural world but also in relationships with others. Nature, through this "most unlikely prodigious pig" (5), affords the family both food and an occasion for affirming friendship and interdependence.

One of Chappell's pervasive poetic concerns has been his resistance to the self-absorption that characterizes so much contemporary poetry, the retreat into the individual psyche that marked the confessional poetry of the late 1950s and 1960s. Despite this concern, the longer narrative poems of *The World between the Eyes* do indeed record the efforts of "the child" to achieve individuation, self-identity. The title poem emphasizes the issue of subjectivity and the child's struggle for selfhood by opening with the boy imagining a scene of troops preparing for battle. Casting himself in the role of "the Swarthy Spy" who "hones a talent for precision" in his reports (12), the child becomes an emblem of the adult poet.

The title of this collection highlights the role that mind and imagination play in shaping the world. But the title also recalls the phrase "a bullet between the eyes," thereby reinforcing the child's sense of being menaced by the world, of being embattled. It is significant that these narrative poems begin with a hog killing and end, in "The Dying," with the death of the boy's sister, while including in "The Father" the child's contemplation of suicide. Death haunts many of these poems, as it haunted Chappell's first three novels. The book's title is open to a third interpretation as well. The world between the eyes is also a world shared among various I's—that is, shared among different people (families, communities) and shared among the different selves (or different voices) that contribute to a single individual's identity. The child shares his world with his ancestors, with the past, as he wanders "the house of his fathers," "rooms of his fathers" (12). He shares it with his father and mother, with the inhabitants of Canton (in "Tin Roof Blues"), with the religious community in which his parents immerse him (in "Sunday"), with his dying sister, and with the natural phenomena portrayed in "The Farm." That poem too, as it moves from the work required by summer haying to the paralysis of winter, is shadowed by death: "Stupor of cold wide stars" (20), "The world, locked bone" (21).

To make a place for himself in such a world, the developing poet must master his memories, must overcome the stasis they often induce, and must come to recognize, like James Christopher of *It Is Time, Lord,* the resources they offer. Even more importantly, he must achieve a vision of the future, grounding that future in an accurate understanding of his past. Over against "things that bloom and burn," the child sets "words [that] bloom / and burn" (13) and embraces "his duty to read aright, / To know" (14). Surrounded by "signs" and filled with a sense of time "charged past endurance with the future" (14), the child of the title poem nevertheless realizes that "he's blest in his skins, an old stone / House, and a sky eaten up with stars" (15). Time and eternity are yoked in the images of house and star, and brooding on both is the figure of the developing poet.

Though Chappell grounds these narrative poems in the rural and in family, he does not idealize either of those subjects. The seasonal progression from summer to winter in "The Farm" makes this attitude clear, as does the difficulty of the work portrayed. The child's relationships with his father and mother, presented in two consecutive poems, the latter at the virtual midpoint of the book, reveal a similar ambivalence. The father's judgmental stance mirrors that of James Christopher's father in the "January" episodes of *It Is Time, Lord.* Yet the boy's success in fulfilling the task his father assigns—to discover a new spring to replenish the family's water supply—leads the child to a renewed sense of life's possibilities. Having rejected the temptation to commit suicide, he feels like "someone who's lived through his death, come out grinning, / Mind surcharged with the future" (27). While this easy confidence is treated ironically, the child does acquire a new sense of equanimity.

Although the boy's mother promptly shatters that equanimity, he is able to restore it, and what makes his resilience possible is humor—humor and a hard-won capacity for detachment. Significantly, it is precisely such a discovery of the usefulness of humor that helped effect the transition in Chappell's fiction from the gloom of *Dagon* to the lighter tone of *The Gaudy Place,* not to mention the broad comedy of many of the poems in *Midquest* and of many of the characters and events in the Kirkman tetralogy. What Chappell says of humor in Carolyn Kizer's poetry seems applicable to his own increasing reliance on humor after the publication of *Dagon:* "Kizer seems to look upon humor as one of the most welcome parts of her personal, as well as her human, heritage. It is for her not only necessary for balance and tolerance, it is a necessity for survival."[12]

For the child in "The Mother," it is humor that enables him to triumph over hatred and rage. Storming out of the house, he longs to "squash it from sight with his palm" (29). Rejecting that option, he retreats to the woods to consider others. Yet the very shapes of his fantasies subvert their appeal: "Could live in the woods and eat bugs! / Or, handily build Snug Cabin, chink it with mud / . . . // Could murder his mother, conquer the world! / Or, rob banks and live rich on the loot" (30). By acknowledging the absurdity of his fantasies, the child manages to return home.

In this poem at the midpoint of Chappell's first book of poetry, the child-poet comes to recognize that the function of the imagination is not to evade reality but to confront it and to illuminate it. The world between the eyes emerges from and engages with the world those eyes observe, not a world they invent. Chappell's later short stories and novels and poems reveal his penchant for fantasy, but it is fantasy in the service of a deeper understanding of life, not fantasy as an alternative to lived social experience. The child in "The Mother" returns home, "his pace . . . deliberately fashioned." Unlike the figure in this volume's "Face to Face," who, standing at his door, decides that "he'll sleep the ditch tonight" (22), the child-poet "stops to take the measure of the family door. / And then he enters" (31). As Byer says of "The Father" and "The Mother," "Each poem concludes with a real, earned breakthrough into a life-sustaining vision."[13] The return home that the latter poem records becomes the pivotal event in the poet's psychological and artistic development.

The eight longer narrative poems in *The World between the Eyes* are linked by repeated images and phrases; by their narrative structure; by the themes of time, mortality, family ties, and the function of the imagination; and, most importantly, by the figure of the boy or young man who appears in each of them.

Although the poems are not presented as a sequence, they can profitably be read as one. Yet as the striking contrast between the endings of "Face to Face" and "The Mother" shows, Chappell has also established connections between several of the shorter poems in this volume and the longer narrative poems as well as connections among some of the shorter poems. Three poems on the poet's son, Heath, for example, serve as a bridge between the title poem and "The Farm," depicting Heath's wrestling with the world of objects and his efforts to acquire a language expressive of his needs and feelings. Five witty poems on baseball are grouped together, illustrating Chappell's skill with figurative language and apt allusions as well as his sense of humor, but those poems fail to contribute to a sense of underlying unity in the book as a whole. Nevertheless, as Byer remarks, "What continues to fascinate any reader of *The World between the Eyes* is the range of voice, tone, and style the book displays."[14]

Such range has become one of the hallmarks of Chappell's achievement, not only in poetry but also in fiction. In other ways too *The World between the Eyes* adumbrates his later poetic forms, themes, and techniques. The ease with which he moves, for instance, from free verse to a variety of rhyme schemes, meters, and stanza structures is amply evident. His extensive use of narratives that focus on childhood memories and experiences provides another example of the continuity between this initial book of poems and his later work. Even the place names in some of these early narrative poems—Smathers Hill, Wind River— either reappear in *Midquest* or anticipate that book's dominant images. The allusiveness of Chappell's poetry, along with its philosophical concerns, is also evident at many points, starting with the volume's second poem, "A Transcendental Idealist Dreams in Springtime," a poem dedicated to James Applewhite. That allusiveness marks even the opening and closing lines of "Third Base Coach," with its references to the ghost of Hamlet's father and to Aeschylean tragedy. Chappell's willingness to address such seemingly unpoetic material and to dignify the products of popular culture is also apparent in a poem like "Weird Tales," with its celebration of the practitioners of horror stories and science fiction. In form, moreover, "Weird Tales" is an epistolary poem, addressed to R. H. W. Dillard, and it thus looks forward to the four letter-poems that play a crucial role in *Midquest.*

Chappell chose to reprint only four poems from *The World between the Eyes* in *The Fred Chappell Reader,* but he selected ten of them (at times greatly revised) for inclusion in *Spring Garden.* While some of the poems—"Erasures," "Guess Who," "The Survivors," and "Northwest Airlines," among others—are indeed slight, a number of the poems remain of interest both for their insights into the poet's later development and for their own artistic merit.

Midquest

In the title poem of *The World between the Eyes,* the narrator remarks of the child-poet, "Of the elements his is water" (14). It was, in fact, to water that Chappell turned in composing his next book of poems, *River* (1975), the first volume of what was to become *Midquest* (1981), his semiautobiographical epic, "something like a verse novel," as he notes in the preface to that book.[15]

Chappell has traced the genesis of *Midquest* to "Familiar Poem,"
first published in *The Archive* while he was a student at Duke.[16]
But he didn't begin working on this material consciously, he
says, until May 28, 1971, his thirty-fifth birthday, when he was
preparing *The World between the Eyes* for publication. Early on
Chappell realized the potential scope of this new body of material: "By the time I'd written the second poem [in *River*] . . . I saw
the shape of the whole thing. Not the exact structure but the
shape of it."[17] Asked by an interviewer, "How old were you when
you found the grain [of your poetic sensibility] and kept going
with it?" Chappell responded, "I was thirty-five. . . . I started
writing *Midquest.* It became important to me. And that became
the theme of the book—to take stock and change directions."[18]
To another interviewer Chappell remarked, "The whole poem,
Midquest, is about rebirth."[19]

Now widely recognized as what Patrick Bizzaro calls "the
structural and thematic centerpiece of Chappell's poetic achievement thus far,"[20] *Midquest* is an extraordinarily ambitious, com-
plexly structured, deeply humane book. Some five thousand
lines in length, it gathers together the four previously published
volumes *River, Bloodfire* (1978), *Wind Mountain* (1979), and
Earthsleep (1980). Each of those volumes consists of eleven
poems, with each volume organized around one of the four elements—water, fire, air, and earth—that Pythagoras and other
ancient philosophers viewed as fundamental to all life. Chappell
allows each of these elements to assume a variety of meanings
and also has them interact with and upon one another, as when
he describes "the burning river of this morning / That earth and
wind overtake" (187) or speaks of "the morning flush of loosed

wind-spirit, exhalation / Of fire-seed and gusty waters and of every dirt" (98). In *Bloodfire* alone, the image of fire is linked to dawn, to a Rimbaudian derangement of the senses, to the Ku Klux Klan's cross burnings, to sexual desire, to spiritual longing, to Pentecost and the Christian symbolism associated with the Holy Spirit, to hellfire, to the violence of war, to martyrdom (political as well as religious), to hearth and home, to the fevers of physical illness, to natural disasters, to Lucretius's *ignis semina* as building blocks of the physical world, to illumination or revelation, to alcohol ("firewater"), to "fire / As symbolic of tortured, transcendent-striving will" (85), and to many other objects and significations. A similar multiplicity of meanings attaches to the other elements, allowing the poet enormous latitude for the exercise of his ingenuity while at the same time insuring a comprehensive and comprehensible focus for the book.

In addition to using the four elements as a unifying device within and between volumes, Chappell conjoins the four books that comprise *Midquest* in a number of other ways. Each volume opens, for instance, with the poet-narrator (Ole Fred) in bed with his wife, Susan, on the morning of his thirty-fifth birthday, and each volume closes with the couple back in bed. Susan likewise appears in at least one other poem in each volume. Ole Fred's grandparents and parents speak at length in various narrative poems throughout the four volumes. Yet another unifying character is Virgil Campbell, the country storekeeper first introduced in *It Is Time, Lord.* One poem in each of *Midquest*'s four volumes is devoted to Virgil, "who is supposed to give to the whole," Chappell states in the preface, "its specifically regional, its Appalachian, context" (x). Each volume also contains a lengthy stream-of-consciousness poem that meditates on such philosophical issues as the relationship between body and mind, flesh and spirit, time and eternity; and each volume contains a poem that portrays a natural disaster appropriate to the element around which that book is organized: a flood, a fire, a hurricane, and in *Earthsleep* death itself. Similarly helping to unify all four volumes are Chappell's varied allusions to and echoes of Dante's *Divine Comedy,* with its quest for moral and spiritual rebirth at the midpoint of one's life. The motif of pilgrimage is implicit throughout *Midquest,* as is Thoreau's idea that "morning is moral reform" (101). Chappell subtitles *Midquest* "A Poem," thus indicating the unity of impression to which the work aspires, and which, I believe, it achieves—a unity amidst astonishing and engaging variety. The careful design of the book infuses in the reader a sense both of order and of the richness of life's possibilities; yet *Midquest* never slights the struggles that are required to attain and sustain such a vision.

Chappell's preface to *Midquest* indicates a great deal about the author's intentions and about the book's design. The preface has generated some controversy, however, because of several inconsistencies between Chappell's statements there and the book's actual structure. Chappell notes, for example, that the sixth poem in each volume is devoted to Virgil Campbell, when in fact Virgil appears in the seventh poem of *Bloodfire* and the eighth poem of *Wind Mountain.* Likewise, Chappell claims that "the fifth poem in each [volume] is given to stream of consciousness" (x), though it seems clear that it is the fourth poem in *Earthsleep,* "The Peaceable Kingdom of Emerald Windows," that parallels the narrator's stream-of-consciousness meditations in *Midquest*'s first three volumes. Chappell also explains in the preface that "each of the volumes (except *Wind Mountain*) is organized as a balancing act. The first poem is mirrored by the last; the second by the next to last, and so on inward" (ix). Although Randolph Paul Runyon has traced many of these parallels, they ultimately seem far less significant than the narrative and thematic momentum of the book as it moves forward through the poems in a given volume and through the entire text. As Runyon himself concedes, "*Midquest* is probably as rich in sequential echoes as it is in symmetrical ones."[21]

Chappell's preface is more useful, it seems to me, in its comments on the poet's general intentions than on the book's details of design. Chappell characterizes *Midquest,* for instance, as "a reactionary work," one that aimed "to restore . . . qualities sometimes lacking in the larger body of contemporary poetry: detachment, social scope, humor, portrayal of character and background, discursiveness, wide range of subject matter" (x). The longer version of the preface that appeared in *The Small Farm*, a year prior to *Midquest*'s publication, helps to clarify to what and to whom the poet was reacting. There he indicates his dissatisfaction both with the autobiographical lyric and with the long poem as represented by Ezra Pound's *Cantos,* William Carlos Williams's *Paterson,* Charles Olson's *Maximus Poems,* Louis Zukovsky's *A,* and Hart Crane's *The Bridge.* These long poems he faults for their "structural failures" as they "limn down to lyric moments stuck together with the bland glue of raw data."[22] It is within the tradition of the long poem that Chappell places *Midquest,* and his achievement within that tradition is truly extraordinary. *Midquest* combines lyric, narrative, and meditative poems to create a larger structure that derives from the epic, most obviously Dante's *Divine Comedy.*

The title of one of Chappell's book reviews, reprinted in *A Way of Happening,* indicates his assessment of the contemporary long poem—"Piecework: The Longer Poem Returns." In that review he speaks of the "mosaic structures" rather than "extended wholes" that the majority of American long poems offer.[23] One of the consequences of such structures, as he points out in *Plow Naked,* is that "whatever the subject matter of the modern epic, and whatever the ostensible and announced themes, three secondary themes will inevitably be articulated[:] . . . disintegration, disconnection, and loneliness."[24] According to Chappell, "It is a wild connect-the-dots scheme, this construction of the contemporary epic," and he contrasts the fragmentation of perception and structure in such works with Homer's "faith that in fashioning a plot from all the random matter [of his world], he would find meaning, and a truth that would have value."[25] In *Midquest* the poet has striven for a sense of design, an architecture, in which "each part supports every other and a homogeneity of interest results."[26] While the resulting poem clearly lacks the narrative flow of *The Odyssey* or *The Aeneid,* it tries to recover the "sense of community with the people of the past" so often absent from the contemporary epic.[27] Instead of portraying Ole Fred in terms of disconnection and loneliness, Chappell presents him as rooted in family and place and as representative of both the folk culture of the Appalachian South and the formal literary culture of the university. The social dimension of Chappell's poetic vision cannot be overemphasized. As Robert Morgan has remarked: "There is an assumption of community in all [Chappell's] work, a sense of belonging not just to a family and a place . . . but also to the terrain of history. It is a community in time that is implied and evoked, a world of parents and ancestors both literal and literary."[28]

Chappell's reservations about the contemporary autobiographical lyric, like his reservations about the modern epic, stem from its loss of community, its creation of intensely private, fragmentary modes of consciousness. He also criticizes such lyrics for their "attenuation of subject matter" and their "phony mysticism, the substitution of excited language for hard-won perception."[29] Shaped by "the Symbolist prescription that the poet should be a seer, a prophet," the autobiographical lyric, in Chappell's opinion, has reinforced the Romantic notion of the poet as social outsider, as social outcast. Too often, then, he adds, "The subject matter to be perceived lay on or beyond the outer borders of common experience."[30]

Chappell's rejection of this last assumption pervades *Midquest.* As Henry Taylor has written, "*Midquest* is a poem celebrating the world most of us live in and the play of mind and language over it."[31] It is to human beings' ordinary yet remarkable relationships and experiences that Ole Fred turns in his portraits of his grandparents, parents, spouse, and friends. The sense of community is fundamental to the book, and that community extends well beyond the mountain setting of Ole Fred's childhood. Similarly, the self the poet portrays is not simply—or even primarily—an autobiographical self. While the figure of Ole Fred borrows heavily from the author's personal experiences, he is meant to be, like Dante the pilgrim or Walt Whitman's persona, "widely representative" (x). Chappell seeks not the novelties of private moments of illumination but the revelations that result from engagement with tradition and with other people. He resists entrapment in the isolated ego and rejects elitist conceptions of art; instead he situates the reader in a vivid social milieu and draws upon the oral tradition and folk materials to underscore his imagination's democratic inclusiveness. As the poet told an interviewer while the book was still in progress, "Although [*Midquest*] is autobiographical, in many ways, the last thing I want it to be about is the self. . . . And a sense of history, a sense of tradition, is one way to get away from the extremely *personal* tone of so much present-day poetry."[32]

While dissociating himself from the intensely subjective autobiographical lyric, Chappell does not—despite his disclaimer in the preface—sacrifice "intensity, urgency, metaphysical trial, emotional revelation" (x). Such qualities are regularly present in *Midquest,* particularly in the opening and closing poems of each volume and in Ole Fred's stream-of-consciousness meditations, but they occur within the larger context of the relationships, the extended sense of community and tradition, that the poem explores. Nor does Chappell abandon the idea of the poet as a seer, though he employs other conceptions of the poet's identity as well in order to recover for poetry the breadth of subject matter it enjoyed in pre-Symbolist eras. Spiritual vision is crucial to *Midquest,* a text in which Chappell affirms what he has called the traditional role of the poet "as celebrator of divinity and of the created objects of the universe."[33] As seer, Ole Fred embraces both body and spirit, sings the physical world without neglecting "the Mountains Outside Time" (169), and wonders whether the "Earthly Paradise" isn't already "among our amidst" (177). The meditative poems in each volume are especially imbued with visionary insights, which manifest themselves at many other points in *Midquest* too.

Part of what distinguishes this book from Chappell's earlier work is its attitude toward the past. For James Christopher of *It Is Time, Lord,* the past was filled with memories of his father's misjudgment of him and memories of burning down his grandparents' house. For Peter Leland of *Dagon,* the weight of the past meant bondage to Mina and ensnarement in a degrading religious cult. Even for "the child" of the narrative poems in *The World between the Eyes,* the past is often tormenting as he struggles to come to terms with his father and mother, with his sense of alienation from community and church in "Tin Roof Blues" and "Sunday," and with the death of his sister. For Ole Fred, however, as well as for his author, the past is a valuable resource, a strong foundation upon which to build. As Chappell says of his persona in the preface to *Midquest,* "He is cut off from his disappearing cultural traditions but finds them, in remembering, his real values" (x). Yet Chappell does not idealize or romanticize that past. The "Georgic center" of Chappell's poetry, in Don Johnson's phrase,[34] may be the farm, but like the Roman poet Virgil, Chappell is keenly aware of the hardships of agrarian living, especially on hardscrabble mountain farms, as a poem like "My Father Washes His Hands" demonstrates. Chappell is not a neo-Agrarian, but he does find in farming a meaningful—though not financially rewarding—lifestyle, one that heightens recognition of humanity's dependence on nature and that encourages both humility and a sense of stewardship. As he declares in his essay, "Poet and Plowman," "[Farming] is the one life besides poetry and natural philosophy that still touches an essential harmony of things, and when a civilization discards that way of life, it breaks the most fundamental covenant mankind can remember."[35] In *Midquest* farming also becomes a metaphor for the cultivation of the physical world that eventuates in spiritual vision. For Chappell, immersion in the physical world, not flight from it, leads to religious insight.

The agrarian tradition is only one dimension of the past that the poet celebrates in *Midquest*. Memories of his grandparents and parents as well as of Virgil Campbell elicit some of the book's most humorous and affectionate poems. Often those poems are monologues spoken by the characters themselves, though a younger Fred may serve as interlocutor. It is in such narrative poems as "My Grandmother Washes Her Feet," "My Father Allergic to Fire," "Firewater," "My Mother Shoots the Breeze," "My Father's Hurricane," and "Three Sheets in the Wind: Virgil Campbell Confesses" that Chappell utilizes most effectively the oral tradition of his native Appalachia. At the same time, these narrative poems, with their vivid characters and incidents and their use of traditional folk materials, were inspired, Chappell says, by his admiration for Chaucer's achievement in *The Canterbury Tales*.[36]

The humor of the oral tradition—especially that distinctively American art form, the tall tale—had a major impact on the development of nineteenth-century literature in the United States, most notably in the writing of George Washington Harris and Mark Twain. Chappell's reading of both authors is apparent on more than one occasion in *Midquest* (and throughout the Kirkman tetralogy). Ole Fred's father's account of the multilay-

ered windstorm in "My Father's Hurricane," for instance, originates in the Washoe Zephyr that Twain describes in chapter 21
of *Roughing It.* And Harris's Sut Lovingood puts words in Virgil Campbell's mouth—"*Feet don't fail me now*"—in "Three
Sheets in the Wind."[37]

Such borrowings and the frequent literary, musical, philosophical, and religious allusions in *Midquest* attest to the poet's
celebration of the past and to the inclusiveness of his sense of
community. His use of Dante's pilgrimage motif and other Dantean materials further affirms the continuity between past and
present, as do the epigraphs he chooses for each of the book's
four volumes, epigraphs taken from Melville, René Char, Dante,
and Hawthorne, respectively. Of this group, only Char represents
the twentieth century. The challenges faced by Chappell's
"widely representative" persona are perennial human concerns.

Even while evoking the immense resources of the past,
Chappell also emphasizes the importance of community in the
present. This emphasis results not only from his attachment to
place and to family but also from the poem's sociopolitical
dimension and from the relationships Ole Fred cultivates with
fellow writers. Sociopolitical issues are raised in each volume of
Midquest, and the responsibilities of citizenship are never far
from the poet's mind because the text's present, May 1971, finds
the United States still fighting a war in Vietnam. "Bloodfire"
deals most directly with that war, referring to its "fire-martyrs,"
"the immolated and self-immolated" (88). But the penultimate
poem in *River* also speaks of "slow rain twitching wounds and
eyelids / of murdered soldiers, / daily snail-white corpses / bloat-
ing the Mekong" (48). The opening poem of *Earthsleep* likewise

notes how "fire colors the military maps, each village a red coal" (145). In addition to the bloodshed in Vietnam, Chappell protests economic injustice, from the paper mill's role in augmenting the flood's destruction in "Dead Soldiers" to the indifference of the rich toward the poor in "Remembering Wind Mountain at Sunset." By making such issues, including the racism alluded to in "My Father Allergic to Fire," a significant part of the book, Chappell indicates that, for him, poetry is a means of confronting sociopolitical realities, not retreating from them into aestheticism.

Yet aesthetics, as distinct from aestheticism, is certainly another of the issues that *Midquest* addresses. The nature and function of the literary imagination have become one of the dominant themes in twentieth-century poetry, as is evident in the poetry of Wallace Stevens, for example. Unlike Stevens, however, for whom this theme is ubiquitous, Chappell assigns it a carefully delimited role in *Midquest,* as if to suggest that, for all its importance to the poet, it is only one of several ways of approaching the work of the mind. The poems in which aesthetic issues receive the most extended treatment are the playlet in which Reynolds Price appears and the four epistolary poems Ole Fred writes to friends and fellow writers Guy Lillian, James Applewhite, Richard Dillard, and George Garrett. Through their epistolary format, the latter poems reinforce the theme of community and help to dispel the image of the writer as *isolato.* These poems also reveal several of the major literary influences that shaped Chappell's imagination, influences he had learned to question. In "Science Fiction Water Letter to Guy Lillian," for instance, the poet recalls his youthful fascination with this genre. Despite his continuing use of science fiction in a story like "The

Somewhere Doors" (*More Shapes Than One*), this poem expresses Chappell's dissatisfaction with the genre, primarily because of its inattention to the physical world, its failure to develop a "feel for pastness," and its disregard for suffering (38–39). After this critique of science fiction, however, the poet proceeds to comment on the plight of contemporary poetry, especially among confessional poets, "still whining, like flawed Dylan records, about their poor / lost innocence" (40). Rejecting such an egocentric stance and its obsession with the personal past, Chappell proclaims, "Fresh wonders clamor for language," and he recommends (as T. S. Eliot's essays do) a return to Andrew Marvell and John Donne and Henry Vaughan, for "they had senses / alive apart from their egos, and took delight in / every new page of Natural Theology" (40).

This poem's emphasis on utilizing the senses to experience creation's abundance is echoed by the critique of the Symbolist sensibility set forth in "Rimbaud Fire Letter to Jim Applewhite." There Ole Fred renounces the derangement of the senses he had practiced so assiduously under Rimbaud's tutelage. What altered his poetic vision, he explains, following his suspension from Duke, was his return to the mountain landscape and then, following his re-enrollment at Duke, his immersion in the writings of Samuel Johnson, Alexander Pope, and other representatives of neoclassical rationalism. Yet Ole Fred signs this letter, only partly ironically, "Yours for terror and symbolism" (61), for symbolism—though not the Symbolist sensibility—informs all of *Midquest.* As for terror, that term, reminiscent perhaps of the emotion prompted by Rimbaud's "Drunken Boat," assumes for Chappell the added meaning of gazing into the abyss of suffering and meaninglessness. As he writes Richard Dillard in another of these epistolary poems, "Our faith must be earned from terror" (87) to be credible.

The aesthetic issues raised in the preceding epistolary poems are recapitulated in "Hallowind" and in the letter Chappell addresses to George Garrett titled "How to Build the Earthly Paradise." The playlet posits a contrast between Fred as poet and Reynolds Price as fiction writer, the former committed to generalizing symbols or archetypes, to a poetry of paradigms, the latter espousing "local clarities" (136) and declaring, "I regard the 'symbol' as a thief" (137). For Price, as Chappell presents him, "Poems are maimed by their timelessness, / . . . / The *symbol* is at last inhuman" (137; Chappell's italics). In actuality, of course, Chappell and Price write both fiction and poetry, and both authors use symbolism extensively. The conflict this poem articulates is intentionally oversimplified. In *Midquest* Chappell creates a text that reconciles the opposing principles the playlet depicts, combining the "local clarities" of the mountain community in which he was raised with the paradigm of spiritual quest limned in Dante's *Divine Comedy,* itself a poem steeped in symbolism and allegory. Chappell's use of the four elements as unifying images also contributes to the symbolic thrust of the poem, its archetypal and mythic dimensions. But at the same time, the images derived from those four elements anchor the text in the material world, in the realm of time and mortality, even as the pilgrim strives to soar toward eternity, toward a vision of the divine. It is precisely the substantiality of the Earthly Paradise— its composition from stone, sand, earth, water, air, plants and animals, men and women and children—that Ole Fred's epistle to

Garrett insists upon. And the last word of that letter, before its valediction, is "yes," a word that voices both persona's and poet's affirmation of "the seething / homebrew of creation creating" (177). For Chappell both spiritual rebirth and authentic poetic insight depend upon this recognition of the wonder and mystery of nature and of human existence itself. As he writes in "Susan Bathing," "Unattending beauty is danger & mortal sin," whereas "speech-praise" is the "instrument of unclosing and rising toward light" (19).

To enter the presence of such light is the ultimate goal of the pilgrim-poet in *Midquest,* as it is of Dante the pilgrim, and Chappell establishes many parallels between the two works. Both pilgrims commence their journeys in their thirty-fifth years; both have guides named Virgil; and both also experience divine love mediated by a woman (Beatrice, Susan). Though Virgil Campbell speaks for far earthier values than the author of the *Aeneid,* both Virgils are storytellers who, in different ways, represent the power of the vernacular. As in Dante's epic, the disappearance of *Midquest*'s Virgil from the text (Ole Fred visits his grave in the sixth poem of *Earthsleep*) is followed by a vision of the Earthly Paradise. Some of Chappell's parallels to Dante's poem occur in humorous contexts, as when Chappell, by adding Casanova, Lord Byron, and James Dickey, updates the Italian poet's Second Circle, where the carnal are punished. Chappell achieves similar humorous effects by using Dante's *terza rima* in Ole Fred's account of his grandfather's decision to hedge "his final bet" by converting from Methodism to "hard-believer / Baptist" (30), a conversion that necessitates baptism by total immersion, in the irreverently titled "My Grandfather Gets Doused." Such humorous adaptations of Dantean materials and poetic techniques are clearly meant to counterbalance the visionary flights of *Midquest*'s persona. Ole Fred lacks the certitude of his Dantean counterpart, and Chappell thus makes his pilgrim's affirmations more credible by detailing the "wilderness of doubt" (56) from which Fred's faith ultimately arises. The poet's skillful use of humor and irony, his perfectly timed moments of self-deprecation and self-mockery, strengthen the book.

"Birthday 35: Diary Entry," the second poem in *Midquest,* marks the point of departure for Ole Fred's spiritual quest and provides an effective example of the poet's self-directed humor and irony.

> Multiplying my age by 2 in my head,
> I'm a grandfather. Or dead.
>
> "Midway in this life I came to a darksome wood."
> But Dante, however befuddled, was Good.
>
> . . . .
>
> I'm still in flight, still unsteadily in pursuit,
> Always becoming more sordid, pale, and acute . . .
>
> (3)

In the book's opening poem Ole Fred is portrayed as "wishing never to wake" (2). His diary entry helps explain this impulse by describing the spiritual wasteland he wanders. Yet Ole Fred's response to this emptiness is not to despair but to pray. "Birthday

35" concludes with a prayer that runs for twenty-two lines. A striking admixture of the humorous, the grotesque, the self-ironic, and the sincere, that prayer distances readers from Ole Fred's longing for rebirth without undercutting the sincerity and significance of his yearning.

That yearning is powerfully conveyed in *Midquest*'s fourth poem too, "Cleaning the Well," with its archetypal descent into the underworld, its confrontation with death. Hauled up into the light, the "most willing fish that was ever caught" (16), young Fred wonders, "Jonah, Joseph, Lazarus, / Were you delivered so?" (16) and remarks, "*I had not found death good*" (17; Chappell's italics). The prospect of death and the possibility of resurrection preoccupy Fred in many of the book's poems, especially in *Earthsleep,* for as his grandmother tells him as early as *Midquest*'s third poem, "It's dirt you rose from, dirt you'll bury in" (12). For her, this thought is more fact than threat, a fact of nature that does not negate her hope of resurrection. Indeed the natural and the supernatural cohabit throughout *Midquest,* as they frequently do in the Judeo-Christian tradition. Each of the four elements around which Chappell organizes *Midquest* assumes religious significance. Water, often a symbol of materiality, becomes an emblem of the intersection of time and eternity in "The River Awakening in the Sea," as in Anne Bradstreet's "Contemplations." Water is also, in baptism, a means of grace, an instrument of spiritual regeneration. Fire is both instrument of divine wrath and means of purification. It witnesses to God's presence in the burning bush from which God spoke to Moses and in the tongues of flame associated with the Holy Spirit. Wind—bodiless, invisible, yet observable in its effects—is similarly linked to the Holy Spirit, and in "Second Wind" it touches Fred's grandmother with "the weight of grace" (106). Chappell regularly associates wind with music as well and has noted that "music probably stands in my poems most of the time for exaltation, exalted spirits, ecstatic visionary knowledge."[38] As for earth, with its gaping graves, it is the foundation of the Earthly Paradise and the soil from which the "Tree of Spirit lift[s] from the mountain of earth" (149) to "the Mountains Outside Time" (169).

Midquest is a poem that evokes the mythos of Eden and "a final shore" (141) beyond the fevered river of time. Implicit in the sleep of *Earthsleep* is the prospect of awakening, and the epigraph from Hawthorne that opens the book's final volume depicts the peaceful transition from waking to the "temporary death" of sleep, comparing that transition to the experience of dying itself. "So calm, perhaps, will be the final change; so undisturbed, as if among familiar things the entrance of the soul to its Eternal home" (143). Hawthorne's "perhaps" in this passage registers the ineluctable mystery of the human encounter with death, and the sketch from which Chappell excerpts this epigraph is titled "The Haunted Mind." Yet while the questions death poses are irresolvable for the mind situated on this side of the grave—as the varied definitions of the term "earthsleep" in *Midquest*'s closing poem indicate—Chappell concludes that poem by invoking Dante's vision of God: "The love that moves the sun and other stars / The love that moves itself in light to loving" (187). The first of these lines translates the final line of the *Paradiso,* while the second is Chappell's attempt to capture the tone and spirit of Dante's poem. In the final line of "Earthsleep"

Fred and Susan lie side by side "here in the earliest morning of the world" (187), an image suggestive not of death but of new life. Dabney Stuart is thus correct when he argues that Chappell is "preoccupied with and hopeful of images of release and transformation, which are Christian in their orientation."[39] The Fred who resists waking in *Midquest*'s opening poem learns to "invite the mornings" (185).[40]

In addition to tracing this explicitly religious quest, Chappell fills *Midquest* with metaphysical speculations of various sorts. For Chappell, the experience of wonder prompts not only spiritual meditation but also the reflections of poet and philosopher alike. Chappell's repeated probing of philosophical issues, what one critic has called Chappell's "abiding concern with Ultimates,"[41] contributes significantly to both the breadth of *Midquest*'s subject matter and the substantiality of its themes. Yet the book does not simply juxtapose humorous narrative poems with more somber meditative poems. Instead, Chappell's narrative poems address philosophical and religious themes while his meditative poems are leavened by a buoyant humor that prevents reader and poet alike from taking themselves too seriously. The book's more lyric poems—those, for example, that open and close each of the four volumes—are similarly infused with philosophical inquiry. In fact cosmogony is a recurring motif in the initial poems of *River, Bloodfire,* and *Wind Mountain,* introduced in each case by references to "how the world was formed" (2, 56, 98). Myths of origin are also evident in Ole Fred's "slightly different Big Bang theory" in "The Autumn Bleat of the Weathervane Trombone" ("In the beginning was the Trombone" [115]) and in the excerpt from his novel-in-progress in "Science Fiction Water Letter" (41–43). Obviously, a concern for cosmogony also underpins Chappell's use of the four elements to structure *Midquest*. Renouncing the abstraction of Plato's realm of Ideal Forms (as he had done in his early poem "A Transcendental Idealist Dreams in Springtime"), Chappell recurs to the pre-Socratic naturalistic era in Greek philosophy. What he offers, finally, is a profoundly incarnational view of the relationship between matter and spirit, time and eternity, a view shaped by Christian thought.

This incarnational perspective is most fully developed in *Midquest*'s four long meditative poems: "Susan Bathing," "Firewood," "The Autumn Bleat of the Weathervane Trombone," and "The Peaceable Kingdom of Emerald Windows." The first two are single-sentence stream-of-consciousness poems, each seven pages in length, and they thus contrast in structure with the greater formal and syntactical clarity of the latter two poems, differences intended to mirror, Chappell says, his pilgrim's progress "as the speaker begins to order his life" (x). To term these poems "interior monologues," however, as Chappell does in the preface, is somewhat misleading, for each includes features of direct address that again reinforce the network of relationships in which the poet embeds Ole Fred.

"Susan Bathing" incorporates both philosophical and explicitly religious themes while also confirming Chappell's claim that *Midquest* is "in its largest design a love poem" (xi). The epigraph to "Susan Bathing," taken from Pope's "Windsor Forest," asserts that harmonious confusion, not chaos, governs the world, and thus underscores the fundamental outlook of *Midquest* as a whole and the artistic impression of order that the book conveys.

The Susan of this poem takes on a variety of identities. On the literal level she is simply Fred's wife, the object of his love, but marriage in *Midquest* assumes a metaphoric significance that extends well beyond its social function. Marriage illustrates the union of apparent opposites: not only women and men but also humankind and nature, as well as in Christian theology, the human and the divine. Susan herself functions allegorically in this poem both as Beatrice and as the Virgin Mary. In "Susan Bathing" body and spirit are conjoined, and Chappell's wide-ranging diction reflects this yoking of the earthy and the ethereal. In addition to her roles as Beatrice and Mary, Susan becomes the poet's muse, her "clean / flesh the synonym of love," eliciting his "speech praise" (23), reminding the poet of his "responsibilities to whatever is genuine" (19). In traditional Christian terms, the poet describes his will as "stricken and contort" and declares that "only intercession from / without can restore it" (21). Through Susan and the outpouring of praise she provokes, he gains access to self-transformation, "for once the mind prepares to praise & garbs / in worshipful robe it enlarges to plenitude" (19), a pleni-tude, as in the annunciation to Mary, "plena gratia" (20), full of grace. Significantly, it is the sight of Susan's body that prompts this epiphany, just as her physical act of bathing promises the poet spiritual regeneration.

In contrast to "Susan Bathing," "Firewood" is less explicitly religious and more overtly philosophical in its exploration of the relationship between flesh and spirit, matter and mind. It too employs the metaphor of marriage, however, and discusses the role of art in bonding humanity and nature. Much more than "Susan Bathing," "Firewood" confronts the fact of death and attempts to reconcile that fact with the longing for immortality. The wood Ole Fred splits in this poem is destined for his fireplace, where the sun (imaged as stored in the wood) will be released as heat and light, "the sun risen at midnight" to ascend "the rose trellis of stars . . . afire" (69). Burning, this wood will become "tree of spirit," with the poet's chimney linking the corporeal and the immaterial and suggesting humanity's dual identity as flesh and spirit—the world of spirit symbolized, here as elsewhere in Chappell's work, by the stars. The chimney "pins our dwelling / to the earth and to the stars equally" (69), the poet observes. Yet despite the beauty and the rhetorical effect of an image like "the rose trellis of stars," Ole Fred remains skeptical, fearful that "the cold dark will tear our tree of fire / away complete" (69) and conscious that Lucretius's "seed of fire ignis semina is seed semina mortuis," that is, seed of death (70). Unable to endorse, as he once did, Rimbaud's conception of "the vatic will" (71) capable of utterly transforming reality through the powers of the poetic imagination, Ole Fred yields to thoughts of death. For a moment he even longs to jettison human consciousness in exchange for the apparent contentment of the animal world. But, finally, he can neither surrender the uniqueness of human selfhood nor evade its often anguished doubts. As he continues to wonder, "but where / shall I sit when once this flesh is spirit?" (73), the reader notices that Ole Fred has undercut the Lucretian view of a purely physical universe in the very formulation of that question. "Firewood" concludes by comparing the ultimately successful splitting of the wood to the annunciation to Mary and by depicting that experience as a kind of baptism: "I'm washed in the blood / of the sun, the ghostly holy of the deep

deep log" (73). The punning religious diction here is meant to resolve, to some extent at least, the tensions between secular and sacred, flesh and spirit, time and eternity, that this poem examines. Yet, as Ole Fred states in the poem's final lines, "It doesn't come easy, I'm / here to tell you that."

What the other two long meditative poems in *Midquest* make clear is that, for Chappell, this "ghostly holy" is not to be sought at the expense of the physical world. To both "The Autumn Bleat of the Weathervane Trombone" and "The Peaceable Kingdom of Emerald Windows," the poet introduces a new character. someone whom Ole Fred refers to as Uncle Body. This figure is intended to subvert the philosophical idealism espoused by Plato, Plotinus, Descartes, and Emerson as well as the otherworldliness of a Protestant Christianity too often misled by Gnostic and Neo-Platonic thought. For the Emerson of *Nature,* personal identity was purely a mental or spiritual phenomenon; even one's body belonged to the category of the "NOT ME."[42] The playfulness and linguistic exuberance of both these poems reflect the expansiveness of the poet's sense of selfhood. In "The Autumn Bleat" fall is less a time of decay than of rebirth. Yellow, gold, and blue are the dominant colors, the last recalling Wallace Stevens's use of blue as the color of the imagination in "The Man with the Blue Guitar." That connection is evident here in Fred's music, a "bluesy A" (115) emerging to drift "the bluebleached air" (114). As the title's term "bleat" implies, that music is scarcely elegant, but the poem provides a cornucopia of sound effects, of levels of diction and allusion too. "There's something in air in love with rounded notes, / The goldenrod's a-groan at the globèd beauty," Chappell writes, in lines of consciously exaggerated alliteration (110). "Bring me my trombone of burning gold, bring me / My harrowing desire," he adds, paraphrasing Blake's *Milton.* Obviously, Chappell takes risks in such passages, as he attempts to communicate Fred's vision of life's fullness; occasionally those fanciful flights collapse under the weight of their distended diction. In general, however, readers are likely to be borne along by the sweeping sense of elation Ole Fred expresses, by the sheer energy and inventiveness of his words.

Like "Firewood," both "Autumn Bleat" and "The Peaceable Kingdom of Emerald Windows" address the fact of death. In contrast to "Firewood" the latter two poems actually contain portraits of the afterlife (as does *Earthsleep*'s "At the Grave of Virgil Campbell"). At times, these visions of the afterlife are wildly comic, verging on the blasphemous, as when Fred states his certainty that there is "Whiskey-after-Death" and refers to God as "the Holy Bartender" (173). But the different versions of the afterlife Ole Fred offers all have in common their being grounded upon human relationships and the physical world. In "Autumn Bleat," for example, he anticipates—with some apprehension—the prospect of spending eternity in the company of his fellow poets. In "Peaceable Kingdom" it is naturalists like Gilbert White and William Bartram, a novelist like Colette, and "rare Ben Franklin" whom he envisions joining, all of them people firmly attached in their earthly lives to the physical world. Moreover, since the phrase "Emerald Windows" refers to raindrops, nature becomes precious in itself, associated through the color green with seasonal rebirth and providing a source of spiritual vision, a window on eternity. At odds with the philosophical idealism of Emerson, Chappell nevertheless seems to concur with the Transcendentalist precept, "Nature is the symbol of Spirit."

Yet while Ole Fred celebrates nature and renounces Nirvana as "a sterile and joyless blasphemy" (113), he is decidedly unwilling to resign himself to physicality alone. He refuses to surrender to matter his powers of mind and spirit. Thus in "Autumn Bleat" he attempts to induce Uncle Body to voyage with him through the realms of philosophical speculation: "To swim from Singapore / To Hermeneutics and through the Dardanelles / To Transcendentalism, back through the Straits / of Hegel" (113). Here, as in many other poems in *Midquest,* Chappell attempts to naturalize metaphysical thought and thus to create for poetry—and for its readers—a commitment to philosophical reflection, to the Socratic ideal of examined lives. Just as the Virgil of the *Georgics* identifies the natural philosopher (along with the farmer and the poet) as one of the three kinds of people most attuned to the harmonies of the universe, so Chappell makes philosophical thought one of *Midquest*'s central activities, along with farming and artistic creation and the religious quest itself.

Perhaps the most persistent philosophical and religious problem Chappell's book addresses, especially in *Earthsleep,* is human mortality, the inescapable reality that Martin Heidegger terms *Sein zum Tod* (being toward death). "The Peaceable Kingdom," the meditative poem in that final volume, includes the statement, "Goodbye I perceive to be a human creature" (156). Yet the tone of that poem is not one of fear or anxiety but serenity. Chappell achieves this effect in part by invoking the utopian vision of the Edward Hicks painting mentioned in the title, in part by making green one of the poem's dominant colors (as that color predominates in several other poems in *Earthsleep*), and in part by organizing the latter portions of the poem around the activity of harvesting hay. That activity, successfully completed despite the threat of rain, lends to the poem an aura of fruition and reaffirms the bonds of family and community which the entire book cultivates. Rejecting again idealism's "sleepy flea market of Forms" (158), Ole Fred emphasizes the goodness of the creation, informing Uncle Body, "All the world is lit for your delight" (159). Integral to this vision of oneness with nature are those passages in which the poet personifies Maude and Jackson, the horses pulling the hay wagon, endowing them with speech. Through this device Chappell bridges the accustomed gap between humanity and nature and suspends the reader's commitment to the purely factual. His appeal to a wider conception of truth encourages the reader to assent as well to his image of the sun nestling "in the form / In the hay in the world in the green green hand" (157).

Clearly the resolution "The Peaceable Kingdom" offers is more emotional than logical. Like the repeated sound of the church bell calling *home, home, home* at key points throughout the last two volumes of *Midquest* (100, 133, 161, 185), it appeals more to the heart than to the head. But Chappell has already conceded as much in "Firewood" in his account of the postlapsarian intellect as "all alert and doubtful" (72). What Chappell manages to accomplish in *Midquest*—and it is no small achievement in what is commonly considered a postmodern, post-Christian age—is to awaken readers to the presence of Spirit, both in nature and in themselves. The *Book of Earth,* as Ole Fred discovers, is "brimming over with matter, / Matter aye and spirit, too, each / And every page is chock to stupefying" (160). Or, as Fred puts it after visiting the site of a burned church in "My Grandfather's Church Goes Up":

> *Pilgrim, the past   becomes prayer*
> *becomes remembrance rock-real   of Resurrection*
> *when the Willer so willeth   works his wild wonders.*
>   (77; Chappell's italics)

Among the types of resurrection to which *Midquest* testifies is that of traditional poetic forms. "My Grandfather's Church" employs Anglo-Saxon alliterative verse; the epistolary poem to Richard Dillard is in elegiacs; the letter to Guy Lillian in syllabics; "My Grandmother's Hard Row to Hoe" uses chant royal. While blank verse and free verse predominate, other traditional forms abound: rhymed couplets in lines of varying lengths, heroic couplets, *terza rima,* Yeatsian tetrameter, even a variation on classical hexameter in "Susan Bathing." The rhyme scheme in the playlet "Hallowind" consists of three successively rhymed tetrameter lines, with the rhymes carrying over from one speaker to the next. In the grandmother's monologue in "Second Wind" the poet uses iambic pentameter octets based on an abba abba rhyme scheme, yet maintains the impression of a vernacular voice. Few poets since Robert Frost have captured the natural speaking voice as effectively as Chappell does in both rhymed forms and blank verse. The book's varied stanza structures—couplets, tercets, quatrains, sestets, octets, verse paragraphs of differing lengths, seven-page single-sentence stream-of-consciousness meditations—help keep the poems continually fresh as the reader accompanies Ole Fred on his quest. As one critic has remarked, "The poems fairly exult in their technical invention. . . . The range is extraordinary."[43] Chappell's skill with such structural matters is especially evident in the epistolary poem to George Garrett titled "How to Build the Earthly Paradise." There the poet creates a nine-line stanza, each end stopped, to represent the blocks of material used to construct this utopia. Each stanza opens and closes, moreover, with a single-syllable line, as if to evince the solidity of the workmanship, and the second and eighth lines contain just two syllables per line. The ponderous rhythms these four lines establish at each stanza's beginning and end suggest the thought and care that underlie the poet's making. Chappell's mastery of his craft is readily, though unostentatiously, apparent throughout *Midquest,* reminding readers of the poetic resources many contemporary poets have neglected in their commitment to free verse.

The revival of the narrative impulse in poetry is another of the aesthetic resurrections that this book attains. As one interviewer has noted, there are at least three kinds of narrative in *Midquest:* "the movement of images," "the repetition of narratives within a poem, the story lines themselves, the plots," and "the whole poetic narrative of the self, a biography of sorts."[44] It is in the second of these categories that the poet allows his gifts for storytelling their freest rein, particularly when his grandparents and parents and Virgil Campbell speak; and it is often in these poems (for example, "My Father's Hurricane" and "Three Sheets in the Wind") that Chappell's comic vision reaches its greatest heights. Because of the accessibility and humor of these poems, general readers as well as critics have sometimes seen them as the most distinctive or original aspect of the book. Yet for all their vividness and directness of appeal, these poems are subsumed within *Midquest*'s larger narrative and thematic structure, which is centered upon Ole Fred's search for moral and spiritual renewal and for a deeper understanding of his place both in the human community and in the cosmos.

Midquest is ultimately most original in its elaborate interweaving of the regional and the universal and in its intricacy of design, a design in which lyric, narrative, epistolary, and meditative poems echo and enrich one another. Chappell's enormous range of allusions ties his individual Appalachian voices to many of the most significant features of the Western literary, philosophical, and religious traditions. To declare, as one reviewer of *Earthsleep* did, that Chappell's "real subject" is "the hard but satisfyingly essential dirt-farming life as it used to be in the South," a subject from which the reviewer felt the poems in *Earthsleep* had strayed, is to badly misread both the poet's intentions and his accomplishment.[45] *Midquest* is a book that requires and rewards rereading. It is, to quote Kelly Cherry, "a terrifically . . . powerful poem, full of the pleasures of surfaces and the deep gratification of complex structure."[46] As the book receives the kind of searching critical analysis its achievement merits, it will increasingly be seen for what, in fact, it is—one of the finest long poems in twentieth-century American literature.

CHAPTER FOUR

"The Singer Dissolved in Song"
Castle Tzingal to *Spring Garden*

Since the publication of *Midquest* in 1981, Chappell has produced five additional books of poems: *Castle Tzingal* (1984),
Source (1985), *First and Last Words* (1989), *C* (1993), and
Spring Garden: New and Selected Poems (1995). Each volume
has been strikingly different from the others in overall design,
poetic structures, and dominant tone. Yet all continue to demonstrate the powerful inventiveness of Chappell's imagination, his
mastery of both traditional forms and free verse, and his profound concern for moral and spiritual values. The humor that
enlivens *Midquest* is absent from *Castle Tzingal* but is amply
evident in the epigrams of *C* and in various poems throughout
the other volumes. The allegorical impulse apparent in his early
fiction and in *Midquest* also operates at numerous points in these
later collections.

Castle Tzingal

Nowhere, perhaps, is that allegorical impulse more evident than
in *Castle Tzingal,* which Chappell subtitles "A Poem" to emphasize the unity of effect he intends the book to achieve. After the
rollicking humor and metaphysical speculation of *Midquest,*
grounded in the twentieth-century mountain South, Chappell
wisely chose to write a book set in an entirely different era, using
a diction equally remote from the folksy vernacular of Virgil

Campbell and the jazz riff wordplay of Ole Fred. Set in the late Middle Ages or early Renaissance, *Castle Tzingal* bears no resemblance to the world *Midquest* portrays, and Chappell thus liberates himself from the obligation to compete with that text. In fact *Castle Tzingal* reads more like a play than a typical poetry collection. Its twenty-three poems are spoken by nine different voices ranging from the king and queen of the castle to the realm's astrologer, his page Pollio, and Queen Frynna's hand-maid. The other characters include a homunculus, Tweak; an unnamed admiral; Petrus, an envoy from King Reynal, half-brother to King Tzingal; and the disembodied voice of the mur-dered harpist-poet Marco, King Reynal's nephew, whose disappearance Petrus has been sent to investigate. When these characters speak, their vocabulary contains many words of four-teenth-century origin or earlier: *assoilment, villeyn, dour, pleachy, frore, throstle, malapert,* and *grutch,* among others. Additional terms are of sixteenth- and seventeenth-century ori-gin: *catamite, fulgurant, suborn.* In setting and diction, then, *Castle Tzingal* immediately distances the reader from the con-temporary world and from the landscape and kinds of characters *Midquest* celebrates.

Part allegory, part murder mystery, part dark fairy tale, *Cas-tle Tzingal* draws inspiration from the Elizabethan revenge tragedy and the myth of Orpheus as well as from such Poe tales as "Hop Frog."[1] Chappell reports that the book's opening poem, "The Homunculus," came to him as "a kind of dream or vision": "I woke up at three o'clock in the morning and wrote it down just like it is, except for changing one or two words."[2] The whole book "took three years of off-and-on labor, very intensive labor in the last six months," he comments.[3] The result is a tale of jealousy, murder, political intrigue, moral corruption, and revenge that is also an allegory about the power and endurance of poetry and of the humane qualities that poetry nourishes. It is a book that fuses the narrative, dramatic, and lyric modes in a startlingly original fashion. As Chappell puts it, "*Castle Tzingal* tells a single story; it's almost like a little novella. In my mind it was a chamber opera, with all the separate poems being arias sung by the different characters."[4] The term "aria" is somewhat misleading, however, since it implies a melody sung by a single voice. Yet among these poems, Chappell includes not only monologues but also explicit and implicit dialogues as well as three poems written as reports from Petrus to King Reynal. As in *Midquest,* the characters of *Castle Tzingal* are portrayed in a network of relationships; they are creatures with a decidedly social identity—though here the society they inhabit is harshly destructive, a realm, as typified by King Tzingal, of hatred, distrust, madness, and murder. Acts of betrayal are not limited, however, to the king. They infect his minions, especially Pollio and Tweak, both of them open to bribes, and the moral void King Tzingal embodies is reflected in the machinations of the astrologer, an eager appendage to the king's will.

As the book's dramatic action unfolds, Chappell again reveals his virtuosity with rhyme and meter by individualizing each of the character's voices. On an iambic base of varying line lengths, he builds verse paragraphs that likewise vary in length. The frequency of the rhymes' occurrence, the proportion of exact to slant rhymes, the placements of caesuras, the poet's use of enjambment, the syntax the speakers employ, their diction—all

contribute to defining and differentiating the characters' personalities, as does the substance of their thoughts. The indentured
servant Pollio's vanity and petty ambitions are quickly sketched:
"How like you this green doublet that I wear?" he asks Petrus,
before telling the envoy, "My loyalty / Cements fast to my new
employer."[5] Queen Frynna's concern for the vanished Marco and
the lovelessness of her marriage, the retired admiral's anguish
over the sailors he has lost at sea, Petrus's distaste for the "ugly
murk of treachery" (13) that pervades the castle, and the murdered poet's own suffering ("Marco's become a monster" [30])
are all evoked in just a few lines. The same is true of Tweak's
pride in his ability as a spy in the volume's opening poem, for the
homunculus thinks of himself as "a whole intelligence force in
minuscule" and is "happy to be set to work, / To know who
knows, and how he knows, and why" (1).

Such comments and Tweak's alchemical origins raise one
of the book's major themes: to what ends knowledge? King
Tzingal uses the information Tweak ferrets out to hold his people in thrall. He uses the astrologer's skills to create Tweak, who
enhances the king's capacity to domineer over others, and to
maim or unmake Marco. Pollio too has information he offers to
Petrus if Petrus will purchase his debenture. "All you / Ever
could desire to know is in my head," he assures the envoy (10).
The hyperbole of this claim escapes Pollio but not the reader, for
what Pollio knows is "a nether history" of the castle and that
only. Is knowledge to be valued primarily as an instrument of
brute political power? Of economic advancement? Of the individual's assertion of control over or independence of others? For
Chappell, this book implies, knowledge—like poetry itself—is

an instrument of revelation, a means of self-understanding rather than a means of manipulating others. *Self*-control, not domination of others, is its aim. Knowledge should eventuate in the wisdom of love and compassion, qualities largely absent from Castle Tzingal and certainly absent from its king.

The presence of alchemy and astrology in this text links *Castle Tzingal* to Chappell's career-long interest in the former and his consistent use of the stars as prominent symbols.[6] Alchemy appeals to Chappell's imagination for several reasons. It represents, first of all, an early stage in the development of science and of the quest for knowledge that the term "science" implies. Secondly, alchemy seeks a formula for transformation, a means of translating a base substance into a precious metal, or a formula for unifying discrete particulars into a meaningful whole, a process akin to the transformations poetry often strives to effect, especially in a book like *Midquest,* with its principal metaphor of rebirth. Thirdly, alchemy interests Chappell because it involves magical and mysterious powers and thus frees the imagination from the mundane and the strictly factual.

In *Castle Tzingal,* however, alchemy is depicted primarily in terms of black magic. The astrologer is a figure of evil, though subordinate to the greater evil of the king. Or perhaps it is more accurate to say that the astrologer, like many practitioners of modern science, assumes a stance of moral neutrality that Chappell finds untenable. Pollio tells the astrologer, "You have no conscience at all" (23), a flaw that explains the astrologer's willingness to put his expertise at the service of the king, even to the extent of "suspend[ing] in fluids beside a gurgling retort / The harpist's comely head," as Tweak tells Petrus (26). Yet despite his terrifying powers, the astrologer—like the king himself, who severed Marco's head from its body—has failed to silence the poet. The harpist continues to fill the castle's nights with song— "a song not counted on" (26).

Tweak's revelations about Marco's fate occur in the book's central poem. The very fact that Chappell discloses this information so early indicates that he is less concerned with how Marco disappeared than with the effects of that disappearance on the other inhabitants of the castle. Characterization and theme take precedence over plot. While Tweak's comments solve the mystery of Marco's absence, the mystery associated with his continuing powers of song remains, a mystery that directs attention to "the poet's role in society," as Patrick Bizzaro notes.[7] Chappell structures *Castle Tzingal* to heighten the impact of Marco's songs, assigning the seventh, fifteenth, and final poems to the poet's "Disembodied Voice." Thus, after allowing time, in customary dramatic fashion, for the exposition of plot and character, Chappell complicates the situation by introducing Marco's songs.

Marco has been murdered because of the king's misguided jealousy, for although the poet had won the queen's heart during his sojourn at the castle the previous year, the pair had not become lovers (25). That Marco's voice continues to fill Frynna's thoughts is apparent—even before Marco's disembodied voice is heard—in the book's second poem. Here the queen addresses the vanished poet and recalls lines from his songs, stanzas that reflect her mental state, particularly her dismay over her loveless marriage. The winter season in which *Castle Tzingal* is set mirrors the icy embrace of the king's so-called affection. Chappell contrasts the happiness of Frynna's childhood with her current situation

amid the "thorny intrigue of a blackguard time" (5). One effect
Marco's songs have upon Frynna is to revive her memory of that
earlier joy: "All I'd unremembered I remembered when / You
struck the harp and sang the old old ballad" (5). Given a poet like
Chappell, whose work regularly draws upon traditional poetic
forms, whether Dante's epic quest or Elizabethan revenge tragedy
or classical epigrams, such a passage testifies once again to the
resurrective powers of art. Marco's songs remind the queen of
life's potential goodness, but in his absence she despairs of re-
attaining that experience. In her first poem she thus welcomes the
prospect of suicide. Chappell assigns Queen Frynna more poems
(five) than any other character and links her repeatedly to the term
"dream" and to the act of dreaming. Even as she dies of the poison she has drunk, she clings to her conception of a world where
love and justice and nobility of character might flourish. Of
Frynna Chappell has said, "The hardest persona [to write] was the
Queen, because the difficulty was not to make her sound whining
but one of verity's heroines."[8] The phrase "verity's heroines"
highlights the moral framework of *Castle Tzingal* and the moral
vision that underlies Chappell's art.

   Allied with the queen, both in his abhorrence of the castle's
corruption and in his choice of suicide to escape that world, is the
admiral. Increasingly haunted by the deaths for which he feels
responsible, he finds in Marco's songs a further prick to conscience. Though he appeals to the fact that "everything I did was
in the line of duty" (21), he gains no comfort from such rational-
izations. After he is publicly accused by the king of pederasty,
the admiral hangs himself. Although this charge links the admiral to the astrologer, Chappell clearly contrasts the two men in

other ways, for the admiral has none of the astrologer's amorality and self-absorption.

The character who stands in sharpest contrast to the evils of the castle, however, is Petrus, whose name suggests his rocklike stability and moral substance. He finds the atmosphere of the castle stifling: "A fortnight here I find myself / Gasping for air like a man in mortal combat," he informs King Reynal in his first report (14). The vision of duality present throughout Chappell's work appears in *Castle Tzingal* in two major ways: as the opposition between the realms of King Tzingal and King Reynal and as Marco's consciousness that "Arcady is fled" (16), that "the happy season of the world has left no mark" (31, 46). As King Reynal's envoy, Petrus uncovers the truth about Marco's disappearance. Although his first report doesn't appear until the volume's sixth poem, Petrus is the unidentified interlocutor to whom both Tweak and Pollio speak in the initial poems assigned to them, and he is likewise the person addressed in the astrologer's initial poem. Petrus is thus a significant figure in four of the book's first six poems. If the queen is one of verity's heroines, he is among its heroes. Petrus's quest for the truth is stymied, however, until Tweak yields to the envoy's proffered bribe of a duchy. Yet it is not the promise of that duchy but rather King Tzingal's scornful remarks to Tweak at a dinner party that enable Petrus to enlist the homunculus's aid in assassinating the king. The simplicity and directness of Petrus's second and third reports, which are among the book's shortest poems, reflect the calm control with which he accomplishes his mission and arranges for the purgation of Castle Tzingal.

As is generally true of allegories and fairy tales, the principal villain of this narrative is readily identifiable. The king is not only thoroughly evil and irrationally jealous but also literally mad, as Tweak confides to Petrus: "His body is a cage, his mind a beast / Harried by phantasms of guilt" (25). Yet the king's consciousness of guilt, unlike the admiral's, never results in self-condemnation or remorse. Significantly, only the king and the astrologer remain oblivious to Marco's voice, which, as Petrus tellingly notes, "was as present with us as our own souls are" (24). King Tzingal prefers to rule by fear, prefers brute power to justice. His contempt for his subjects suffuses the one poem Chappell assigns to the king, a poem that opens with the line, "I am the toads' great lord, hating the toads" (34). But that disdain is also apparent in his remarks at the dinner reported by the astrologer. On that occasion, which precipitates many of the key events in the last half of the book, including the king's poisoning by Tweak, Tzingal accuses the admiral of pederasty, the queen of adultery, Petrus of spying, and the astrologer of self-betrayal. He concludes his tirade by disparaging Tweak as an "insect, animalcule. Toad!" (28), insults that prompt Tweak's willingness to serve Petrus's cause.

Despite the king's madness, the one poem in which he speaks directly is the most formally structured in the entire volume. That poem is, in fact, a variant on the sestina, and its repeated terms include "toads" and "fire," the former alternating once with the word "turds," the latter twice replaced by the word "fear" and also by the words "four" and "fair," though "fire" appears in the first and final two stanzas. The opening stanza's

end-stopped lines emphasize the king's abrupt shifts in thought
and mood, his hostility toward others and his fear of them:

> I am the toads' great lord, hating the toads.
> Under the snow are many eyes.
> A legion of foot-slither must me surround.
> The burning salamander attacks the raven-holt.
> Every heart unsheathes its dagger now.
> Fire.
>
> (34)

"Fear," the next stanza begins, in a parallel one-word line.
And as the king's monologue proceeds, Chappell subtly includes
the reader among those who must learn fear of the king's arbitrary, unpredictable wrath. Whereas the poem initially uses the
pronoun "them" to refer to the king's subjects, in the fifth stanza
Tzingal unexpectedly shifts to the second-person pronoun: "That
hour will come when I shall gnaw *your* eyes" (34; italics added).
This shift in pronouns is reinforced by the imperative with which
stanza six opens. In a society devoid of moral or political principles, Chappell implies, every citizen is a potential victim of the
presiding tyrant.

That recognition seems among the motives that lead Tweak
to ally himself with Petrus to overthrow the king. The minatory
vow with which Tzingal concludes his poem—"And soon I'll
sear with fire these lordly toads" (35)—ironically produces "the
raveling fire" of the poison Tweak administers. The term "fire"
appears as often in the homunculus's final poem as in the king's
one speech, and Tweak insures that Tzingal's "last earthly sight

is fire" by igniting the tapestry that celebrates the king's coronation, both symbolically and literally terminating Tzingal's reign.

Although it is tempting to read *Castle Tzingal* as a political fable, especially given its 1984 copyright date, Chappell has tended to discourage such an approach to the book. "The closer [*Castle Tzingal*] verges toward political allegory and satire," he said in an interview, "the weaker it is, it seems to me. And the more fairy-tale the atmosphere, the more successful it is."[9] Perhaps the major character reinforcing that fairy-tale atmosphere is Marco, the harpist-poet. Baffled by and sorrowing over his fate, Marco persists in singing, sometimes involuntarily, at other times to promote the achievement of justice. His voice, despite its anguish, represents the power of memory and conscience, of lost but not irrecoverable innocence, as is apparent when he comments, "Arcady is fled and gone / *Until I rend* the guilty sleep / Of Castle Tzingal" (16; italics added). Marco's voice sings of love, of hope amidst suffering, and of humanity's dual identity as both spirit and flesh. The persistence of that voice after Marco's death, what the harpist calls "the singer dissolved in song" (15), becomes emblematic of the triumph of poetry over death, of art's capacity to transcend time.

Like Chappell himself, Marco sings in a broken world, seeking means of healing, aspiring to visions of wholeness. Yet *Castle Tzingal* never realizes such a vision. Instead the melancholy tone of Marco's epilogue concludes the volume in a minor key. At least for the moment, as in the final act of *Hamlet,* the knowledge of waste and loss outweighs the potential for rebirth implicit in the death of the old order. Yet the poet's song endures, testimony to the "light [that] informs the sunlight," the "beauty [that] has no body" (15)—a light and beauty that, in Chappell's view, poetry has an "unanswerable duty to sing" (30).

Source

Whereas *Castle Tzingal* is an extended narrative embedded in a dramatic structure, *Source* is a collection of mainly lyric poems, almost none over two pages long. It is the most conventional of Chappell's books of poetry since *The World between the Eyes,* conventional in the sense that it gathers together a variety of previously published material: thirty-six poems in all, including a seven-part lieder cycle titled "The Transformed Twilight." Five of the poems are reprinted from the fifteen that appeared in the 1979 chapbook *Awakening to Music.* Most of the others first appeared in various literary journals. Yet as with all his books of poetry after his first, Chappell structures the poems in *Source* in such a way that the volume achieves a sense of focus, of thematic unity, often lacking in typical collections of poetry. According to its author, "*Source* is organized around the idea of folk myth and folk motifs, the origins of narrative."[10]

The book is divided into four titled sections: "Child in the Fog," "Source," "The Transformed Twilight," and "Forever Mountain." As it progresses, the book moves broadly from childhood through adulthood to death. As that movement might suggest, *Source,* like *Midquest,* pursues the theme of transformation. Yet while in *Midquest* transformation was viewed primarily in terms of the potential for rebirth, in *Source* the kinds of transformation portrayed are more varied—and often fearfully destructive. The title of the collection indicates Chappell's ongoing concern with ultimates, and it recalls the cosmogonies and fables of origin scattered throughout *Midquest.* The singular noun of the title points to a single source, but the sections into which the book is divided, as well as particular poems, emphasize the diverse formative experiences that shape human identity, both individually and collectively. Among the most important to these poems are childhood, nature, encounters with the divine, music and story, war, and the mystery of suffering and death.

The first of these originative experiences, at least chronologically, is childhood, and thus it is with childhood that *Source* begins, specifically with the title poem of the opening section. Though written from the perspective of the adult poet, the poem effectively reflects the child's outlook: "It was the first day of school and Mama / Had betrayed me to the white fog leopard, / Tree-croucher to eat my bones."[11] The fog becomes a metaphor for all those things that obscure the child's vision, that limit his understanding, and it also attests to the fundamental mysteries that attend human existence, for adult as well as child. The fog provides a lesson in the insubstantiality of the physical world; it mediates an experience of flux and of blindness. In the poem's opening lines the child is immediately put on the defensive: "Did the ghosts watch my prayers when the strange / Fat hats of everything attacked? / Or was it the fearful Nobody?" (3). Although exaggerated, the child's fears in this passage foreshadow the encounters with death and nothingness that later poems in *Source* will depict.

The childhood detailed in the initial section of *Source,* like that portrayed elsewhere in Chappell's writing, is rural, grounded in an agrarian lifestyle. The child's attachment to nature is a key element in defining his sensibility, as is evident in "Nocturne," "A Prayer for the Mountains," "A Prayer for Slowness," "Here" and "Awakening to Music." This last poem focuses not, as the reader might expect, on musical compositions of human origin but rather on memories of "a whiteface heifer" and the daily chore of milking cows. The speaker's memories, however pastoral, are scarcely idyllic. In fact the poem opens by recounting the boy's efforts to retrieve the escaped heifer in a harsh winter landscape. "I'd curse to melt the snow in air," he remarks (10). Nevertheless it is through the activity of milking the cow that the boy comes "to the pulsing green fountain where music is born" (11). That mundane activity nurtures his imagination, salves his spirit. Yet the poem concludes, for the adult poet, with a sense not of fulfillment but of loss. "How would I get it back?" he asks; "How can I wake, not waking to music?" (11). This poem, Don Johnson has suggested, is Chappell's version of Keats's "Ode to a Nightingale."[12]

Many of the first two-thirds of the poems in part 1 convey a sense of peace, of gentle ease, that is reinforced by images of people and animals at rest and of "the deep Bible" lying open "like a turned-down bed" (9). Religious consciousness is integral to these poems, invoked both by the three poems that are identified as prayers (5–7) and by the poem titled "Humility," which closes with the image of the Bible just quoted. These poems project a world from which the fears expressed in the opening lines of "Child in the Fog" have been banished.

These visions of a landscape where even "the milk-flecked fawn [may] lie unseen, unfearing" (5) give way, however, to "the terrors" the poet must confront in parts 3 and 4. Even the last few poems in part 1, like the opening chapters of Genesis, tell a story of exile. Indeed the poem immediately following "Awakening to Music," with its evocative closing questions, is titled "Exile." It recounts a courtroom scene in which the judge's sentence is exile and the accused's childhood is "confiscate[d]." The succeeding poem, "Abandoned Schoolhouse on Long Branch," underscores this sense of the displacements wrought by time, for the schoolhouse's "final scholar" is a blacksnake whose enormous length is intimated by the nine-line sentence describing it with which the poem begins. Chappell reinforces this sense of childhood's departure by concluding part 1 with a lightly revised version of "Seated Figure," one of the last poems in *The World between the Eyes,* a volume for which memories of childhood are crucial and in which "the child" is arguably the central character. The seated figure of this poem may represent the quality of endurance, but she also manifests a stolidity that might be as readily associated with Fate itself as with human personality. Moreover, by portraying this seated figure's unwavering focus on her needlework even after the wind tears the roof from her home, Chappell uses this poem to anticipate the folktale and mythic elements of many of the poems in part 2.

The second section of *Source* is its longest and its most varied in subject matter and tone. Although its bears an epigraph from the Brothers Grimm, this section opens not with a fairy tale but with a nightmare vision of human existence following a nuclear holocaust, the allegorical "The Evening of the Second Day." In this poem Chappell reminds his readers that humanity has now developed the power to *undo* creation, to annihilate the sources that have sustained human beings for millennia. The agrarian landscape so beautifully imaged in part 1 is here utterly transformed with "*sacred fields in ashes,*" "bat-spattered shell casings [not harvested crops] stacked in the barn loft," "The only green things the scattered bales of money" (17; Chappell's italics). Instead of the luminous landscape of "A Prayer for the Mountains," the reader encounters an ominously "glowing mountain" irradiated by nuclear warheads. Instead of the comforting shadows of hill and barn in "A Prayer for Slowness," the reader hears of a shadow that so frightens the survivors of this holocaust that they march two miles out of their way to avoid it (18). The poem is horrifying enough in itself, but read in the context of the earlier poems in *Source,* its impact intensifies. In addition the poem's narrator thrusts the reader inside this experience of desolation by using "your" and "you" ("After your sister on all fours has died fearing water"). *Devolution,* not evolutionary progress, is at the poem's center, for children are referred to as "cubs," "females groom for lice," and society has reverted to warring tribal groups: the One Eyes, the Screechers, the Knee-walkers, the Wallowdogs. The narrator's tribe has a soothsayer ironically named Blindboy, and the poem concludes with the narrator insisting, "Time now to choose one of us for stoning" (18). While some of the ironies here are rather heavy-handed, the haunting details of this six-part poem demonstrate Chappell's skill with dystopian fantasy and fable, a mode to which he returns in the short story "Alma" in *More Shapes Than One.*

The catastrophe envisioned in "The Evening of the Second Day" modulates into the bloodless departure of "The Lost Carnival," the second poem in part 2, which presents another trope of vanished—though not unblemished—beauty. The third poem in part 2, "Music as a Woman Imperfectly Perceived," marks an abrupt shift in tone, as Chappell revels in music's capacity to transform and invigorate human lives. Just as in *Wind Mountain* music is the voice of spirit, one of the ways the transcendent becomes manifest in the temporal world, so here music is linked to the image of a woman as physical being who also represents the poet's muse. Each of the four numbered sections of this poem adopts a distinctive form and style: elegant unrhymed quatrains and tercets in section 1; unrhymed couplets in a question-and-answer format in section 2; a jazzy long-lined prose poem in section 3, filled with exuberant alliteration and assonance and internal rhymes; and a madrigal-like ten-line rhymed stanza in section 4. Chappell here writes both a love poem and a paean to music's transfiguring powers. In the catechetical second section, music is personified (with a nod to Wordsworth) as "the Queen of Intimations." When the speaker inquires about her "azure country," asking, "Are there many great dangers?" the response is: "*You will tremble but not in fear*" (21; Chappell's italics). When he asks, "Can we return alive?" he is told, "*Alive, but not unchanged.*" Throughout Chappell's work music is a fundamental source of revelation and transformation. Like the woman imperfectly perceived to whom music is compared in this poem, music "sheds such grace / Upon this place / Of darkness, that every flower burns brightly in her face" (22). As Chappell's collection of short stories, *Moments of Light,* demonstrates, the classical concept of the music of the spheres functions importantly in his writing. For this author, music is a "*Natural* Resource," as the title of the subsequent poem in *Source* indicates, not simply a *human* artistic creation (my italics), an idea emphasized as well in section 1 of "Music as a Woman Imperfectly Perceived." To be aligned with music and nature does not, however, exempt one from mortality, from time's most devastating change, as the poem "Transmogrification of the Diva" reveals.

"Transmogrification" and "Latencies," terms that underscore *Source*'s theme of transformation, appear in the titles of consecutive poems just before the midpoint of the book. The word "latencies" originates from the Latin *latére,* to lie hidden, and is related to the Greek *lanthanein,* to escape notice. One of the poet's principal functions is to observe, to engage in acts of attention that bring the often overlooked to light. Poetry thus becomes an instrument of revelation—and hence, like music, of change. In "Latencies" Chappell notes the ambiguous nature of change, its potential for destruction as well as growth. While a window may be "a latent religion" ("Thrust it open, and / what new knowledge, new immanence, pour in upon us"), a young man gone to war becomes "a latent garden of terrible American Beauty roses" (25). This view of latency emphasizes the importance for Chappell of the choices people make, the futures they envision and invite.

At the center of part 2 is a series of poems focusing on varieties of folk narrative and on the imagination's role in defining and explaining the human condition. "The Story" gives precedence to oral narratives and, with playful self-deprecation, comments on the debilitating effect poets have had on story, "drench[ing] it with moonlight and fever," then abandoning it to novelists (26). "Fox and Goose" is an explanatory fable designed to account for a constellation called The Fox Forestalled, and Chappell situates the speaker squarely in the Appalachian storytelling tradition by opening the poem with the line, "Fox took him a yearn for honey" (27). "Trolls" and "Silent" evoke Norse legends, while "Narcissus and Echo," one of the most beautiful and accomplished poems in the collection, retells the Greek myth in two voices, Echo's formed, appropriately, by repeating at each line's end syllables or sounds Narcissus speaks in that line. For Chappell, the self-absorption of Narcissus remains one of the permanent flaws in human nature—and in modern poetry, especially so-called confessional poetry.

Some of the shifts in subject and tone in part 2 come too abruptly to leave the reader with a sense of coherent progression among the poems. "Recovery of Sexual Desire After a Bad Cold," for example, is delightful in itself, but its placement in the book seems somewhat arbitrary, though a case might be made that its line, "I am a new old man," with its echo of Saint Paul, both anticipates the biblical allusion of the following poem, "Rib," and raises the moral issues addressed more directly in "The Virtues." But the poem's humorous focus on *recovery* of physical health and sexual potency seems out of tune with part 2's closing poem, "Source," the title poem for both this section and the book itself. Set in an unspecified past of perfumed barges, viceroys, and peasants, "Source" deals directly with death. "An ancient wound troubles the river," the poem begins (36), recalling the conventional use of the river as a symbol of temporality. The experience of mortality inspires stories and fables, myths and songs, poems and novels and musical compositions. It also promotes philosophical reflection and religious beliefs. "Source" thus serves as an apt conclusion to part 2, while at the same time it introduces readers to the twilight world of part 3 and the terrors and consolations of part 4.

"The Transformed Twilight," the lieder cycle that composes part 3, arises out of the war in Vietnam, as do several of the poems in *The World between the Eyes* and *Midquest.* The poem's central character, a sculptor, is a veteran of that war, haunted by the brutality he witnessed there, especially the violence inflicted on children: "Villages of children lift their ruined faces in the bedsheet" (43). The carefully wrought formal structure of "The Transformed Twilight" (seven numbered sections of twelve lines each divided into unrhymed quatrains) contrasts with the sculptor's emotional turmoil and the poem's at times surrealistic images.

Chappell's choice of the lieder cycle as a model for this series of poems derives from his lifelong interest in the connections between poetry and music and from his fascination with the music of words. The specific inspiration for "The Transformed Twilight," Chappell has said, was Arnold Schoenberg's *Gurrelieder,* and Schoenberg has been among Chappell's favorite composers since the author first read Thomas Mann's *Doctor Faustus* in high school.[13] The dissonance that Schoenberg's music often contains is particularly appropriate to the psyche of the sculptor in this sequence of poems. In "The Transformed Twilight" Chappell occasionally shifts from first- to third-person point of view to mirror the sculptor's disorientation, his sense of "Polaris unfixed" at "the planet's unsteady margin" (39). Conscious that he "can imagine no brutal history that will not be born" (43), the sculptor labors in vain to recover a vision of wholeness, to reaffirm what Chappell calls the artist's "pact with unbroken eternity" (40). The sculptor is left instead with his memories of "black terror" in Vietnam and his impression of the contemporary world as "a nebula / Of accident" (45), "my hand the chisel of shadow" (44). The transformation to which this poem testifies has been devastating, not inspiriting.

Part 4 of *Source,* "Forever Mountain," opens with a poem that extends the bleak mood established in part 3, a poem titled "The Capacity for Pain." The opening line of this poem—"I am changing shape again" (49)—confirms the book's focus on transformations of various kinds. Like the sculptor of part 3, the speaker in this poem confronts the violence of human history. Yet he also voices a courageous desire not to evade the knowledge of that brutality, imaging that courage as a willingness to eat "whatever detritus the troopers' boots grind down." "Whether it is tatters / Of holy books or the torn blood of children, / I will eat that," he vows, for he wants to understand what he ironically terms "civilization."

Five of the six other poems in part 4 address death and suffering, and three of them include the term "terror" or the phrase "the terrors," a word that concludes the fifth poem of "The Transformed Twilight" as well. Like the speaker in "The Capacity for Pain," like the Lucretius portrayed in "Urleid" who "*walked out far to view the Gorgon / Terror*" (54; Chappell's italics), like the Thomas Hardy who provides the epigraph to part 4, Chappell never dodges or slights pain and anguish. As Ole Fred says in *Midquest,* "Our faith must be earned from terror" (87). It is toward faith, toward affirmation, that part 4 moves, as its title poem intimates, yet not without acknowledging the many times when "the prayed-for transformation / remains stone"

("Windows" 50). In "Urleid," a German word suggesting ancient or aboriginal sorrow, Chappell focuses, as already noted, on Lucretius, the Roman philosopher and poet who numbered the soul among material things and thereby sought to liberate people from fear of divine punishment in an afterlife. Chappell lightens the mood of this poem by inserting humorous anachronisms. He has Lucretius deplore, for example, the mysticism of "the detestable Rilke: those angels" and proclaim, "The silliest *movie* is that empty drawing room farce / They call Olympus" (53; italics added). While some critics have contended that Chappell's outlook in *Source* is itself essentially the atomism of Lucretius's *De Rerum Natura,*[14] the poem's closing lines, addressed to the philosopher, suggest otherwise: "We saw you in the white fountain of delirium / Burning but not purified" (54). These lines allude to the legend that Lucretius died in fiery pain after being given a poison assumed to be a love potion.

The following poem, "Message," dedicated to fellow poet David Slavitt, whose mother had been murdered in her home by an intruder, uses the very angel image Lucretius rejects. And although "Message" starts with "The first messenger angel . . . / purely clothed in terror" (55), the poem progresses to a moment of revelation when the message's recipient "is transformed head to foot, taproot to polestar. / He breathes a new universe . . ." (55). Here, in contrast to the closing lines of "Windows," transformation does occur. The basis of Chappell's faith in such transformation is implied in *Source*'s penultimate poem, "O Sacred Head Now Wounded," which takes its title from a hymn on which Bach based one of his cantatas. In keeping with the generally somber tone of part 4, Chappell presents a portrait of the suffering Christ and the Bosch-like fleering faces that surround Him. This poem consists entirely of sentence fragments, as if to mirror the broken condition of the soon-to-be-executed Jesus. Crucifixion, not resurrection, is the focus of this poem. And yet, Chappell seems to suggest, there is implicit consolation here, for Christianity witnesses to a God who is not remote from human history and human suffering but who has entered the world of time and embraced suffering. Pain and death remain, but so does the promise of resurrection, a promise inextricably bound up, for Christians, with the crucifixion.

It is that promise of resurrection which Chappell emphasizes in *Source*'s final poem, "Forever Mountain," dedicated to the memory of his father. "Now a lofty smoke has cleansed my vision," the poem opens (57), a clarifying smoke in contrast to the obscuring fog of the book's initial poem. The tranquil mood of the poem and its exquisite images of nature's beauty set it apart from all the other poems in part 4. The poet envisions his father climbing Pisgah, a mountain not far from Chappell's Canton but also the mountain from which Moses viewed the Promised Land (Deut. 34: 1–4). The steady ease with which the poet's father ascends the slope, "taking by plateaus the mountain that possesses him," lends an air of assurance, a quiet certitude, to this vision. Chappell concludes the poem with the italicized line, "*This is a prayer,*" and he thus links this poem to the gracefull prayers of part 1 and to the religious conviction that underlies his work, a faith that he repeatedly tests and refines in the fires of suffering and death and doubt.

Not all the poems of *Source* sustain the level of artistic excellence and the thematic significance of the book's finest work. Yet the best of these poems—"A Prayer for the Mountains," "Humility," "Awakening to Music," "Music as a Woman Imperfectly Perceived," "Latencies," "Narcissus and Echo," "Urleid," and "Forever Mountain"—are superb, and many others are almost equally good. Moreover, even the slighter poems (e.g., "Charge" or "Rib") have a role to play in the book's thematic design and gain power from the contexts in which they appear. To appreciate Chappell's artistry readers must recognize such thematic structures and the principles of organization the poet has employed.

First and Last Words

The title of this volume reflects the fact that the first section consists of nine poems conceived as prologues to other works of art while the third section contains nine poems conceived as epilogues. Between these two stands a central section of sixteen poems aptly titled "Entr'acte," a term that designates not simply an intermission between the parts of a performance but a dance or musical composition or play presented in that interval. The very format of this collection, with its prologues and epilogues, presupposes the ongoing relevance of the past to the present and assumes, as *Midquest* does, a community of mind that transcends place and time. Like *Midquest, First and Last Words* is committed to conserving a rich heritage of human aspiration and expression. "These poems are the product," Chappell has said, "of my thinking over the years about the books and authors I've been teaching and the books I've read to prepare to teach. You could say it's a kind of homage to Western Civilization."[15]

One of the most striking qualities about this book's subject matter—and thus, in part, about Chappell's reading—is its range. The poet writes prologues and epilogues not just to literary texts but to books of the Bible, Goethe's *Theory of Colors,* Kant's *Prolegomena,* Einstein's *Relativity,* and the United States Constitution. He also provides responses to Copland's *Appalachian Spring,* to the film *The Cabinet of Dr. Caligari,* and, in "Entr'acte," to paintings by Rubens and Vermeer and to the music of Anton von Webern and his teacher, Arnold Schoenberg. The writers included span the period from roughly the sixth century B.C. (the Book of Job) to the twentieth century (Allen Tate's 1938 novel *The Fathers* being the most recently published text). The prologues are arranged chronologically from most ancient written text to most recent; the epilogues, in contrast, are less precise in their individual ordering but generally move backwards in time, in groups of three poems each, from the twentieth century to the eighteenth century and then to the broadly defined ancient world of *De Rerum Natura, Beowulf,* and the Gospels. The loosely structured "Entr'acte" provides the book with sufficient flexibility to avoid a rigid pattern. Yet Chappell connects this middle section directly to the prologues and epilogues by having "Entr'acte" begin with the poems on Rubens and Vermeer and end with "Webern's Mountain."

In many respects, then, *First and Last Words* is a bookish, highly allusive text, one that, like *Midquest,* lends credence to George Garrett's observation, "Fred Chappell is the best-read person I know."[16] Some of these poems clearly demand a well-educated reader, a person familiar with the works the poet is examining. Yet many of the poems present self-contained psychological portraits or meditations on a theme that enable them to achieve vitality apart from their sources. As Henry Taylor notes, "Chappell makes us at ease with what he is talking about, however familiar or unfamiliar the works he addresses."[17] Moreover, as Peter Makuck points out in his discussion of "Subject Matter," Chappell's epilogue to Goethe's *Theory of Colors,* these poems often resemble those of W. H. Auden, whom "Subject Matter" depicts as composing a "bookish poem // that seemed somehow not bookish at all. / Seemed instead a colloquy."[18] There is indeed a conversational quality to many of the poems, a quality reinforced in "Subject Matter" by Chappell's addressing the reader as "you" *after* the word "colloquy" appears in the text. More importantly, "Subject Matter" even implies that the reader need not have read the text under discussion. With a guide as skilled as Auden (or Chappell),

> You'd come away
> believing you *knew* the book you hadn't read
>   half through, and that something had been said
>   that made the stubborn Ocean of the Past
> whiffle with a bit of zephyr from Today
>   as the poet chatted.
>
> (47; Chappell's italics)

The reader feels that bit of zephyr throughout *First and Last Words,* and as in "Subject Matter," so in other poems, the presumed inspiration for the text is not always the principal focus of the poet's remarks.

Whereas folk and fairy tale motifs underlie many of the poems in *Source,* Chappell has said that *First and Last Words* is a book with "less use of folk material."[19] Nevertheless, as Don Johnson remarks of this volume and others, "Chappell's poetry . . . remains firmly rooted in the homeplace soil of the southern Appalachian mountains."[20] The first prologue, in fact, is titled "An Old Mountain Woman Reading the Book of Job." A meditation in stately blank verse and one of the most moving pieces in the entire collection, this poem links *First and Last Words* to *Source* not only in setting but also in theme, for Chappell again raises the mystery of suffering that recurs throughout part 4 of *Source.* The widowed mountain woman recalls the suffering of her dead husband, "whom the Lord like a hunting lion / Has carried off" (6). Although, like Job, "she never shall curse God," Chappell also writes of her:

> She will not suffer
> A God Who suffers the suffering of man,
> Who sends the fatherless their broken arms,
> Who sends away the widows empty as faith.
>
> (6)

"Tonight's no night for the heartless bedside prayer," the poem concludes, recognizing perhaps, in its use of the word "tonight," that the woman may be reconciled with God some other day.[21] But on this occasion she remains adamant, rebelling against humanity's inexplicable burden of pain and loss.

A number of other poems in this book share the regional setting of *Midquest* and of such poems in *Source* as "A Prayer for the Mountains" and "Forever Mountain." "The Gift to Be Simple" is a prologue to Aaron Copland's *Appalachian Spring,* for example, and both "Patience," a prologue to Virgil's *Georgics,* and "Scarecrow Colloquy," the epilogue to the Gospels that concludes *First and Last Words,* invoke the agrarian landscape of *Midquest.* Chappell is careful, however, to avoid pastoral primitivism. In "Patience," which employs a hexameter line inspired by Virgil's classical meter, Chappell undercuts the utopian outlook presented in the poem's opening section by beginning the second section with the statement, "Always the Poet knew it wasn't that way" (9). The lines that follow this statement largely translate the final lines of Book I of *The Georgics,* where Virgil describes a world immersed in bloodshed, a violence into which the farmer is conscripted. The agricultural life endures, for people must eat; but according to Virgil, farmers must labor strenuously if they are to succeed. In the third section of this three-part poem, the reader senses Chappell's *im*patience with the marginalizing of the farmer and of agriculture not only in Virgil's day but also in our own. Like "The Transformed Twilight," "Patience" might be numbered among Chappell's political poems.

In fact, many if not all of these prologues address three major themes: the nature of evil; the often frustrated quest for peace and justice in a world rife with war; and the varied human responses to suffering and injustice. Such concerns are obvious features of "An Old Mountain Woman" and "Patience" and of the intervening rhymed poem "The Watchman," a prologue to Aeschylus's *Oresteia.* While the Book of Job in "An Old Mountain Woman" deals with what philosophers call *natural* evil, "The Watchman" deals with moral evil, with evil that originates in human conduct.

"The Watchman" introduces the subject of war, which is

pursued in "Patience," in "Legions" (a prologue to the Roman historian Livy), and in each additional prologue, either explicitly or implicitly. That topic appears more implicitly than explicitly in the two poems that follow "Legions," the first drawn from Tolstoy's diary, the second a prologue to his novella *The Death of Ivan Ilych.* Yet Tolstoy is also the author of *War and Peace,* and both poems revolve around intense conflicts. In "Tolstoy's Bear," for instance, Chappell begins with a passage from the writer's diary that focuses on Tolstoy's sense of moral struggle, his attempt to "set down new Rules / Of Life" in the manner of Benjamin Franklin's *Autobiography* (12). The principal event in the poem is Tolstoy's encounter with a huge bear that attacks him during a hunt. The poem thus incorporates both humanity's conflict with an often hostile natural world and the individual's internal moral struggles. Chappell's use of this incident from Tolstoy's life seems to have been influenced by Delmore Schwartz's symbolic equation of bear and body in "The Heavy Bear Who Goes with Me," a poem that ends with the line, "The scrimmage of appetite everywhere."[22] Given Chappell's preoccupation with the tension between will and appetite, Schwartz's poem is likely to have had a special resonance for him.

The prologue to *The Death of Ivan Ilych,* "Meanwhile," also centers upon intense conflict, in this case Ivan's confrontation with human finitude. Yet Chappell attends less to death itself than to the choices people make before death strikes. "A man must get ahead in the world," the poem opens (13), its neatly ordered unrhymed quatrains contrasting with the loss of control Ivan experiences. Like Tolstoy, Chappell underscores the tension between one's *career* and one's *life.* "A man must get ahead in the world," the poet repeats from Ivan's point of view in the text's penultimate line, "The world that breaks its first and only promise," the author concludes. Yet the poem, like the Russian novella on which it is based, produces an awareness more of self-betrayal than of external treachery.

Chappell does not, however, simply dismiss Ivan's complaint. Instead he returns to it again in the subsequent poem, "Stoic Poet," a prologue to Thomas Hardy's *The Dynasts.* Hardy's consciousness of human suffering and of the universe's indifference to it leads him to compassion, not to insensitivity. Although "Terrors assail him," he retains "his human sympathies" (14). Like the Lucretius of *Source*'s "Urleid," Hardy represents qualities of courage and endurance amid "the wounds of the world's every crime." Through Hardy's example Chappell affirms the capacity for moral conduct and humane values even in a universe that the Victorian author perceives as amoral.

Just as Chappell plays Hardy's personality off against that of Ivan Ilych, so he contrasts Hardy's experience of glacial chill ("our stars implacable and indifferent") with the vision of "A natural transparent Open Harmony" (15) in "The Gift to Be Simple." The tone and meter and exact rhymes of this prologue to *Appalachian Spring,* based on a Shaker hymn tune, differentiate it from all the other poems in the book's opening section. Chappell's frequent anapests create a lilting rhythm that belies the music's composition in 1943–44, at the height of World War II. At times that rhythm appears to be used for ironic effect, and yet the words of the poem attest to the power of music, imaged as "that Valley of love and delight." Here as elsewhere in Chappell's work, music is linked to "Order" (with a capital *O*) and is credited with helping us "straiten our Lives." The ability of the arts, both literary and nonliterary, to engender and sustain moral insight, to effect moral change, is one of the principal tenets of Chappell's artistic credo. Still, the optimism of this poem's closing quatrain is sharply qualified by almost all the other prologues.

The final prologue, "Afternoons with Allen," masterfully integrates the major themes sounded throughout the book's opening section. The Allen of the poem's title is Allen Tate, a one-time colleague of Chappell at the University of North Carolina–Greensboro and one of the major figures in Southern writing in the first half of the twentieth century. By presenting this poem as a prologue to Tate's Civil War novel, *The Fathers* (1938), Chappell again invokes the theme of war, a theme further reinforced by allusions to Homer and to Virgil, both appropriate figures given Tate's own classicism in such poems as "Aeneas at Washington" and "The Mediterranean." "Afternoons with Allen" concludes, in fact, with a quotation from Book II of *The Aeneid,* the book in which Virgil has Aeneas recall the Trojan War that was Homer's principal subject. The poem thus looks back to "The Watchman," "Patience," and "Legions," all grounded in classical literature. Ironically, the urbane conversations between the poet and Tate occur against the backdrop of televised professional football, a species of ritualized war.

The particular game referred to involves Vince Lombardi's Washington Redskins and an unnamed opponent. One critic has suggested that Chappell's emphasis on Tate's "pale pale eyes" is meant to recall the struggle between the "palefaces" and Indians in American history.[23] Whether or not this meaning was part of Chappell's intention, the reference to Lombardi is itself significant, for during the one year when Lombardi coached the Red-skins, he was afflicted with as yet undiagnosed cancer, a disease emblematic of the physical evil that nature dispenses not just to Lombardi but also to the husband of the old mountain woman reading Job, to Ivan Ilych, and to the innumerable anonymous recipients of Hardy's sympathies in "Stoic Poet." It is for Lombardi that Tate cites the poem's closing line from *The Aeneid,* a line that Chappell uses to foreshadow Tate's own death as well: "*Forsitan et, Priami fuerint quae fata, requiras?*" (16). As Peter Makuck has pointed out, in Virgil's epic this line occurs after the Greek warriors have breached King Priam's palace, and the Roman poet pauses to address the reader: "Perhaps now you will ask the doom [or fate] of Priam?"[24] The king's response is to take up arms in a futile attempt to defend his city and to avenge the death of the son who is killed moments later before his eyes. In this poem, then, rich allusiveness and the mundane details of Sunday afternoon football combine to produce a text that reca-pitulates the major subjects of the preceding prologues. At the same time, "Afternoons with Allen" clearly demonstrates how the world of literature and the world of daily living interpenetrate and enrich one another, a theme Chappell explores at greater length in "Entr'acte."

The longest and most varied section in this book, "Entr'acte" opens with a three-part poem whose title reflects the cross-fertil-ization of art and life, "My Hand Placed on a Rubens Drawing." Here the interconnection of the two is made palpable by the poet's gesture of resting his hand on the drawing. The poem focuses ini-tially not on Rubens's art but on the poet's hand, and its opening lines can be read as an invitation to the reader to join in a spirit of attentive wonder, of glimpsed possibilities: "It is what it is, / And being what it is, is something more" (19)

In part 2 of the poem, Chappell turns to Rubens's drawing itself. "Not the usual Rubens woman," he notes in a series of musical metaphors:

Rubens for once is not sounding the whole
Outsized orchestra of Flemish flesh,
The tuba bellies and thighs, kettledrum buttocks,
The pale blond appogiatura breasts.

She is chamber music.

(20)

The appropriateness of this exuberant figurative language is apparent to anyone familiar with Rubens's luscious nudes. Yet despite the delicacy and refinement attributed to this woman through Chappell's reference to chamber music, her hands evince her farmer ancestry: "The smell of earth about them, undertone / Of cabbage, onion, potato, the branmeal loaf" (21). Such vivid, earthy images evoke the agrarian lifestyle not only of "Patience" but also of Chappell's own childhood, so that this young woman becomes the poet's counterpart, as Rubens himself does too when the poet proclaims, "Rubens sinks the piers of vision deep / Into the earth" (21). Surely the same is true of the author of *Source* and even more so of *Midquest,* with its use of the four elements and its portraits of Virgil Campbell and Uncle Body.

"My Hand Placed on a Rubens Drawing" concludes with a brief coda consisting of two rhymed quatrains that contrast stylistically with the loose blank verse of the preceding sections. These last eight lines emphasize the spiritual dimension of Chappell's view of art. Pulling back from the drawing itself, the poet generalizes, as he does so effectively at many points in his work.

> The ages work toward mastery
> Of a single gesture. . . .

> Fragments that might still add up
> To compose a figure of the perfected soul . . .
>
> (21)

Chappell rhymes "soul" with "whole" in the second quatrain and thus underscores the integrative thrust of his art, his longing to reconcile opposites, to create a unified and unifying vision.

Though some of the poems of "Entr'acte" (for instance, "Slow Harbor," "A Prayer for the Hanged Man," and "Score") are only loosely related to the book's principal themes, the four poems that cluster at the center of the volume are essential to the interpenetration of literature and life—and of past and present texts—that *First and Last Words* posits. These four poems are titled "Word," "Literature," "The Reader," and "The Garden," with "Literature" standing exactly at the midpoint of the volume's thirty-five poems, on a facing page with "The Reader." Far lighter in tone than most of the prologues, these poems fancifully explore the centrality of word and story in defining both self and world.

In "Word," for example, Chappell highlights the rejuvenating power of literature, its ability to make new identities possible, "a clean snowfield into which we march like children, / printing our fine new names" (27). In "Literature" Chappell traces a double, or actually triple, movement that balances the impulse to realism against the impulse to idealism. "The girls and flowers keep changing into literature," the poem begins, and they thus enact literature's desire to achieve a transfiguring moment "when all the world becomes a picture catalogue of gardens" (28). In Chappell's view, however, that ideal realm must be regularly regrounded in actualities lest it attenuate into airy nothing. Chappell rejects Wallace Stevens's tendency to substitute what Stevens called "the planet on the table" (the book) for the natural world. Yet he also criticizes people's failure to look beyond the immanent to the transcendent, their inability to find in literature a deeper vision of the human experience that will enrich their lives. In the poem "Literature" the planet created by literature's abstracting and idealizing impulse "throbs in its orbit like a hive of sleepy bees" and is "a world prepared for men." Yet "no one comes," the closing lines of the poem remark, "each reader still entranced / by the courtly chronicle of his native world" (28). Given the wonders of the physical world, such entrancement is understandable, Chappell implies—but it is ultimately impoverishing.

Both "The Reader," dedicated to the poet's mother-in-law, Helene Nicholls, and "The Garden" involve similar dialectics and paradoxes. In the former the first stanza ends with a surprising personification: "The books read into her long through the night" (29). In this poem, instead of people opening books, the *book* opens the reader. Moreover, the story the reader encounters is one "that has no end," though any particular text clearly has a terminus. "[Books] bring the world—or some outlook of its soul— / Into her small apartment," the poet observes, again combining the temporal and the spiritual through his diction. The elegance of such lines as "a light / The color of cool linen bathes her hands," creates a mood of calm reflection and intense emotional fulfillment. Chappell attains comparable effects in "The Garden," a poem that employs what has steadily become one of the governing metaphors of his entire body of work: from the Edenic images *Midquest* evokes at key moments, through the ravaged garden of "The Overspill" (the opening section of *I Am One of You Forever*), to the garden's structural and thematic function in the new and selected poems of *Spring Garden,* and on into the rose and garden imagery of *Look Back All the Green Valley.* Biblical in origin, this garden metaphor is perhaps most directly inspired in Chappell's work by Dante's mystic Rose in the *Paradiso.* But it is a metaphor that enables Chappell to embrace both the immanent and the transcendent in a balance toward which his writing repeatedly aspires.

"The Garden" opens by stating, "The garden is a book about the gardener," and continues by elaborating on this initial figure of speech.

Her thoughts, set down in vivid greenery,
The green light and the gold light nourish.
Firm sentences of grapevine, boxwood paragraphs,
End-stops of peonies and chrysanthemums,
Cut drowsy shadows on the paper afternoon.

(30)

These lush images link nature and art, but the poem's opening statement may also be read as a version of one of the five classical proofs of God's existence, the argument from design. Such a reading is reinforced by the subtle paradox of Chappell's closing lines: "The book is open once again that was never shut. / What now we do not know we shall never know." These lines anticipate "After Revelation," the final story in *More Shapes Than One,* while functioning here to undercut the invitation to logical proof of God's existence that the argument from design presumes to offer. Between these opening and closing statements Chappell inserts another paradox by reversing the terms of the poem's initial line, declaring instead, "The gardener is a book about her garden." The end-stop in both lines gives each an aura of quiet certitude despite their apparent contradiction. This ability to grasp conflicting or opposing ideas and to hold them in fruitful tension is one of the qualities Chappell's poetry nurtures in its readers even as it aspires to an ultimate reconciliation of opposites.

The final poem of "Entr'acte" is titled "Webern's Mountain." The mountain image of the title, while recalling the landscape of the poet's birth and of the volume's opening poem, also suggests the heights of spiritual and artistic vision—"the perfect nobility of true Idea," according to the poem (37). While the title refers to Webern, the poem focuses not on that composer but on his teacher, Schoenberg, for *berg* means mountain in German and *Schoen* means beautiful. Schoenberg thus is "the lovely mountain [that] fled to America, / The beautiful mountain that was Webern's father," in the poem's closing lines. While Schoenberg escaped Nazi Germany, Webern remained in his homeland, to be killed accidentally by an American soldier after the cessation of hostilities. The wartime context of this poem relates it to Chappell's prologues, while its floral imagery extends the garden motif of the central poems in "Entr'acte." Of Schoenberg's artistic quest, Chappell writes:

> Might he not find among these terrible peaks
> The flower that Goethe postulated, Ur-plant,
> Theme for the infinite variations that greenly
> Populate the world and all its mind?

> (37)

Though Schoenberg seeks an "order consecrate by Origin," his search for such an absolute is shattered by Hitler's tyrannical "Ordnung for the blond millennia," an Ordnung opposed as well to the Order depicted in "The Gift to Be Simple," the other poem in this collection that directly addresses the art of music. The desire for order, Chappell implies, must not displace the quest for social justice, for what the poem calls "the true nobility of perfect freedom."

The third and last section of the book, "Epilogues," continues the prologues' exploration of war, the quest for justice, and the struggle against evil, both internal and external. But this section is unified less by its treatment of these themes than by its analysis of the tension between subjectivity and objectivity and of the mind's or imagination's crucial role in defining reality. This section's opening poem, "Caligari by Dreamlight," an epilogue to the German film *The Cabinet of Dr. Caligari* (1919), is linked by nationality to the closing poem of "Entr'acte" and by its use of popular culture to the final prologue, "Afternoons with

Allen." The title's term "dreamlight" emphasizes the subjective, as does Caligari's descent into madness, signaled by the poem's abrupt shifts in point of view.

It is the third epilogue, "Observers," based on Einstein's *Relativity,* that voices most explicitly the modern era's preoccupation with subjectivity, its recognition of the limits of human knowing, its conviction that "all the consistent systems lie to one another" (43). That conviction is intensified, of course, in the dogmas of postmodernism. According to "Observers," it is Einstein's speculations on the relativity of space and time "that allow us to say / *Let us suppose*" (43; Chappell's italics). Yet as the poet intimates in the preceding poem, "Years Afterward," an epilogue to *The Wind in the Willows,* and in the later poem, "Subject Matter," the literary imagination has long played "let us suppose" without surrendering thereby its commitment to objective realities beyond the imagination and the thinking self. In "Years Afterward" that objective reality is a cultural artifact, the children's book itself. In "Subject Matter" that objective reality is both a cultural artifact, Goethe's *Theory of Colors,* and another human being, the poet Auden, whom Chappell praises not only explicitly, through the poem's content, but also implicitly, through its Audenesque formal structure. In "Observers" too it is toward such objective realities that the poet moves the reader, specifically "the blackened matchstem that was Nagasaki" in the poem's final line (44). To ignore the consequences of ideas, to fail to recognize the implications of our supposings, is more than dangerous; it can be fatal, Chappell insists.

While Chappell is deeply aware of the complex interrelationship between the subjective and objective, in these epilogues, as elsewhere in his writing, he seems most concerned with the loss of objective reality posited by philosophical idealism and its postmodern variants. "Ideally Grasping the Actual Flower," an epilogue to Kant's *Prolegomena to Any Future Metaphysics,* returns to the images of garden and rose in "Entr'acte." Yet Kantian idealism relegates the "real" flower to a realm remote from sensory experience, a realm, Chappell notes ironically, "As empiric as the faultless Empyrean" (46). Similarly, the human figure in the poem, whom Chappell has identified not as Kant but as Wallace Stevens,[25] is depicted as "at large in the garden which perhaps he postulates," where he is paradoxically "determined to picture this *rose* as pictureless" (45). According to Chappell, Stevens shares with Kant philosophical premises that tend to sever humanity from nature. The recovery of the actual, of the concrete physical world, is a recurring theme in Chappell's poetry. In fact Chappell directs the reader's gaze not toward the "arbitrary starlight" of "Observers" (44) but toward "the cathedral of starlight" in "Slow Harbor" (24). He invites the reader on a pilgrimage "directly to the source / of light, where an endless sheet of stars / burns palpitant and interweaving" (48).

Significantly, the final poem in *First and Last Words,* "Scarecrow Colloquy," presents the title character as a "Sentinel of the Stars" (56). Labeled an epilogue to the Gospels, this closing poem is a companion piece to the book's initial poem on Job. Together these two poems attest to the religious dimension of both Chappell's work and the Western literary and philosophical tradition. Yet like "An Old Mountain Woman Reading the Book of Job," "Scarecrow Colloquy" is a poem of doubt as well as of faith. In fact, as Makuck has remarked, "The poem can easily be seen as dialogue between Faith and Skepticism,"[26] with the scarecrow representing faith and his unnamed interlocutor representing skepticism. The latter speaks first, in tercets that alternate with the quatrains assigned to the scarecrow. Chappell thus not only allows the scarecrow to speak at greater length but also provides him with the last word—indeed, the "last words" of the entire collection. The scarecrow's poignant longing for a decisive revelation of the divine is among the most moving elements in this poem. But that revelation never occurs, and the reader may seem to be left with a portrait only of the scarecrow's fidelity, his patient endurance despite the silence and absence of the God he yearns to hear. Ultimately, however, the scarecrow may be more than an embodiment of faith. He also appears to be an image of the crucified Christ, Eliot's hanged man. If so, then the "hard farmer" may be less an emblem of an indifferent God and more a symbol of humanity's failure to accept the possibility of redemption inherent in Christ's self-sacrificial death. As the anonymous interlocutor tells the scarecrow, albeit ironically, "This disaster they call a world might find a pivot / if you but stand outlined within the sunrise" (56).

The ambiguity here is characteristic of Chappell, as is the impulse to allegory that lends the poem its evocative power. The scarecrow's closing words, with their allusion to Isaiah 40 and to the legend that Jesus was crucified on the same spot where Adam was buried, suggest that more than human fidelity is at stake in this poem:

I have spoken in the field till my voice became an owl.
I have surveyed the horizon till I lost my buttons.

The fieldmouse heard my silence and gnawed my flesh of
    grass.
And still I stand here, guarding the bones of Adam.
                    (57; Chappell's italics)

While Isaiah 40: 6 avers that "all flesh is grass," that chapter of
Isaiah's prophecy also declares, "The word of our God will stand
for ever" (v. 8), like the figure of Chappell's enduring Scarecrow-
Christ. Moreover, the word that Isaiah 40 proclaims is one of
comfort and pardon and divine love even when it appears to Israel
that God is absent or unseeing (vs. 1–2, 27–28). Although Chappell's poetry gives voice to doubt, it does so largely within a biblical tradition. Makuck errs, therefore, when he contends that this
book's closing poem "endorses a Hardyesque world" in which
the scarecrow's "inexhaustible voice [is] still talking to its self-
made Other, whistling in the dark."[27] Much of Chappell's poetry,
in contrast, presents not a self-made Other but the God manifest
in the Judeo-Christian tradition, a divine presence as objectively
real for the poet as nature itself—and often equally inscrutable.
Makuck correctly perceives, however, the essentially religious
outlook of Chappell's poetic sensibility. "In the best sense of the
word," Makuck observes, "Fred Chappell is an old-fashioned
poet, one for whom writing is a spiritual project. . . . Chappell's
poems implicitly argue against the current literary/philosophical
notion that words are problematically referential, or don't have
meaning, or don't mean much. Chappell knows they mean plenty
and, skillfully used, are capable of providing sustenance and
solace."[28]

    First and Last Words serves to remind the reader of many of the sources of such sustenance throughout the Western tradition, not only in literature and art and music but also in philosophy and religion. The volume accomplishes that purpose with astonishing breadth of intellect and singular artistry, qualities that make it one of the author's best books.

C

The publication of *C* in 1993 marked both a new development in Chappell's poetry and a confirmation of long-standing tendencies in his career. After the demands he imposed on his readers in *First and Last Words,* Chappell turns in *C* to poems that are substantially shorter, much more humorous, and far more accessible in diction and subject matter. Yet, as in his preceding volume and in *Midquest,* Chappell draws on earlier writers to establish a community of mind and imagination that interfuses past and present—in this case by utilizing the classical and neoclassical tradition of the epigram. Other twentieth-century American poets have composed epigrams, of course, most notably J. V. Cunningham and Howard Nemerov, but *C*, like *Midquest* and *First and Last Words,* derives more from the broader Western literary tradition than from any distinctively American influence.

The title *C* announces the book's connection to the classical world, for "C" is the Roman numeral 100, and *C* consists of one hundred poems. But the title assumes other meanings as well. "C" is the poet's initial, after all, and spoken aloud the letter also represents, says Chappell, the imperative mood of the verb "to see."[29] David Slavitt links the title to Wallace Stevens's poem, "The Comedian as the Letter *C,*" and Chappell has said, "I became interested in epigrams because I'm interested in humor in writing."[30] Humor becomes a major feature of Chappell's work after 1970, and the poems that comprise *C* were written over a fifteen-year period starting near the end of that decade. "Some . . . I did in a few minutes; others I kept polishing for up to 10 years," the poet has remarked.[31]

So short a title is certainly appropriate to a book of epigrams, a poetic form noted for its compression, its wit, and its careful crafting. Many readers assume that epigrams must have a satirical edge, for the epigram in English has generally followed the example set by the Roman poet Martial. *C* includes a number of poems of this sort, particularly those aimed at literary critics, physicians, and politicians (among them, Jesse Helms in "El Perfecto"). But in conceiving this book, Chappell has clearly drawn on the broader epigrammatic tradition of *The Greek Anthology,* that gathering of some four thousand works by classical Greek poets, with its wide range of subject and tone and formal structures. In *C,* as in *The Greek Anthology,* the lyric impulse is almost as prominent as the satiric, with the elegiac impulse also much in evidence. Chappell's epigrams vary greatly in rhyme scheme, length and structure as well as in subject matter and tone. Twelve of the poems are composed of just two lines, but only six of those use rhymed couplets in iambic tetrameter or pentameter. One of the two-line poems, a translation from the twentieth-century Italian writer Giuseppe Ungaretti, simply reads, "Immensity / Illumes me."[32] While three of *C*'s poems consist of a single line (LXIV, LXVI, LXVII), others are substantially longer than readers might expect of the stereotypical epigram. Seven run to at least fourteen lines, with the longest, "The Ubi Sunt Lament of the Beldame Hen," extending to twenty-eight lines.

Even when these poems employ quatrains (as customary as the couplet in traditional English epigrams), Chappell achieves a variety that prevents monotony. Poems XV–XIX, for example, consist of a single quatrain each. Yet Chappell alters the rhyme schemes and the meter from poem to poem and also varies each poem's appearance on the page. Though most of the lines in these five poems are end-stopped, enjambment is another device Chappell uses effectively to differentiate the poems' aural effects. The same is true of the number and placement of stressed and unstressed syllables in each line. Iambic tetrameter predominates in this series of poems, but poem XIX, "Toadstool," relies on a strikingly different meter, with its alternating trimeter and dimeter lines.

He's the oddest fellow
  Ever was made,
Lifting his white umbrella
  To ward off shade.

(8)

The heavy initial stresses in the first three lines of "Toadstool" are also one of Chappell's characteristic devices in *C*. Such line openings command attention, pulling the reader into the poem. In its subject matter "Toadstool" indicates something of the unexpected range of material Chappell incorporates in these epigrams. Indeed *C* encompasses many of the poet's recurring concerns, among them nature, love, literature itself, religion, and death. Sometimes these subjects are treated satirically, but often the poet merely invites the reader to *see* them in new ways, as in "Toadstool," a poem reminiscent of Emily Dickinson in its whimsical personification and its paradoxical angle of vision.

C begins with "Proem," which invokes Martial, and three of the next four poems are translations, two of epigrams by Martial. The fourth of these poems paraphrases Juvenal and refers to other satirists like Aristophanes and Terence. Initially, then, Chappell places *C* squarely in the tradition of the satiric epigram as it was established by Martial. Yet by including in this opening group of poems the already quoted text by Ungaretti, Chappell enlarges the book's range of subjects and tones and also aligns himself with twentieth-century poets, not just with classical precursors. Moreover, Ungaretti's lines, "Immensity / Illumes me," testify to the sense of wonder and the promise of illumination that underlie Chappell's whole poetic enterprise.

A quarter of the poems in *C* consist of translations, an art to which Chappell has found himself increasingly attracted, as the various prologues in *Spring Garden* also attest. Michael McFee explains the presence of so many translations in *C* by noting, "An epigram is part of an ongoing literary conversation, an exchange of quick minds and pens, where the point is not the individual who wrote the poem . . . but rather the truth and pithy eloquence of what's said."[33] These translations tend to confirm Chappell's belief in the persistence through time of fundamental human experiences that literature attempts to clarify as well as his commitment to ongoing dialogue with other writers, both past and present.

In *C* Chappell uses several important devices to enliven that dialogue. One is anachronism of the sort he employed in *Source*'s "Urleid." In "Proem," for instance, where Martial speaks, Chappell has him compare forceful epigrams to telegrams, since both can "deliver intelligence / With such a sudden blaze / The shine can make us wince" (1). In *C*'s second poem, "Small Is Beautiful," a translation of Martial, Chappell inserts the term "Silly Putty," and in "How To Do It," another translation from Martial, he has the Roman poet address him as "Chappell." That poem, which deals with the things that make life blessed, is followed by "Rejoinder," in which Chappell enumerates the things that make life boring. Such a pairing of poems is another device Chappell uses to enhance the sense of dialogue with the past and to expand the scope of the traditional self-contained epigram. Other paired poems include XI and XII, LXVI and LXVII, LXXXI and LXXXII, and XCVI and XCVII. The second of those pairs, "Definition" and "Corollary," includes two of the book's three one-line poems. They read, respectively: "The only animal that dares to play the bagpipes." "Or wants to" (32). These lines, in turn, echo in structure if not in sentiment, Mark Twain's strictures on humankind: "Man is the only animal that blushes. Or needs to."[34] Here again Chappell engages with one of his major influences— and one of the great satirists of the American literary tradition— though Chappell's lines are more humorous than satiric, less biting than Twain's.

Many of the poems in *C* do bite, however, do aim to make their targets wince. Four consecutive satirical epigrams about physicians, for example, poems XLI–XLIV, attack one of the favorite subjects of the humorists of Twain's era but also of far earlier satirists—three of these poems are translations from Martial, Lucilius, and Ausonius. Yet the hyperbole of Ausonius's "Memorial" is as characteristic of the tall tale as of ancient Greece or Rome, again confirming the timelessness of the epigram as a literary form:

In the plaza Dr. Shaddoe
Found the memorial to General Hyde.
Where he touched, the stone turned black.
Two weeks later the statue died.

(XLIV)

Chappell's satire is equally keen when directed at literary critics in poems XXIII–XXIX. The couplet that constitutes XXVI simply states, "Blossom's footnotes never shirk / The task of touting his own work," while XXIV reads:

Dr. Cheynesaugh has one rule
That makes all others void and null,
Embodying this sentiment:
Guilty till proven innocent.

The names the poet invents for these critics—Strychnine, Blandword, Professor Pliant, Dr. Cheynesaugh (pronounced *chainsaw,* presumably)—are part of the pleasure of these poems, as is his use of such a term as "hermeneuter." But Chappell does not simply write poems *about* literary critics; he writes poems *of* literary criticism, including "First Novel" (XIV) and "Upon a Confessional Poet" (XV):

> You've shown us all in stark undress
> The sins you needed to confess.
> If my peccadilloes were so small
> I never would undress at all.

In addition to satirizing others Chappell includes such self-deprecatory poems as "No Defense" (XVII), "Epitaph: The Poet" (XI), and "The Epigrammatist," *C*'s concluding poem: "Mankind perishes. The world goes dark. / He racks his brain for a tart remark."

Although tart remarks obviously abound in *C,* augmenting the humor of this text, clustered at the center of the book is a series of poems about women, sexuality, and love. Some of these poems are satiric—"Epitaph: The Playboy" (LI), "Epitaph: Lydia" (LIV), and "Sex Manual" (LV)—or comically exuberant in the manner of "A Glorious Twilight" (LXI). But many are wistfully lyric, marked by an awareness of love's fragility. The poignancy of "Ave Atque Vale" (LVIII) and "I Love You" (LIX) once again subvert common preconceptions about epigrams, as do the immediately preceding translations from Paul Éluard and Petrarch and the translation from Hölderlin that follows, a poem titled "Midway in This Life." That title recalls both Dante's *Divine Comedy* and Chappell's own *Midquest* and thus serves to remind the reader that *C* resembles the hanging lamp depicted in poem LXV: "A playful serious purpose informs the whole." Illumination, not mere diversion, is the book's intent. For Chappell, the exposure of folly, however entertaining, is subordinate to the quest for "the things that make life blest" (3).

While laughter is certainly one of life's blessings, along with literature and other works of art, *C* also celebrates love and nature and prayers that help to establish a relationship with God. As early as poem VII—well before, that is, the love poems at the book's midpoint—the poet invites his wife Susan to take a morning stroll around a lake.[35] And that poem is followed by three others that emphasize the wonders of nature: "Daisy," "White Clover," and "Chipmunk." In each Chappell personifies the object identified in the poem's title, thus enhancing that plant or animal's vitality and creating a kinship between nature and humanity. The daisy remarks,

> Men build Parises and Zions;
> I, wide meadows of Orions.
> Rome took two thousand years, but in one day
> I built a Milky Way.
>
> (5)

The contrast Chappell draws between the trimeter closing line and the preceding pentameter line suggests the ease of nature's creative outpourings. Moreover, by linking the Daisy to Orion, Chappell yokes nature to the heavens, creation to Creator, a conflation of images that is repeated in poems XXXVIII (where the snowflake is a "Sugar-star"), XLVI, and XLVII.

It is from nature that the poet obtains the dominant metaphor of "Wedding Anniversary" (LXII)—a tree that drought and frost almost destroyed but that "in its thirtieth year / . . . blooms like a candleflame, / And puts its youth to shame." But nature, in *C* as in *Earthsleep,* also speaks the lesson of mortality. In "Dandelion" (XXI) the weed of that title proclaims, "Ponder, friend, in me / Mortality," and in "Autumn Oaks" (XCIV) Chappell writes, "Our trees, those brides, are stripping now to skeletons. / And so shall I when I am wed to Winter."[36]

Despite the humor of many of its poems, *C* is a volume filled with memento mori. In fact the book contains six poems labeled epitaphs and another, "For the Tomb of the Little Dog Zabot" (XLV), that constitutes an epitaph. The epitaph is one of the epigram's conventional forms, so it is not surprising to find it among the poetic structures Chappell employs in *C.* In addition the epitaph is a device Chappell had used to delightful humorous effect earlier in his career, both in *Midquest*'s "At the Grave of Virgil Campbell" and in his portrait of Uncle Runkin in *I Am One of You Forever,* as Michael McFee has also noted. Here, in combination with such poems as "Dandelion," "Autumn Oaks," "The Intimation" (XL), "Foreshadowing" (XLIII), "The Old Actor" (LXXX), "Villon" (LXXXIII), and "The Ubi Sunt Lament of the Beldame Hen" (LXXXIV), poems sprinkled throughout the collection, Chappell's epitaphs highlight human finitude. The consciousness of time passing is reinforced by the book's structure, for despite occasional exceptions, the poems of *C* move from morning to night, from summer to winter, and from relative youth to old age. The earlier "Aubade" (VII), inviting Susan to walk outdoors, is balanced by "Serenade" (XC), which states, "Let's stay at home tonight." The three blessings said before meals (XXXIII–XXXV) are paralleled by three bedtime prayers (XCI–XCIII). As winter has banished summer, so the moon displaces the sun.

The imminence of death—not only in the volume's closing poems but also throughout the book—is meant to remind the reader that, in inventorying the things that make life blest, Martial (and Chappell) had concluded with, "A death not longed for, but without dread" (3). To reconcile the reader to the fact of mortality has been one of the consistent aims of Chappell's poetry and of much of his later fiction as well. In *C* that intention is particularly evident in the paired poems, "The Moon Regards the Frozen Earth" and "The Earth Replies" (XCVI–XCVII). In these two poems near the book's end, Chappell contrasts two opposing outlooks on life. The recriminatory moon, on the one hand, represents a narrowing of expectations, a retreat from experience into a fruitless asceticism; the earth, on the other hand, speaks for openness to experience, for an expansive celebration of life, including the gains and losses that attend mutability. It is, after all, the moon that is forever frozen, while the earth's winter will yield to spring. Chappell gives the earth almost twice the number of lines allotted to the moon, thus weighting the argument in the earth's favor. And the lighter tone of *C*'s last three poems seems meant to imply that the poet has indeed adopted earth's viewpoint.

It is tempting to attribute the poet's equanimity in the face of death to his religious convictions, especially given the prayer poems he incorporates in *C.* Yet as in the opening and closing poems of *First and Last Words,* so here, Chappell sets up a dialectic between faith and doubt. "Bless us who pray, bless us who can't," he writes in one of the graces said before a meal (14), including himself in both categories. Similarly, in "Dodder" the title suggests unsteady movement accompanied by trembling or shaking. But the term "dodder" also refers to a genus of parasitic vines belonging to the morning-glory family, vines deficient in chlorophyll and thus having scales instead of leaves. Given this definition of "dodder," the poem becomes more obviously a part of the series of three poems on natural objects—"Toadstool," "Honeysuckle," "Dandelion"—that precedes it. At the same time, "Dodder" extends the philosophical and theological concerns raised in "Dandelion," which insists that "even the yellow sun / Dwindles from the One" (9).

C is clearly, then, a book of far more than the satiric remarks many readers customarily associate with the epigram. Although the book opens and closes with poems about the epigram as a literary form, poems in which the terms "wince" and "tart" recall the satiric thrust of traditional English epigrams, Chappell's poems are as often lyric as satiric. The poet's choice of the epigram as his genre sets *C* apart from all his preceding collections, especially from the epic structures and motifs of *Midquest.* Yet in its themes, in its careful design, and in its creation of a sense of literary community across time, *C* embodies Chappell's major aesthetic commitments.

Spring Garden

When Chappell published *Spring Garden: New and Selected Poems* in 1995, he included twenty-five of the one hundred epigrams in *C.* The book also reprinted, usually greatly revised and sometimes retitled, ten poems from *The World between the Eyes,* over a third of the poems in *Source,* and just over half the poems in *First and Last Words.* From *Midquest* came only two poems: "Susan's Morning Dream of Her Garden," *Spring Garden*'s opening selection, and "My Grandmother Washes Her Feet," the latter present, Chappell has said, because it was the first of the narrative dialogue poems he wrote and thus marked a distinct turning point in his poetic career.[37] *Spring Garden* reprints no poems from *Castle Tzingal* because that book's dramatic structure did not encourage excerpting. In addition to the selected poems, *Spring Garden* contains nineteen new or previously uncollected poems,[38] together with a general prologue, an epilogue, and separate prologues for the seven sections into which the book is divided.

For a poet as attentive to his books' principles of organization as Chappell has been, preparing a volume of selected poems must have been a daunting and painful task, since poems had to be removed from the contexts into which they had been carefully placed. Chappell confirms this assumption in his interview with Resa Crane and James Kirkland. The first version of the book submitted to Louisiana State University Press seems to have followed the traditional pattern of most new and selected volumes, with the poems grouped according to their original place of publication. Copyediting the manuscript, Chappell was extremely disappointed, he reports: "It was like a book that was snippets of other books. I decided I had to do something with the whole thing . . . something to draw the poems together."[39] His solution, inspired by the French Renaissance poet Pierre de Ronsard (1524–1585), was to organize the book around the motif of a garden and to compare the selecting of the poems to the gathering of herbs depicted in Ronsard's poem "*La Salade.*"[40]

While this strategy may strike some readers as highly artificial, it has the benefit not only of providing a structural principle but also of grounding poetry—and human identity—firmly in nature. As David Middleton comments, "Chappell's metaphorical linking of poetry with specimens from the natural order is more than a convenient fancy; it represents a deep understanding of the relationship between the pastoral dream, the agrarian insistence on the binding of culture to agriculture, and the poet's double-rootedness in the eternal ground of being and in a postedenic earth."[41] On a more mundane level, moreover, *Spring Garden* is an apt title because it is part of the address of the university where Chappell has taught for more than thirty-five years.[42] A spring garden, then, is not only the book's principal setting but also its dominant metaphor, representing fecundity, harmony, and the promise of rebirth while evoking memories both of Eden and of the Earthly Paradise which Dante portrays in the closing cantos of the *Purgatorio.* Early in *Spring Garden,* Chappell refers to the book's setting as an "enchanted grove" (10). Yet Chappell's garden, as Middleton notes above, is decidedly postlapsarian. Consciousness of time passing and of death's approach pervades the volume. At times that concern with mortality seems excessive, almost morbid, considering the fact that Chappell was not yet sixty years old at the time he published the book. Nonetheless, the *carpe diem* motif is one of this volume's major unifying devices. Significantly, the pleasures the poet urges the reader to seize are not those of body alone; they also embrace the delights of the intellect, the imagination, and the spirit.

The poems of *Spring Garden* are divided into seven unnumbered sections of varying length: "In the Garden," "The Good

Life," "The Garden of Love," "Poems of Character," "Poems of Fantasy," "Epigrams," and "Poems of Memory." There is nothing mutually exclusive about these categories. That is to say, a poem like "Humility," which opens "Poems of Memory," might as readily appear in the section titled "The Good Life," while "Afternoons with Allen" might easily have been categorized as a poem of character rather than a poem of memory. But the titles of these sections obviously reflect many of Chappell's major preoccupations over the course of his career, from his stance as moralist/philosopher ("The Good Life") to his interests in fantasy and the epigram. Of these groupings Chappell has said, "The organization is just an accident of poems composed over many years that happened to fall into these different categories."[43] Yet such topics as love, character, and memory are not simply arbitrary classifications appropriate to this particular poet's output; they are perennial human concerns, just as the locus of the garden in Western literature and in the Judeo-Christian tradition assumes archetypal significance. It should be noted, moreover, that Chappell places the "Poems of Character" at the center of this series, as if to underscore the humanism that infuses his work. That section, the longest in the book, contains twenty-three poems—as many as the preceding three sections *combined.* The number seven itself, of course, carries connotations of the sacred because of its association with the account of creation in Genesis, but that number also suggests the theme of mutability, the inexorable advance of time as the days of the week unfold.

In addition to providing a general prologue and an epilogue, Chappell writes a separate untitled prologue for each of these seven sections. In all this material it is Fred Chappell the formalist poet who steps center stage, using an iambic pentameter eight-line stanza rhymed abbacdcd (except in the appropriately brief four-line prologue to "Epigrams"). Equally evident, however, is Fred Chappell the translator, whose first major appearance came in *C,* though he was also present in *Midquest*'s "In Parte Ove Non È Che Luca" and in the second section of "Patience" in *First and Last Words.* Scattered throughout these prologues (again, except for the prologue to "Epigrams") and the epilogue are a dozen poems translated from Latin, Italian, and French. Chappell's inclusion of such poems has the obvious advantage of enabling him to vary the prologues' eight-line stanzas with other verse forms, while it also establishes a sense of the larger literary community out of which the poet's work originates and to which it is indebted. Three-fourths of the translated poems are by French authors, with four of them by Ronsard—though the last of Ronsard's is itself a translation of the emperor Hadrian's sole surviving poem.

In many ways Ronsard is the presiding spirit in *Spring Garden.* Called by his contemporaries "the prince of poets," Ronsard was the chief poet of the Renaissance in France, the leader of the group of seven poets known as the Pléiade.[44] Like Chappell, Ronsard was deeply committed to a literature informed by the writing of the past, especially classical and Italian models, and like Chappell, he explored a wide variety of poetic forms. Both poets share an intense interest in music, Ronsard composing many of his poems to be set to music, and both are attentive to the musical effects of rhyme and rhythm, assonance and alliteration. Chappell and Ronsard likewise share a propensity to pursue moral and philosophical and religious themes, and both celebrate the diversity and vitality of nature and the power of love, human and divine. What K. R. W. Jones says of Ronsard often applies to Chappell's poetry as well: "[Ronsard] draws on all his vast reading, his sense of the concrete image, of colorful and elaborate detail, and his feeling for myth, symbol, and allegory animated by narrative, humor, and his musical verse to produce something uniquely his own."[45] By invoking the spirit of Ronsard, Chappell simultaneously invokes the Renaissance itself, with its openness both to the classical past and to new developments in science and the arts, its sense of hopefulness and new beginnings consistent with the governing metaphor, the spring garden, of Chappell's book. References to other Renaissance writers abound in *Spring Garden.*

The volume's various prologues and its epilogue deserve further comment. Not only do they posit—through Chappell's translations and allusions—a profound sense of literary community across time, but they also set forth the literal framework of the poems that follow and reveal many of the poet's most important aesthetic principles and beliefs. Significantly, the poet is not alone in his literal and metaphoric garden. He is accompanied by Susan—wife, lover, muse, and the Beatrice of *Midquest,* though here that last role appears less integral than in the earlier book. In the general prologue, the epilogue, and four of the untitled prologues, Susan is addressed by name so that these poems become implicit dialogues, and the herbs gathered become ingredients for "our anniversary déjeuner" (133). But these prologues and the epilogue also enter into dialogue with the reader as the poet clarifies his literary predilections and prejudices and urges the reader, as well as Susan, to seize the day.

At most points in these materials, Chappell's tone is conversational, familiar, playful—no small accomplishment considering the formal rhyme scheme and meter amid which that informality is achieved. Take, for example, the general prologue's opening lines:

> This morning in the wellspring month of May
> Let's take our coffee out beneath the sky,
> Observe the laurel blooming contentedly,
> And make our plans for this Memorial Day.
> The year's at spring, but I no longer am.
>
> (3)

While Susan tends the garden's literal flowers, the poet will "winnow through" his verses, seeking those "suitable for a volume Old and New" (3). Despite the theme of mortality sounded by the narrator's reference to his age, the pace of the prologues is leisurely, allowing for digressions, illustrative translations, extended commentary, even a ballade contra fantasy (written by Chappell but attributed to Donald Hall) and a humorous rendition of Baudelaire's sonnet "*Les Chats*" under the title "*Les Cochons.*" At times such material grows somewhat self-indulgent and may strike the general reader as simply opaque. In the prologue to "Poems of Fantasy," for instance, which includes several obscure references to Lovecraft's fiction, Chappell also refers to *Codex Dagonensis, Urtica garrettensis,* and "Spreading Gioia" (90), allusions to *Dagon, nettle*-some George Garrett, and Dana Gioia, a fellow poet with some of whose assumptions about poetry Chappell disagrees.[46] At other points in a few of the prologues Chappell's poetic line becomes all too prosaic, as when he justifies his vocation by noting, "Someone has to dream the dreams and write / Them out in the best language they can find" (154). Yet while there is more flaccidity in some of these prologues' connective tissue than one might prefer, the prologues offer a great many delights and surprises as well.

Among the liveliest of these, though many readers may overlook it, is Chappell's effective use of rhyme for both humorous and serious purposes. When, for instance, he offers a mock apology for citing the currently unfashionable poets of the Renaissance, writers who "surrendered to the sweet pursuit of pleasure, / Tippled till they could hardly walk erect, / And—worst of all!—wrote poems in rhyme and measure" (3), his rhyming of "pleasure" and "measure" mirrors his own satisfaction with rhymed metrical forms. What might have been a commonplace rhyme expresses a literary principle. That rhyme may also be meant to suggest the need to moderate pleasure, to seek the measured way of the classical golden mean, which Renaissance writers were rediscovering. Elsewhere in *Spring Garden,* the poet delights in composing such comically ironic rhymes as "art" and "Fart" (in the self-mocking phrase "Old Fart"), and "Good" and "nude" (with the former term appearing in the phrase "Plato's Theory of the Good").

Chappell's comic inventiveness is not limited to matters of rhyme, of course. It manifests itself in his characterizing some writing as so bland that it has "all the pungence of Velveeta cheese" (53) and in his explaining, "The flowers I pretend to cultivate / Are metaphorical: line after line / Whereon critics, like passing collies, micturate" (9). Hyperbole, as in his already quoted condemnation of Renaissance poets, likewise regularly contributes to the book's humor. The prologue to "Poems of Fantasy" contains the greatest concentration of such material, from its opening mock-epic apostrophes, through its "Ballade of the Skeptic Donald Hall" and its redaction of Baudelaire's "*Les Chats,*" to its esoteric allusions. The pleasure of such tonal and structural variety within the overarching formal design of the prologues is felt again when the prologue to "Epigrams" begins with the iambic pentameter line used in the others but then modulates into iambic trimeter in the second and fourth lines—before coming to a complete and unexpected stop:

> The rose is valued for its gorgeous blossom,
>   Watercress for its leaf;
> The ode embodies noble resonance,
>   The epigram is brief.

(117)

The prologue to "Poems of Fantasy," in addition to being the most comically inventive, is one of the two or three prologues in which Chappell makes most explicit a number of the tenets of his artistic credo (as he does in the epistolary poems and the playlet in *Midquest*). Rejecting the assertion he attributes to Donald Hall that "the vein of Fact is the only vein to mine" (87), Chappell responds, "—Well, there go Chaucer, Shakespeare, Spenser out / The window, not to mention poor John Keats" (88). "All writing needn't tour main-traveled roads" (89), he comments, alluding to

Hamlin Garland, apostle of "veritism," nor need it pursue the Naturalism of Ambrose Bierce. Neither Melville nor Poe, Chappell adds, conforms to so constricted a view of literature's function.

In his epilogue Chappell rejects what he considers another unnecessarily limiting conception of the writer's identity: the notion that the writer must be politically engaged, must be a social activist. Like the Emerson of the "Ode, Inscribed to W. H. Channing," Chappell refuses to be consigned to such a role—in part because he had already played it in the 1960s and early 1970s. "Pursuit of wisdom" (153) is the poet's true work, a wisdom articulated, for Chappell, by this garden's "centerpiece medallion with its grave / Beloved quotation from the Florentine" (151). That quotation from Dante is, "*L'amor che move il sole e l'altre stelle*" (151), the closing line of the *Paradiso.* That quotation does actually appear on a similar medallion in the poet's garden in Greensboro, and its presence there, in the closing lines of *Midquest,* and in the epilogue to *Spring Garden* should again remind the reader of the religious sensibility that shapes Chappell's writing. That religious perspective is reinforced by the translation that concludes the epilogue, Ronsard's "*A son âme*" ("To His Soul"), itself a translation of Hadrian's "*Animula vagula, blandula.*"

The first and last translations of *Spring Garden* are thus from Ronsard, both of them emphasizing human finitude. The final poems in sections 4 through 6 also sound this theme, while the seventh section, in contrast, ends with "Forever Mountain" and the hope of resurrection offered by that poem. The references to Dante and the soul in the epilogue make it clear that, for Chappell, the theme of mortality arises in a larger context that includes both the divine love to which the Florentine attests and the power of human love—and of art itself—to transcend death. "Now I lay me down to sleep" is *Spring Garden*'s final line, Chappell's translation of Ronsard's "*Je dors.*" But that statement is also the opening line of a well-known children's bedtime prayer. The simple faith evoked by such a conclusion reflects the poet's quiet trust in divine grace, though elsewhere in *Spring Garden* that faith encounters severe challenges, as it generally does in Chappell's poetry and fiction.

Although the prologues and the epilogue rarely contain the finest poetry in this volume, they do serve, as should now be apparent, a variety of important functions while displaying Chappell's multifaceted artistry and diverse literary impulses. A similar variety is evident in the book's opening section, "In the Garden," which sets the scene for subsequent sections and demonstrates the thorough process of revision that many of the book's selected poems have undergone. A detailed analysis of that process is beyond the scope of this study. Readers of *Spring Garden* need to be aware, however, that its reprinted poems— except those from *C*—have almost all experienced some revision.[47] Much of that rewriting is far more extensive than Chappell's casual remarks in the epilogue about this single "day's fair work, / Selecting each poetic salad green, / Pruning surplusage, trimming the borders clean" (151), might lead one to assume. A few poems—"Voyagers," "The Reader," "Narcissus and Echo," and "Humility," for instance—from collections other than *C* remain unchanged, while the most sweeping revisions have generally been made to the poems drawn from *The World between the Eyes.* But even a poem as brief as *Source*'s "Latencies," just sixteen lines long, can have as many as twenty changes. Most such changes involve diction and punctuation, though sometimes they include lineation, at other times the addition or deletion or rewriting of entire stanzas (for example, "Susan's Morning Dream of Her Garden," "Pierrot Escapes," and "Score"). Although some of these revisions will strike readers as insignificant, even finicky, most improve the poems. Often the changes tighten a poem's diction, making it more concrete or more exact, as in the substitution of "arrives" for "gets here," "restored" for "brought back," or "badinage" for "chat and clutter" ("badinage," a term of French origin, proving particularly appropriate to the poem in which it appears, "Pierrot Escapes"). In other poems an image pattern or surrounding terms, together with a consciousness of rhythmical effects, has prompted a change, as when "floating down / *Mothy* on the shallow *end* of sleep" becomes "floating down / *Mothlike* on the shallow *ebb* of sleep" (50). Attention to sound effects also influences Chappell's revisions. All in all, Chappell's reworking of these selected poems tends to confirm the latter half of his otherwise overly modest self-appraisal: "I really don't think I'm a very good writer, but I'm a terrific goddam reviser."[48]

The fourth and fifth stanzas of the prologue to "In the Garden," as Susan Underwood was the first to point out, set forth the topics which subsequent sections will address.[49] This prologue also introduces, through a translated poem by Jean-Antoine de Baïf, Ronsard's contemporary and another member of the Pléiade, the image of the rose, one of *Spring Garden*'s major unifying devices and a recurring symbol throughout Chappell's career. As a natural object of extraordinary beauty appropriate to a garden setting, as an emblem of romantic love, and as a symbol of spiritual perfection (Dante's mystic Rose), this flower operates on many levels of meaning, later becoming the subject of one of the volume's new poems, "The Rose and Afterward," which appears among the "Poems of Fantasy." But de Baïf's rose is primarily an image of mutability:

The rose is the loveliest kind of bloom
If we gather it in time.
See it luminous with dawn?
By this evening it will be gone.

(10)

These lines remind Chappell's readers that the garden they have entered is neither Eden nor Paradise but a landscape subject to time and decay and death. At the same time, it is a garden both literal and metaphorical—"quite practical and yet quite visionary"—where Susan's physical labor produces not only "pleasure the body takes" but also "murmur that speaks / To spirit" (9).

It is the visionary aspect of this setting that Chappell emphasizes initially by making "Susan's Morning Dream of Her Garden" the book's first selected poem. Besides having undergone various revisions in diction and phrasing, this version of the poem omits the final three stanzas originally printed in *Midquest,* stanzas that showed Susan awakening from her dream. Thus the ejection from the garden portrayed in the original is here suppressed—though the stylized artificiality of Susan's dream-garden evinces its unreality even without those stanzas. "In the Garden" also contains three poems from *First and Last Words,* three of the nature epigrams from *C,* and one poem from *The World between the Eyes,* the heavily revised "The Farm" (here titled "The Fields"). That last poem, as was mentioned in chapter 3, traces the seasonal progression from summer to winter, thereby subverting the pastoral myth of "Susan's Morning Dream." The same is true of the poem that follows "The Fields," "Patience," Chappell's homage to Virgil's *Georgics.* In combination here at the beginning of *Spring Garden,* "The Fields" and "Patience" enable Chappell to expand the purview of his garden motif so that it encompasses the agrarian experience of his childhood and of his mature literary vision.

The complexity of response to the garden motif that characterizes the book's opening section and the dynamic interplay of poems that results from the order Chappell assigns them are typical of his artistry throughout *Spring Garden.* Three of the eight poems reprinted in "In the Garden" refer to roses, for instance, and that section concludes with the poem "Literature," whose first line reads, "The girls and flowers keep changing into literature." That line testifies to the fertile intersection of life and literature, nature and the imagination, that is fundamental to Chappell's poetry and to the metaphorical structure of this entire book.

The scope of this study precludes detailed assessment of each section of *Spring Garden.* Instead the remainder of this chapter will briefly survey several of the nineteen new or previously uncollected poems in the book's six remaining sections.[50] As might be expected, those poems are marked by Chappell's customary diversity of forms, among them the "Dialogue of Naughty and Nice," in which each speaker is assigned two eight-line iambic pentameter stanzas of varying rhyme schemes; "The Fated Lovers," the longest new poem in the collection, its seven parts influenced by the traditions of ballad and song; "The Presences at Sunset," a poem in rhymed couplets; "The Voices," a sonnet composed of a single sentence and "The Bible of the Unlucky Sailor," a second Italian sonnet; free verse poems like "The Sea Text," "(Prologue)," and "Rider"; the allegorical "The Transformations: A Fairy Tale" with its rhymed stanzas of varying lengths and its evocatively named central characters, the Impressario of Moons and the Maestro of Carouses; and the epigrammatic "U.S. Porn Queen (Ret.)" with its iambic tetrameter quatrains rhyming aabb. Absent from most of them, however, is the blank verse line that Chappell uses so effectively in many of the poems of *Midquest* and *First and Last Words.* But the variety of forms among both the new and selected poems, as well as among the translations, witnesses not only to what might be called Chappell's aesthetic inclusiveness but also to the richness and diversity of life itself. Implicit in this profusion of forms and techniques, as Underwood suggests, is Chappell's insistence on the possibility and significance of choices, in life as well as literature.[51]

The largest number of these new poems (seven of the nineteen) appear in "Poems of Fantasy," confirming the impression conveyed in the prologues that a spirit of playfulness, of zestful creativity, oversaw much of the design of *Spring Garden,* despite the book's recurrent focus on the theme of mortality. Six new poems occur among the "Poems of Character," but there they represent only a quarter of the texts in that longest section, whereas the new work in "Poems of Fantasy" provides fully half the poems in that section. Chappell connects these two parts of the book through a pair of new poems with similar titles and settings: "The Bible of the Unlucky Sailor," which concludes "Poems of Character," and "The Sea Text," which opens "Poems of Fantasy." Both poems depict drownings, both point to the potential for transformation that arises from that experience, and both allude to Shakespeare's *Tempest,* whether implicitly or explicitly. In addition both suggest the power of books to reshape, not simply to describe, reality. "The Bible of the Unlucky Sailor," like "An Old Mountain Woman Reading the Book of Job" and "Windows," confronts the mystery of death without resolving it. The poem thus serves as one of many memento mori in *Spring Garden.* Yet in its juxtaposition with "The Sea Text" and its allusion to *The Tempest* in the phrase "a sea-thing strange beyond surmise" (84), this poem leaves open the possibility, if not the likelihood, of resurrection. For when Prospero "drowns [his] book" in the second of these poems, "the sea begins to change" (92). Infused with the force of human imagination "that knows long grief and fear and every human ache," the sea—symbolic of materiality and mortality—"begins to evolve new sorcerers," new agents of transformation.

Among the other new poems "The Presences at Sunset" is especially well realized and merits quotation in full both for its beauties of diction and phrasing and for the thematic implications of its structure.

"Halfstep by palsied halfstep she has come
As if compelled by a remembered dream."

"A shawl about her shoulders, a gnarly stick
To search the path that wends so rough and black."

"The years have settled on her like the silence
Of a shuttered house that once knew violence."

"She rarely lifts her head. The setting sun
Is thin and strange on the scarred horizon."

"Now she arrives, a weary penurious widow,
Where shadow reigns, where all light is shadow."

"A stand of alders guards the deep still pool.
No stars, no moon. The lengthened hour grows cool."

"Why does she come here? This water like dull slate
Can hold no image of a human fate."

"She comes because a half-lost memory
Whispers to her like a distant sea."

(63)

Based on an untitled etching by Mary Anne Sloan, "The Presences at Sunset" is the sort of poem that Chappell had already written so ably in "My Hand Placed on a Rubens Drawing" and "Voyagers," both originally published in *First and Last Words* and both reprinted in "The Good Life" section of *Spring Garden.* In contrast to those poems, however, in which a drawing or painting is described from a single individual's point of view, here Chappell presents, in eight closed couplets, a series of comments by a chorus of voices. Some of the comments are descriptive; others are speculative or interpretive; one is interrogative. Yet from those remarks a coherent narrative emerges, a poignant interpretation of the etching's images. The viewers animate those images, endowing them with meanings that are temporal and causal, that transcend the spatial coordinates of the etching itself. The poem thus becomes a statement about the quest for meaning in interpreting both art and life. The variety of voices, the choral effect Chappell achieves, reflects his characteristic emphasis on community—here a community of interpretation—and the poem's modulation from slant rhyme in the first two couplets to exact rhyme in the last three implies a developing confidence in the interpretation offered. In addition to being a remarkable poem in its own right, "The Presences at Sunset" contributes to the book's theme of mutability, most obviously through the poem's setting at sunset and its central figure's widowhood.

Like *C* in its overarching temporal structure, *Spring Garden* moves from morning in the general prologue to evening in the epilogue. Given the volume's frequently elegiac tone and its pervasive sense of the hurtling passage of time, it is entirely appropriate that the book's final section be devoted to "Poems of Memory." The prologue to this section opens with a translation of one of Verlaine's prison poems, thus recalling Chappell's early literary career, both his use of the relationship between Verlaine and Rimbaud as a substructure for *The Inkling* and his immersion in Rimbaud's poetry as an adolescent and young adult. Eight of this section's thirteen poems are reprinted from *Source*,[52] a title that emphasizes Chappell's concern for origins. Moreover, the opening poem, "Humility," establishes a religious tone that is extended by the following poem, "A Prayer for the Mountains," and echoed by the section's final poem, "Forever Mountain," which the poet also labels "*a prayer*" (147; Chappell's italics).

It is with a sense of fulfillment and reconciliation that "Forever Mountain" and "To His Soul" conclude this volume. Like Chappell's earlier books, *Spring Garden* demonstrates his moving and skillful articulation of all the "effable emotions" (141). As Middleton notes in his review, "Few poets have written verse as wise, humane, and poignant as this."[53] Although *Midquest* remains Chappell's most accomplished single volume, *Spring Garden* is a major achievement. Future students of this poet's work are likely to turn to it repeatedly for the lessons it affords in poetic craft—an artistry evident not only in individual poems but also in the larger design of the book and in Chappell's process of revision.

CHAPTER FIVE

The Short Stories
Moments of Light and *More Shapes Than One*

"Of all the forms I have attempted," Chappell has remarked, "the short story is the most difficult. . . . It is the prose form I most admire."[1] Although he has published only two collections in this genre, *Moments of Light* (1980) and *More Shapes Than One* (1991), he has been steadily writing short fiction since at least his high school days. Moreover, as many reviewers and critics have observed, his novels in the Kirkman tetralogy that began with *I Am One of You Forever* often read more like volumes of interrelated short stories than like traditional novels, an assessment that underscores the importance of this genre in Chappell's total writing career.

As early as 1965, just as *The Inkling* was about to appear, Chappell offered Hiram Haydn, his editor at Harcourt, Brace and World, a manuscript of fourteen stories under the title "The Thousand Ways." According to Alex Albright, Chappell received a contract for that book of stories, but Haydn later persuaded the author to substitute a contract to publish *Dagon*.[2] Over half of those stories were subsequently printed in magazines and literary journals, but only two, the title story and "January," found their way into *Moments of Light*. By 1980 Chappell had published some three dozen stories from which to draw the selections for that volume.

As in his collections of poetry, in his books of short fiction Chappell strives to create an impression of unity among the individual stories. The ordering of the stories, their temporal and thematic progression, and their recurring motifs are central to each book's meaning. And as in his poems, so in his short stories, Chappell writes in a wide variety of literary forms in these two volumes: mythic fable ("The Three Boxes"), tales of horror and fantasy ("Weird Tales," "The Somewhere Doors"), tall tales ("Mankind Journeys through Forests of Symbols"), fictions involving historical figures, ghost stories ("Ember" and "Miss Prue"), straightforwardly realistic fiction ("Duet"), and texts that blend two or more of these genres. This impressive variety of forms is matched by an equal diversity of voices and tones and styles. As in *Castle Tzingal,* Chappell is wonderfully adept at using a diction and syntax appropriate to the historical period in which a work is set and to the specific characters he depicts. Humor, satire, and parody regularly lighten the tone of these stories, especially in *More Shapes Than One.* Yet the playfulness of Chappell's imagination is almost always in the service of substantive themes, if not in each story individually, then in the collection as a whole. Chappell the moralist is never entirely absent from these fictions no matter how comically exuberant or whimsical they may be, for Chappell numbers himself among those authors and citizens "seriously concerned about the tone of our literature and the tenor of our lives."[3]

One of the major subjects in these two books is the partnership of the sciences and the arts in ordering the world and endowing it with meaning. Chappell's use of historical figures like Benjamin Franklin and William Herschel, like Franz Joseph Haydn and Carl Linnaeus and the composer Jacques Offenbach, both reinforces his characteristic insistence on the value of the past and reflects his desire to bridge the gap between the arts and sciences posited by C. P. Snow in his influential book *The Two Cultures.* Chappell seeks to reconcile these two modes of acquiring knowledge by featuring scientists and artists, not just the historical figures cited but also characters like Stovebolt Johnson of "Blue Dive," Kermit Wilson of "Duet," and Arthur Strakl of "The Somewhere Doors." Chappell's interest in promoting greater understanding of science, evident in the Kirkman tetralogy as well, stems from his recognition that much of the general populace "thinks of science as incomprehensible, unapproachable, elitist, and inhumane."[4] For Chappell, in contrast, "Both science and art are humanist endeavors."[5] In a number of his essays he has dealt with the interrelationship of science and the arts, especially in their search for truth, their usefulness in enlarging and refining our senses and our sympathies, and their promotion of curiosity and wonder. His portraits of men like Herschel and Linnaeus are meant to humanize science and scientific research while emphasizing the fundamental human yearning for truth and order and beauty.

Moments of Light

The eleven stories that comprise *Moments of Light* dramatize this quest for truth, moral order, and spiritual transcendence. As the title indicates, many of these stories offer epiphanies, instants of illumination, that transform the characters' and/or the readers' outlook. The world Chappell portrays is clearly postlapsarian, a "stricken world," as the narrator of "The Weather" puts it.[6] Yet the acceptance of moral responsibility remains both possible and necessary. Chappell insists that human beings have the capacity to act justly despite their fallen condition, and it is that capacity—not the recovery of a specious innocence—on which the stories focus.

Writing six years after the book's publication, Chappell stated that "*Moments of Light* may well be my favorite child among my books of fiction."[7] Reviewers were equally enthusiastic. One said, "Chappell's stories are consistently thought-provoking and well written," while another called the book "a memorable . . . collection." Yet a third praised it for being "as satisfying a moral fiction as we can find in contemporary literature, . . . a remarkable collection."[8] Such comments are well deserved in light of the volume's originality of conception and high level of achievement both in characterization and in theme, qualities warmly acknowledged in Annie Dillard's foreword to the book.

In its chronological structure *Moments of Light* moves from an explanatory fable set in mythic time and a brief first-person account narrated by Judas to three stories set in the eighteenth century and six set in the twentieth. This temporal progression does not trace a simplistic history of either decline or progress; instead Chappell emphasizes the perennial nature of the moral challenges human beings face, the individual's recurring opportunities to enact justice or to reject its claims, to embrace or to betray love. Yet Chappell does seem to sense in the modern world a lack of commitment to active pursuit of the good, a failure of will that Dante's age identified as *acedia,* spiritual sloth. In Chappell's view, moral lassitude rather than outright evil characterizes the modern age, as an increasingly secularized culture obscures the very existence of values beyond material interests. *Moments of Light* thus recalls the reader to the possibilities for self-realization and self-transcendence in art, love, and the quest for justice.

The book's opening story, "The Three Boxes," based on a folktale Chappell found retold in Simone Weil's *Notebooks,*[9] deals directly with the quest for justice and the need to affirm individual and collective moral responsibility. At the same time, "The Three Boxes" makes use of the archetypal journey motif, which recurs in various forms in seven of the remaining ten stories, and introduces music as a means of transcendence, thereby anticipating the role music plays not only in the title story but also in the book's final story, "Blue Dive." For Chappell's characters, the journey usually leads to heightened moral and spiritual insight, because they are pilgrims rather than merely travelers.

"The Three Boxes" attests to Chappell's religious concerns not only by using this metaphor of pilgrimage but also by numbering God among its characters. Annie Dillard refers to the story as "a hieratic parable" (ix–x), one that addresses racial differences. Each of the three men presented in the opening paragraph assumes a different racial identity as he swims across a river emblematic of time. Once across the river, he is permitted to open one of three boxes. The man who turns black is the last to traverse the river, and he discovers in his box not the treasures afforded the Caucasian and Asian figures who precede him but chains and branding irons and hang nooses, instruments of oppression. Pain and suffering all but fill the box, though patience and endurance and music are also among its contents. While this story seems to originate in a troublingly Eurocentric conception of African culture and history, Chappell is writing primarily in the context of the African American experience, in which slavery was the predominant reality. When God appears to this black man, the man rightfully protests the injustice of the gifts' distribution, and God concedes, "It is not fair."

> "The reason the distribution is not fair," God said, "is that the principle of justice is not yet established in the world. I—even I—cannot act justly until justice itself comes into being."
>
> "When then will justice happen?"
>
> "Justice will not happen," God said. "Justice must be created, and it is you who shall create it."
>
> . . . .
>
> "But there have fallen to me only the means and emblems of injustice."
>
> "Out of these justice shall be created. For it cannot come into being in the abstract, by fiat. It can inhabit only the human soul and the human body." (12)

In this dialogue Chappell raises perplexing issues about the principle of justice, issues as complex as those that attend divine command theory in the realm of ethics. Chappell's main point, however, seems to be that just as God cannot compel people's love without violating their freedom, so God cannot create justice by fiat, cannot compel just action. As "The Three Boxes" concludes, the black man journeys forth to find his companions and to present them with "the gift of justice, the one thing in the whole world worth knowing that can be learned in the world, and is not divinely revealed" (14). The last five words in this quotation point to the problem of evil that Chappell also confronts in such poems as "Windows" and "An Old Mountain Woman Reading the Book of Job."

The gift of freedom makes possible the abuse of that gift, and it is to such abuse that Chappell turns in the volume's second story, "Judas." Less than three pages long, "Judas" recounts its title character's reasons for betraying Christ. It wasn't the money, he declares. It was the "insupportable feeling of responsibility" that Jesus engendered (17). The figure of Judas is meant to contrast with the black man of "The Three Boxes," who accepts the burden of striving for justice despite the world's inequities. These two characters represent, respectively, fidelity and betrayal, the acceptance of moral responsibility and its rejection, and they enable Chappell to measure the characters in many of the subsequent stories against the conduct these two display. Among the characters found wanting are Blackbeard of "Thatch Retaliates," Mark Vance of "The Thousand Ways," the narrator of "Broken Blossoms," and Locklear Hawkins of "Blue Dive."

"Thatch Retaliates" is one of the three historical fictions Chappell sets in the eighteenth century, commonly called the Age of Reason or the Age of Enlightenment. It is, indeed, enlightenment on which he focuses in the first and third of these stories, "Mrs. Franklin Ascends" and "Moments of Light." The former was Chappell's first effort in the genre of historical short fiction, a text he wrote, he explains, to give his students in an American literature survey some understanding of the personality of Benjamin Franklin and some sense of the texture of eighteenth-century life.[10] One of the main pleasures of this story, however, is the portrait it provides of Deborah Franklin, who is far more complex than Dillard suggests when she says, "Sweet Mrs. Franklin is, I'm afraid, as simple and material as a bolt of cloth" (x). The repartee between the Franklins is echoed by the playful tone of the story itself, which culminates in a comic anticlimax when Deborah awakens to what she perceives to be celestial music and mistakenly assumes that she and Ben have died—only to discover that the music originates from the *armonica* her husband has brought back from England and is playing in their attic. In the person of Ben Franklin, Chappell unites the scientist and the artist, suggesting that both are inspired by the quest for order, the quest for harmony, symbolized here by Ben's new musical invention.

Between the comedy of "Mrs. Franklin Ascends" and the book's title story falls the shadow of "Thatch Retaliates." The title character, Blackbeard, parallels Judas as a figure of evil and challenges the eighteenth century's assumptions about the innate goodness of human nature and the power of reason to guide human conduct. Chappell effectively contrasts the setting, events, and tone of this and the preceding story. Instead of focusing on domestic life, as does "Mrs. Franklin Ascends," "Thatch Retaliates" opens in "the primeval Carolina forest" amid "the discomfort of wilderness travel" (29) before shifting to the primitive colonial town of Bath. The story's main characters, in addition to Blackbeard, are Toby Milliver and Hyde Prescott, the former a bookseller intent on founding a print shop and bookstore in Bath. Toby, the spokesperson for education and reason, believes that "the great flaws of personality both in the state and in the individual [are] historical products rather than inbred propensities" (34). Thus, through Toby, Chappell invokes the mythos of the New World as a second Eden and the American as a new Adam liberated from the errors and evils of the past. In Hyde Prescott, in contrast, Chappell creates an opposing voice, one that undercuts the myth of American innocence, that insists "that the old Adam [is] still heartily at work in every man" (34).

In "Thatch Retaliates," as in *The Inkling* and *Dagon,* Chappell's outlook is closer to Hawthorne's than to Toby Milliver's. Indeed "the heavy American darkness" through which Prescott and Milliver travel resembles "the benighted wilderness" of "Young Goodman Brown." Yet unlike Brown, Toby has his shattering experience in town, not in the wilderness, for within hours of his arrival in Bath, he is shot to death by Blackbeard. Despite this violent rebuttal of Toby's assumptions about human nature, the young optimist retains the reader's sympathy. Lying on his deathbed, Toby continues to identify himself as "a friend to Reason in this place" (48), a statement that Chappell might well make about himself. What is needed, Chappell implies, is not an abandonment of reason but a renewed commitment to cultivating its strengths while acknowledging its limitations. In this story Blackbeard comes to represent what Melville called in *Billy Budd* "the mystery of iniquity." For Chappell as for Melville, the eruption of moral evil is an irreducible fact of human experience, one that appears to lend credence to the theological concept of Original Sin.

As this collection's title story makes clear, however, the quests for truth and goodness and spiritual insight persist despite such eruptions of evil. While "Thatch Retaliates" bears witness to the presence of irrational evil even amid the Age of Reason, Chappell's placement of that story between two that highlight the pursuit of science and music demonstrates the fundamental hopefulness of his artistic vision. In "Moments of Light" Chappell brings together the astronomer William Herschel and the composer Franz Joseph Haydn, describing their meeting in 1792 during Haydn's first London sojourn. In addition to linking science and art, this story emphasizes the compatibility of science and religious faith.

Chappell's convincing portraits of both Herschel and Haydn, his skillful use of a secondary character like Doctor Burney, his subtle re-creation of the style and temper of the eighteenth century, and his effective blending of historical fact and visionary fancy— these are among the qualities that make "Moments of Light" one of the finest stories in this collection. Equally significant are the themes this story develops and its use of the stars, one of the prominent images throughout Chappell's writing, as a symbol of eternity and of spiritual realities. Haydn conceives of astronomy as a matter of "searching out new moments of light" (56), an apt definition of literature's function as well. In this story, science and art join forces in their effort to illuminate the human condition. Herschel, himself both an oboe player and a former organist, praises the scientific insights provided by such poets as Lucretius and Homer and Virgil. And he rejects Doctor Burney's suggestion that modern science makes untenable the ancient notion of the music of the spheres. For Chappell, as for Herschel, "the Harmony of the Universe . . . is surely the conception of greatest grandeur the ancient world could claim" (55), a conception to which Chappell continues to give his allegiance through his repeated references to music in both his poetry and fiction. But Haydn's acts of creation, as Chappell points out, ultimately derive not from his imagination alone but from the divine fiat that, according to the Judeo-Christian tradition, gave rise to the universe: "Let there be light." The artist's and scientist's quests for illumination are thus mutually grounded upon that primordial act. Like Chappell himself, both figures seek to assert harmony and order, a vision of wholeness, without denying the contradictions and complexities, the real chaos, that also attends human experience.

It is chaos rather than order that Chappell emphasizes in "The Thousand Ways," the first of six stories set in the twentieth century. This story, the longest in the book, takes its title from the lyrics of a popular song that serve as the story's epigraph: "Love, O love, O careless love, / You broke my heart a thousand ways" (71). Yet this story and those that follow deal not so much with outright betrayals of love as with *care*-lessness, with moral lassitude. To underscore the distance between the world of "Mrs. Franklin Ascends" and "The Thousand Ways," Chappell sets the latter in 1962, two hundred years after the 1762 date of Franklin's homecoming. The change in emotional and intellectual climate is apparent in Chappell's shift from the "deep certitude and serenity" of Haydn's temperament (53) to the "indecision and dismay" (71) that characterize Mark Vance, the would-be poet who is the protagonist of "The Thousand Ways." The setting in which Mark finds himself, a cheap hotel room where "no light burned," also contrasts with both the domestic comforts of the Franklin household and the emphasis on light throughout the title story. Though Mark eats in the Venus Grill, that name functions ironically, for Mark is shown, over the one-day span of the story, struggling to extricate himself from a loveless affair with Norma Lang, a forty-five-year-old alcoholic divorcée nearly twice his age. The physical disorder in Norma's home mirrors the moral and emotional chaos of both her life and Mark's. In their mutual lack of direction these two characters typify an aimlessness that promotes self-betrayal as well as disregard for others. "The Thousand Ways" opens and closes with Mark alone in bed in his hotel room, a circularity of structure that confirms the characters' entrapment in their lives. Yet the story ends, significantly, with Mark's thrice-repeated whisper of the word "Help," the words functioning as a largely unconscious prayer. Like the final gesture of "Moments of Light," Haydn's pointing of his baton toward heaven, Mark's whispered plea orients him toward something beyond the self.

The three stories that follow "The Thousand Ways" are first-person retrospective narratives that depict childhood experiences. The first, "January," which was also incorporated in three variations in *It Is Time, Lord,* returns to the theme of injustice raised in "The Three Boxes" and "Thatch Retaliates." At the same time, "January" extends the book's concern with moral responsibility. Like "Judas," this story is just three pages in length, another instance of Chappell's striking economy of storytelling. Yet it is among the most evocative and ambiguous texts in *Moments of Light,* its very ambiguity one measure of the complexity of moral judgment. Is the narrator guilty of neglecting his three-year-old sister's welfare? Are the assumptions his parents make accurate? Has he done all he could to protect his sister from the harsh winter weather? And what is the meaning of the boy's remaining silent before his parents and of his blotting out the moon with his frosty breath upon the window pane? The boy clearly feels the injustice of his parents' attitude, for he has not been trying to hurt his sister but to help her home. Yet his response to the men in the barn, "I told her not to come" (103), sounds too glibly self-exculpatory. The winter weather points to a physical cold that requires the warmth of human compassion to combat it, the capacity to recognize and then to alleviate others' suffering. On this occasion, then, the boy's blotting out of the moon, a common symbol of the imagination, may reflect his failure of empathy, his lack of moral imagination.

"The Weather" and "Broken Blossoms" raise much more directly this issue of moral lassitude, of an innocence that consists of inactivity, of a withdrawal from the world that unintentionally abets injustice. The narrator of "The Weather" acknowledges his preference for passivity, while the narrator of "Broken Blossoms" exhibits an inattentiveness, a "dreaming reverie" (129), dangerous not only to others but also to himself. In the latter story Chappell vividly re-creates the perspective of an imaginative yet self-absorbed child. This story stands out from the others in *Moments of Light* because it deals with an extended time period, nearly a year rather than the twenty-four- to forty-eight-hour time frames of almost all the other stories. "Broken Blossoms" is also one of the two stories, along with "Thatch Retaliates," that most clearly evoke the biblical account of the fall. When the narrator, searching for a rare stamp that he imagines will bring him fame and fortune, breaks into a locked trunk belonging to his parents, he unwittingly comes upon a box of blasting caps, which he gently shakes before returning the box to the trunk. The child's father learns what has happened and asks the hired man, Mr. Cody, to show the boy the blasting caps' destructive power. Mr. Cody lodges one of the caps in a disfigured apple tree and, from a safe distance, fires a bullet into the cap. The resulting explosion destroys the tree. "From this instant I can date my awkward tumble into the world," the narrator remarks (133).

Together with the stars and light itself, this tree is one of the book's major symbols, reminiscent of Eden's tree of knowledge but also of the duality of human nature itself. Mr. Cody's lesson forces the child to recognize that inaction and passivity also have consequences, that self-absorption and inattention are among "the thousand ways" to betray love. Chappell's sense of the insidious appeal of irresponsibility can be gauged by his adult narrator's admission that, despite what he learned from Mr. Cody, "If I could get it back, if I could return, I would undo it all. I would wrap myself in dream ever more warmly and would sink to the bottom of the stream of time, a stone uncaring, swaddled in moss" (133). Resistance to moral awakening is fierce, Chappell concedes, but awakening remains possible, even for someone as inclined to sleep as this unnamed narrator, whose very anonymity makes him a representative figure, an everyman.

The need for such wakefulness, for moral alertness, is underscored in "Children of Strikers," the succeeding story. Almost as brief as "Judas" and "January," this story provides a third-person account of two children's confrontation with evil. Chappell sets this encounter alongside a mill town's "black chemical river," thus highlighting the paper mill's pollution of the physical environment, but the strike of the story's title also suggests a context of social and economic injustice. The children's discovery of a doll's severed foot introduces yet a third species of evil, individual cruelty of the sort embodied in Blackbeard, for the children realize that only an adult could have used a knife so skillfully. Thus the maimed doll comes to symbolize what Chappell calls the "unguessable violence" of the mill town itself. Once again in this story, Chappell leaves the principal characters nameless, hence widely representative. Minimalist in length, "Children of Strikers" resonates powerfully both in its own right and in the framework of the entire collection.

The concluding story, "Blue Dive," is another third-person narrative that focuses on injustice. Its protagonist, Stovebolt Johnson, is an African American blues guitarist recently released from prison who is looking for a job he was promised three years earlier by the owner of the Blue Dive. That owner is gone, however, and the new owner, an African American named Locklear Hawkins, has no interest in the kind of music Johnson plays. Though "Hawk" gives Johnson an opportunity to audition and though Stovebolt wins the patrons' approval, Hawkins's decision is already made: "There is no room in this nightclub for any Rastuses or any Sambos. . . . And there's no room for anybody named *Stovebolt*" (165; Chappell's italics).

Chappell's use of both music and African American characters in this final story links it to "The Three Boxes," while his use of music and of star imagery also connects "Blue Dive" to "Moments of Light." Ironically, the injustice Stovebolt experiences here comes not from whites but from another African American. The tellingly named Locklear Hawkins fails to grasp the significance of the blues, deriding them as "those old-time nigger whining songs" (158). He ignores their function as a means of transcending suffering and injustice and as a means of ordering and understanding experience through the power of art. For novelist Ralph Ellison, in contrast, "The blues is . . . an assertion of the irrepressibly human over all circumstance whether created by others or by one's own human failings."[11] Of the blues as an expression of freedom and transcendence, Hawk knows nothing, and he thus epitomizes those who abandon the cultural resources of the past without ever understanding what it is they are discarding. *Moments of Light,* like *Midquest* and *C* and *Spring Garden,* is structured to affirm the ongoing value of the past. The lives of Judas and Blackbeard, of the Franklins and Herschel and Haydn, all speak to contemporary human conduct and values, though in different ways. Among the most important elements in "Blue Dive," then, is its implicit critique of the modern world's willingness to jettison the traditional. Hawkins, while obsessed with the new, seems finally to be the same old Adam of whom Hyde Prescott spoke.

One of the other major strengths of "Blue Dive" is its sensitive portrait of Stovebolt himself. As Dabney Stuart has noted, in addition to musical skill, "Stovebolt has more important qualities to recommend him: decency, delicacy, balance, dignity, a sense of proportion and humor and perspective."[12] Despite the insulting treatment Stovebolt receives, he retains something of the serenity Chappell associates with Haydn. Walking away from the Blue Dive late at night, Stovebolt is also linked with Haydn through the stars he observes. "There was one clear yellow star," Chappell writes, "that stood in the sky directly behind the twiggy tip of a wild cherry tree. As the wind moved, the tip kept brushing through the light of it. But, Stovebolt knew, it was never going to brush that light away" (166)

On this note of affirmation *Moments of Light* concludes. Justice has not been established, nor has fallen humanity returned to innocence. The fall is an absolute in Chappell's fiction, a fundamental datum. At book's end humanity, in the person of Stovebolt, remains a pilgrim. But the stars still shine, emblems of the mysterious source of life, with their promise of illumination and revelation. Moreover, the "falling star" of the toppled candle that marks Toby Milliver's death (48) is here replaced by the star whose permanence Stovebolt emphasizes. Like Haydn at the end of the volume's title story, Stovebolt looks heavenward, another of the many sentinels of the stars that fill Chappell's work and testify to its moral and spiritual concerns.

More Shapes Than One

The book that ultimately became *More Shapes Than One* had been conceived as early as 1983, at which time it bore the title "Waltzes Noble and Sentimental."[13] Among the Chappell papers at Duke University there is a table of contents page for this projected volume, showing that the author made a number of major changes before the book appeared in 1991, including the deletion of two of the eleven stories in the original manuscript and the addition of four new stories: "The Adder," "Ember," "Duet," and "Miss Prue." Chappell also altered the tenor of the collection substantially by choosing to omit "Bloodshadow"—a tale of witchcraft, an indelible bloodstain, and cosmic convulsion—which had originally been intended to conclude the book. Several of the stories were also retitled. Chappell's dramatic transformation of "The Sleeping Orchid" into "The Somewhere Doors" is one measure of the care and skill with which he revises as he moves from periodical to book publication.[14]

The thirteen stories of *More Shapes Than One* are preceded by an epigraph from Milton's *Areopagitica* that provides the volume's title. That epigraph again directs attention to Chappell's moral and religious concerns as well as to his commitment to what might be called literary pluralism, that is, his willingness to embrace the genres of popular culture and folk culture, not just the genres of canonical literature. The passage Chappell draws from Milton reads in part, "For who knows not that Truth is strong, next to the Almighty. She needs no policies, nor stratagems nor licensings to make her victorious. . . . Yet is it not impossible that she may have more shapes than one."[15] The diverse stories that follow confirm the variety noted in the book's title. At the same time, by invoking Truth with a capital *T,* Chappell suggests that the quest for knowledge has a spiritual dimension, that it aims to achieve an ultimately unified and unifying vision. As the mathematician Feuerbach declares in one of these stories, "The mind makes no mistake in intuiting intimations of a high and eternal order" (36–37), although the precise nature of that order may elude the mind's grasp.

In addition to containing two more stories than *Moments of Light, More Shapes Than One* differs from Chappell's first collection of short fiction in several other significant ways. First, it contains a greater range of stories, a variety evident not only in their literary forms but also in their historical settings and casts of characters. Second, *More Shapes Than One* includes more historical fictions and a larger number that deal with scientists (Linnaeus, Maupertuis, Feuerbach), though Chappell continues to examine artist figures as well, composers like Jacques Offenbach and writers like Lovecraft and Hart Crane. A third difference between the two volumes is the latter's more detailed use of the mountains of western North Carolina as a setting. But the most striking difference arises from Chappell's extensive use of fantasy in *More Shapes Than One,* a literary strategy already apparent to readers of *I Am One of You Forever* and *Brighten the Corner Where You Are,* both published before this second collection of stories.

The prominence of fantasy elements in *More Shapes Than One* tends to underscore the playfulness and inventiveness of Chappell's imagination. Yet that appearance of whimsicality should not lead readers to overlook the thematic substance of such tales. For Chappell, fantasy is not escapist. Instead it is a means of seeing reality anew. "Our problem is not that we imagine too much, and therefore become unreal," Chappell told an interviewer, "but that we don't imagine fully enough, and don't understand the reality that's out there. . . . We discover the world by imagining it."[16] The writer who diverges from factual accuracy, Chappell observes, does so "in order to illuminate, and not to deceive."[17] His interest in fantasy and in what he calls visionary fiction has been evident throughout his career, and he has commented on what he sees as critics' arbitrary division of his stories into two types, the realistic and the fantastic: "For me there's no important difference between them in terms of treatment; . . . both ways of writing are ways to try to deal with reality on the plane of literature."[18] The mimetic aim of fantasy in Chappell's hands is implicit in the verbal interplay of his title "Fantasia on the Theme of Theme and Fantasy," an essay in which he identifies as works of fantasy not only science fiction and horror stories but also texts by E. T. A. Hoffmann, Nathaniel

Hawthorne, Lewis Carroll, Henry James, Franz Kafka, and Thomas Mann.[19] Such folk traditions as fairy tales and tall tales also involve fantasy, but Chappell traces the *literary* ancestry of contemporary "visionary fiction" to such varied sources as Genesis and Revelation, *The Odyssey, The Faerie Queene, A Midsummer Night's Dream,* the Gothic novel, and narrative poems like "The Rime of the Ancient Mariner" and especially *The Divine Comedy,* which he calls "the single most important influence."[20] "What is most at stake" in such visionary literature, says Chappell, "is a transfiguration of quotidian *secular* life,"[21] a renewed awareness of the immanence of the sacred.

It is precisely such a visionary moment that Chappell celebrates in the opening story of *More Shapes Than One,* "Linnaeus Forgets." By focusing on the eighteenth-century Swedish botanist who established the system of binomial nomenclature, Chappell immediately introduces the theme of the quest for order in nature, a major subject of both science and art. Yet the story turns not on the discoveries of empirical science but on the fantastical vision Linnaeus experiences while studying a plant sent to him from the South Seas. Examining that plant, the scientist observes within its leaves "a little world . . . in which the mundane and the fanciful commingled" (13), a world that revolves around a pageant procession honoring the goddess Flora.[22] This vision of harmony and beauty grows so intense that Linnaeus faints, awakening later to find that the plant has disappeared and that the notes he made during this experience are unreadable. The very effort to decipher them causes the entire scene to vanish from his memory. Yet this visionary interlude does have enduring effects. Linnaeus's "love for metaphor sharpened"

(18), Chappell writes, linking scientist and artist as he does Herschel and Haydn in "Moments of Light." The vision also instills a new confidence in Linnaeus, whose theories about the sexuality of plants were extremely controversial and sometimes subjected him to accusations of immorality. The story concludes by affirming Linnaeus's newfound confidence: "He was finally certain that the plants of this earth carry on their love affairs in uncaring merry freedom, making whatever sexual arrangements best suit them, and that they go to replenish the globe guiltlessly, in high and winsome delight" (18).

Although the details of Linnaeus's vision recall the Golden Age, this opening story clearly contrasts the paradisal condition of nature with what Linnaeus himself thinks of as "the fallen world of mankind" (7). Plants and animals exist apart from the moral order that originates in humanity's capacity to reflect, to empathize, and to act in accordance with the dictates of conscience. The very fact that Linnaeus *forgets* his extraordinary experience may be meant to indicate the distance between physical nature and human nature, between the kind of innocence that nature possesses and humanity's consciousness of moral evil. Humanity's expulsion from paradise is apparent or implied in many of the book's subsequent stories, most notably in "Weird Tales," "The Adder," "Ember," and "After Revelation." *More Shapes Than One* thus continues to investigate "the stricken world" of human conduct that Chappell also explores in such stories as "Judas," "Thatch Retaliates," and "Broken Blossoms" in *Moments of Light.*

In other ways too "Linnaeus Forgets" introduces major figures and themes that help to unify the book. The figure of the scientist, for instance, reappears not only in some of the volume's additional historical fictions but also in the concluding story, "After Revelation," whose narrator has been imprisoned "for practicing science" (186). The scientist as seeker after truth is associated with various artist figures in stories that analyze the origins of artistic creativity ("Barcarole," "Duet," and "Mankind Journeys through Forests of Symbols"). "Linnaeus Forgets" also raises at least three themes developed in subsequent stories. First of all, this opening story reminds the reader of humanity's dependence on nature, no matter how much human consciousness transcends the capacities of physical nature. In both "The Somewhere Doors" and "Duet," the protagonists' moments of insight stem from contact with nature (96–97; 141–42), from their awareness of what Linnaeus calls the "ordinary amazing errands" of nature's creatures (11). The awakening of a sense of wonder and reverence and gratitude is among the primary aims of Chappell's writing, here and elsewhere. Secondly, despite the verb in the story's title, "Linnaeus Forgets" paradoxically demonstrates the need to *remember.* As in *Moments of Light,* the historical figures in the first five stories of *More Shapes Than One* affirm the temporal continuum of which the present is a part. Just as Linnaeus's scientific studies require the collection and classification of specimens, so Chappell's art involves acts of *re*collection, of memory as well as invention. To ignore the past Chappell repeatedly implies, is to lose much of the potential of the future.

Yet a third major theme introduced by "Linnaeus Forgets" involves love and sexuality. The volume's second story, "Ladies from Lapland"—along with "Ember," "Miss Prue," and

"Alma"—reveals that *human* sexual relationships are far more complicated than those Linnaeus observes in his botanical studies. The transition Chappell creates between these first two stories demonstrates his usual care in structuring a collection of poems or short fiction. The protagonist of "Ladies from Lapland" is Pierre de Maupertuis, a French mathematician, biologist, and physicist, the leading Continental proponent of Newton's theories. Maupertuis is linked to Linnaeus not only because both are scientists but also because both conducted research in Lapland during the 1730s. But Chappell's account of Maupertuis focuses not on the latter's scientific pursuits but on his sexual exploits in Lapland, conduct satirized by Voltaire in *Micromégas.* Maupertuis's behavior highlights his egotism and his general disregard for the scientific responsibilities that brought him to Lapland, research that others must complete for him.

As a mathematician, among other things, Maupertuis in turn anticipates the central character in this volume's third story, "The Snow That Is Nothing in the Triangle," which traces the mental disintegration of the nineteenth-century German mathematician Karl Wilhelm Feuerbach, originator of the Feuerbach Theorem on the nine-point circle of a triangle. Yet Chappell's portrait of Feuerbach is obviously meant to contrast with his sketch of Maupertuis. The Frenchman's self-centered conduct is juxtaposed with Feuerbach's conviction, after his arrest on charges of anarchy, that "if one man die, the others shall be freed" (37), a belief that leads him to two attempts at suicide while imprisoned. His willingness to sacrifice himself for others clearly differentiates him from Maupertuis, as does his inability to forget, once he is released from prison, the death of his fellow mathematician and presumed co-conspirator Klaus Hörnli. Chappell uses Feuerbach to re-emphasize the quest for order that is one of the central themes of *More Shapes Than One*. Feuerbach is astounded that a geometer should be accused of anarchy since for him, "the propositions of Euclid follow as inevitably from one another as the roses spring from the vine" (35), an analogy that reminds the reader of Linnaeus's similar confidence in a divine order underlying the natural world. Feuerbach points to the snowflake, another striking example of "more shapes than one," explaining that "in the snowflake nature reaches out to us as if it were reassuringly . . . suggesting that the mind makes no mistake in intuiting intimations of a high and eternal order" (36–37). The image of the snowflake recalls the story's title, which conjoins natural and geometric forms but which may also be meant to affirm nature's own creation of beauty and order. The boundary between the products of nature and the products of human artifice blurs when we consider such a geometric form as the circle, for circles abound in the natural world. Both scientist and artist build upon designs or structures inherent in nature itself, as Feuerbach avows and Chappell intimates.

While Chappell shifts from scientists to artist figures in the book's other two historical fictions, the concern for moral responsibility introduced in "Ladies from Lapland" recurs in both. Like Feuerbach, the composer Offenbach of "Barcarole" reveals a concern for others that Maupertuis lacks. In fact "Barcarole," set in 1871, opens with an encounter reminiscent of the parable of the Good Samaritan when Offenbach discovers a dying violinist, Rudolf Zimmer, lying on a sidewalk in Vienna. Momentarily mistaking the stranger for his brother Julius, Offenbach also discerns his own features in Zimmer's face. Using the literary motif of the double, Chappell stresses the imagination's role not, in this case, as an instrument of scientific research or artistic creation but as an instrument of moral vision, of compassion in its root sense of "suffering with" others.

"Barcarole" is a superb example of Chappell's skill in selecting and developing the figures who populate his historical fictions, in dramatizing the events that befall them, and in establishing a broad network of thematic implications and allusions that tie a particular story to others in *More Shapes Than One.* Given Chappell's own interest in popular literary forms, Offenbach is an apt choice as protagonist because of his contributions to such musical genres as the operetta, which he helped to popularize internationally. Like much of Chappell's writing, Offenbach's compositions are marked by their gaiety and tunefulness. Moreover, at the time of his death, Offenbach was working on a comic opera based on the tales of E. T. A. Hoffmann, whose fiction shares Chappell's predilection for the fanciful and the supernatural in this book. Hoffmann was himself a musician as well as a writer, and Chappell's work repeatedly exhibits its author's love of music.

Thematically, "Barcarole" not only extends Chappell's treatment of moral responsibility but also initiates a new theme, the origins of artistic creativity, a theme pursued in several subsequent stories set in the twentieth century. The dying Zimmer's gift to Offenbach is a copy of the one piece of music the violinist ever composed, a waltz tune that has long haunted Offenbach because his sisters had hummed it to him in his childhood. That tune, which inspires the famous "Barcarolle" in Offenbach's *Les*

Contes d'Hoffmann, was prompted by the death of Zimmer's fiancée Rosalie. Grief, intense suffering, Zimmer says, is the origin of his art, perhaps of all great art. "For another song like this one to be written," he declares, "another Rosalie would have to die" (55). Like the Wallace Stevens of "Sunday Morning," for whom "death is the mother of beauty," Zimmer seems to ground artistic creation in the experience of loss. This viewpoint is reinforced in the later story "Duet," whose protagonist traces his success as a country music singer to the death of his best friend. Yet this assumption about the necessary connection between art and suffering is challenged in other stories in *More Shapes Than One,* especially in "Weird Tales" and "Mankind Journeys through Forests of Symbols."

"Weird Tales," the book's final historical fiction, deals with events that occur in the 1920s and 1930s, but it is narrated, as the final paragraph makes clear, from some point in the future, after the Old Ones of Lovecraft's Cthulhu mythos have seized control of the world from humankind. The story's title is also the name of the pulp magazine that began publishing Lovecraft's fiction in the 1920s, one of the magazines which the adolescent Chappell read avidly and for which he aspired to write. Like *Dagon,* then, "Weird Tales" is in part a tribute to Lovecraft and the kind of horror fiction Lovecraft popularized. "The visionary poet Hart Crane and the equally visionary horror-story writer H. P. Lovecraft met four times," the story begins, but its focus soon shifts away from Lovecraft himself to Sterling Croydon, a member of Lovecraft's circle, who suffers a ghastly death as a result of his experiments with "spatial emplacement," a concept derived from one of Lovecraft's own stories, "The Dreams in the Witch

House," to which Chappell refers in "Weird Tales." Similarly, the Antarctic setting of Croydon's death stems from Lovecraft's use of that region in his novel *At the Mountains of Madness.* Chappell obviously relishes the opportunity to create a horror story to rival one of Lovecraft's own and to fill it with details from Lovecraft's fiction.

"Weird Tales" is more, however, than a *jeu d'esprit* in the horror genre. In fact the story raises questions about the struggle between free will and fate that are fundamental to the very possibility of moral choice. The implied narrator of this third-person tale (which shifts to first-person plural only in its closing paragraph) shares the pessimism bred by Lovecraft's mythos. "Lovecraft," writes the narrator, from whom Chappell distances himself, "described a cosmos that threw dark Lucretian doubt on the proposition 'that such things as . . . good and evil, love and hate, and all such local attributes of a negligible and temporary race called mankind, have any existence at all'" (60). The words quoted by the narrator in this passage are taken from one of Lovecraft's letters to Farnsworth Wright, the editor of *Weird Tales.*[23] In the context of Lovecraft's mythos, the narrator presents Hart Crane's suicide as a surrender to the prehistoric gods, represented by "the immense serpentine manifestation of Dzhaimbú, . . . *this fabulous shadow only the sea keeps*" (70). The last phrase, which serves as the closing line of Crane's poem "At Melville's Tomb," seems intended to remind readers of the Old Testament's Leviathan, God's archetypal enemy, personified for Melville's Ahab in the white whale, while the "serpentine" shape of Dzhaimbú recalls Satan's disguise in Genesis.[24]

But Chappell's mythos is not Lovecraft's. Nor does he share

Croydon's theory that "all human speech [is] merely the elaboration of an original shriek of terror" (63). For Chappell, literary creation often seems to originate in delight, in the exuberant playfulness of the artistic imagination. Instead of invoking the cruel prehistoric gods of Lovecraft and Croydon, Chappell's fiction and poetry are informed by the Christian mythos, with its emphasis on the radical distinction between good and evil, its ethic of self-sacrificial love, and its sense of the crucial role choices play in defining moral character.

This issue of choice is also central to "The Somewhere Doors," the first of the book's nonhistorical fictions. Like "Barcarole" and "Weird Tales," this story deals with an artist figure, Arthur Strakl, a writer of science fiction. In German the verb *strakln* means "to stretch" or "to stretch one's arms," and one of the effects of Strakl's fiction, like Chappell's itself, is to enlarge the reader's mind and imagination and heart. The plot, as is appropriate to a science fiction tale, involves a visitor from another dimension, a person who calls herself Francesca and who announces that Arthur will soon be receiving two doors. He is to choose between them, entering a new world from which he can never return. One of the doors will open on a pastoral paradise, a second Eden, with Arthur its only inhabitant. The other door will give him access to a utopian civilization of "great cities." Ultimately—and perhaps too predictably—Strakl recognizes a third option: to remain where he is, to embrace earthly existence. Before Francesca's appearance, however, Strakl had tended to disdain the earth. "Arthur did not read invasion stories," Chappell writes; "he could not imagine that Earth . . . would be a desirable prize" (72). Like Virgil Campbell and

Uncle Body in *Midquest,* though without their bawdiness, Strakl learns to celebrate the physical world. As with Linnaeus, Strakl's moment of insight occurs in the presence of nature, amid sights he has long overlooked, sights "he could remember . . . and yet he would always mostly forget" (97). Such forgetfulness seems to constitute one major category of error, if not of sin, in the moral universe Chappell's fiction postulates. It is thus significant that Strakl rejects both "paradise" and "utopia" because they "could not remember. They were eternal and unaging and had no history to come to nor any to leave behind" (97). Chappell concludes "The Somewhere Doors" by inviting his readers to make a choice, an interpretive choice involving the story's final image: Strakl "weeping aloud like a child deceived or undeceived."

This story earned Chappell the 1992 World Fantasy Award, an award he won again two years later for the chapbook publication of *The Lodger.*[25] Despite its award-winning status, however, "The Somewhere Doors" is too schematic and didactic to reach the level of artistry Chappell achieves in "Linnaeus Forgets" and "Barcarole" and "Weird Tales." The story is also flawed by a sentimental subplot involving Arthur's relationship with his employer. Yet Chappell endears Strakl himself to the reader, in part by referring to the protagonist by his first name after using surnames for the characters in the five historical fictions. "The Somewhere Doors" plays a key thematic role in the book, moreover, by underscoring the primacy of choice, by enlarging Chappell's cast of artist figures, by insisting on the importance of memory, and by again distancing humanity from paradise.

That distance is re-emphasized in the volume's seventh—and thus central—story, "The Adder," which is narrated by a book dealer in Durham. Like "Weird Tales," this story invokes Lovecraft's mythos, for its title refers to *The Necronomicon,* a book of black magic invented by Lovecraft, who attributed it to a fictitious Arabic author, Abdul Alhazred. In contrast to "Weird Tales," however, with its visions of violent destruction, the tone of "The Adder" is more comic than minatory. Although *The Necronomicon*'s presumed capacity for evil is immense, Chappell focuses specifically on the book's power to alter other texts and even people's memories of those texts. The narrator discovers this power when he conceals the book beneath a tattered copy of Milton's poems, only to find that the opening lines of *Paradise Lost* and of Milton's sonnet on his blindness have been grotesquely distorted. The variant readings Chappell cites are themselves delightful parodies: *"When I consider how my loot is spent"* (108), *"When I consider to whom my spode is lent"* (109), among several others. But Chappell does more than entertain. "The Adder" also makes clear that language and literature are not exempt from moral categories. Nor is the writer, as Chappell's use of Milton, both here and in the collection's epigraph, appears to suggest. Whimsical as this story is, it limns a world well east of Eden. To paraphrase Melville's assessment of the Encantadas, "In no world but a fallen one could such [a book] exist." It is Chappell's conception of literature's moral responsibilities, its role in preserving and promoting humane values, that accounts for his placement of "The Adder" at the very center of *More Shapes Than One.*

Like "The Adder," four of the book's final six stories use first-person narrators. These narrators range from a jealous lover who has just killed his sweetheart ("Ember") to a persecuted practitioner of science ("After Revelation"), from a country music star still mourning the death of his best friend ("Duet") to a frontiersman in an unspecified era who abhors "the woman trade" as it is practiced by his contemporaries, for whom women are so much livestock ("Alma"). Chappell individualizes each of these narrators, endowing them with personalities as varied as those of the volume's earlier historical figures. Although several of these later stories are set in the North Carolina mountains, Chappell usually avoids nonstandard English except in spoken dialogue. When his narrators address the reader or another silent auditor (as Bill Puckett does in "Ember" or Kermit Wilson does in "Duet"), it is their diction, syntax, and figurative language that reflect the stories' mountain settings. Puckett says, "My face got laid open by a bramble or a twig" and reports how he struggled through a laurel thicket "as puzzledy as a roll of barbwire" (124, 125). He sees "a little old granny woman" transformed into something "all gnarled and rooty like the bottom of a rotted oak stump turned up" (126). Such images and expressions derive from authentic regional dialect and the circumstances of mountain life without reinforcing regional stereotypes.

In a third-person narrative like "Mankind Journeys" Chappell both exploits and subverts such stereotypes. Sheriff Balsam and his deputies, "tall tobacco-chewing mountain boys," seem initially the stock-in-trade of Southern fiction. Yet one of the deputies, as it happens, is a closet symbolist poet who can identify the French wine (Château Beychevelle '78) in a soupçon of barbecue sauce. "Mankind Journeys" is the most wildly humorous of all the stories in *More Shapes Than One.* Part parody, part satire, part sheer comic extravagance, it draws on both the tall tale tradition and the exotic fabulations of an author like Donald Barthelme. By taking the story's title from Baudelaire's famous poem "Corréspondances" and by parodying Symbolist poetry, Chappell also pokes fun at his own youthful literary influences, as he did in *Midquest*'s "Rimbaud Fire Letter." At the same time, this story presents variations on the artist and scientist figures who appear throughout the volume.

The story's opening paragraph illustrates Chappell's seamless blending of fantasy and realism when an immense dream, "about two stories tall and five hundred yards wide," is discovered blocking a highway. To remove this obstruction, the sheriff eventually learns, he must sponsor a poetry contest, for the dream originates in the unconscious or blocked work of deputy Bill's poetic imagination. In "Mankind Journeys" Chappell hilariously interweaves a frustrated artist figure, a pseudoscientific expert, and French Symbolist speculations on the origins of literary creativity. Unlike Linnaeus, Dr. Litmouse, the scientist in this story, is caricatured. After ingesting a piece of the dream to determine its composition, Litmouse spouts several lines of Baudelaire's poem, then collapses, the apparent victim of a Rimbaudian derangement of the senses. Moreover, his quart jar of what the sheriff assumes to be secret formula turns out to be barbecue sauce. Part of the pleasure of this story stems from Chappell's outlandish comic similes, as when he echoes one of Apollinaire's definitions of surrealism by stating, "Dusk had come to the mountains like a sewing machine crawling over an operating table" (160). But Chappell also uses this story to puncture the Symbolists' conception of the suffering artist, the poet *maudit*. His hyperbolic account of the deputy's agonizing efforts to complete his poem serves to undercut the views of Rudolf Zimmer in "Barcarole" that artistic creation arises *only* amid anguish.

"After Revelation," the final story in *More Shapes Than One,* looks back to "Linnaeus Forgets" by focusing on a botanist and looks forward to the extraliterary world to which the reader will return beyond the text's epiphanies. Set in a vaguely European locale at an unspecified time in the future, the story might be labeled an eschatological fable. It opens in medias res with the words, "Then one evening I woke from a nap to find the door of my cell open and I walked out" (186). The narrator, George, owes his liberation to the return of "the Owners" of the human race, whose presence on earth ultimately prompts him to become a pilgrim in search of his Owner. This quest motif, treated comically in "Mankind Journeys," recalls both *Midquest* and *Moments of Light.* Significantly, the arrival of the Owners does not negate the fact of death. Indeed the narrator's beloved, Larilla, dies "of happiness" in the company of her Owner. The initially disconsolate George is placed at a table, given a loaf of bread and a cup of water, and urged to rest, eat, and remember (196), images and commands (though wine is absent) similar to those involved in the sacrament of Communion. Religious revelation does not, Chappell implies, enable believers to evade suffering and death, nor does it free people from the continuing need to make complex moral choices and to search for truth. The same obligations attend those who are the beneficiaries of the epiphanies offered by the arts and sciences.

This concluding story also clarifies the moral implications of Chappell's earlier portraits of Maupertuis, Feuerbach, and Offenbach. "The Owners are, I believe," says George, "those who can pay full attention to someone else" (191). Here is the heart of Chappell's moral vision, and herein, he suggests, lies the principal challenge and achievement of literature. Chappell's fiction and poetry strive to become such acts of attention, enabling their readers to share the experiences of others and thus nurturing understanding and compassion. His work promotes respect for the resources of the past while recognizing the reader's need to act in an extraliterary present. "After revelation, what then?" asks George in the story's—and the book's—final sentence. By juxtaposing this story with "Alma," whose narrator has had a revelation about the injustice of the woman trade and vows to free the brutalized women he encounters, Chappell underscores the ethical implications of both extraliterary experience and the experiences mediated by literary texts. Literature, he insists, illuminates the world, enlarging our conception of reality, but it does not replace that world.

More Shapes Than One was widely and enthusiastically reviewed. Michael Dirda, who called the stories "terrifically enjoyable," remarked that "these entrancing pages deserve all the readers they can get," while Orson Scott Card concluded his review by observing, "You'll be glad to have [this] book on your shelf, and even gladder to have Fred Chappell's sweet and searing stories in your memory."[26] Jacqueline Adams spoke of the collection's "13 marvelous stories" and stated, "Chappell is a talented writer who deserves a wider audience."[27] Yet it seems uncertain that Chappell's volumes of short stories will gain the broad readership both Dirda and Adams recommend, for as Chappell himself has noted, historical fictions, especially those about scientists, have "limited audience appeal,"[28] and both his collections contain such work. Allusive as those stories may be, however, they are among Chappell's finest and most thought-provoking short fiction. They appear, moreover, in volumes that offer an impressive variety of stories. What Francesca says of Arthur Strakl's fiction in "The Somewhere Doors" can be said with even greater justice of Chappell's own stories; they afford "many fine pleasures" (77).

CHAPTER SIX

The Kirkman Tetralogy

The four novels that Chappell has devoted to Jess Kirkman and his family—*I Am One of You Forever* (1985), *Brighten the Corner Where You Are* (1989), *Farewell, I'm Bound to Leave You* (1996), and *Look Back All the Green Valley* (1999)—are meant to parallel the four books of verse that compose *Midquest,* "surrounding that poem with a solid fictional universe," Chappell explains.[1] The first of these novels grew out of material generated during the composition of *Midquest,* material which the poet had not been able to use in that volume but had turned into fiction. From 1982 to 1984 at least eight of the ten chapters of *I Am One of You Forever* appeared as short stories in various literary journals. Another, "The Wish," originated in a much earlier story, "Gothic Perplexities," published in *Red Clay Reader* in 1966. It was these stories, combined into what Chappell has called "a deliberately episodic novel something like *Winesburg, Ohio*"[2] that launched the Kirkman tetralogy.

Like Ole Fred of *Midquest,* Jess Kirkman, the tetralogy's narrator, is a semiautobiographical figure who shares many of his author's life experiences, as the similarity between the names Kirkman (*church*man) and Chappell (chapel) suggests. In fact, in *Look Back All the Green Valley,* the reader learns that the adult Jess has become a poet who teaches at the University of North Carolina at Greensboro and publishes his work under the pen name Fred Chappell. But Chappell's extensive use of fantasy and the tall tale in these four novels precludes any simplistic identification of author and narrator. More important is the reader's recognition that Ole Fred's family in *Midquest,* especially his grandmother, father, and mother, is the same family that sustains Jess.[3] The J. T. of *Midquest* becomes the Joe Robert of the tetralogy, and many of the events recorded in the poem are recounted in the tetralogy too. The principal setting remains a mountain farm not far from a paper mill town (called Tipton in the tetralogy), and Virgil Campbell is once again a significant character. Yet whereas Ole Fred's quest for rebirth stands at the center of *Midquest,* Jess often occupies a more peripheral place in the tetralogy. His narratives frequently focus on the actions and thoughts of others, though the impact of these stories and experiences on Jess is clearly an important part of Chappell's larger artistic design.

The structural symmetry evident in the four volumes that compose *Midquest* is apparent in the tetralogy as well. Each novel consists of ten chapters, together with three italicized episodes at the beginning, middle, and end of each book. As in the four volumes of *Midquest,* each novel is dominated by one of the four classical elements arranged in the order that obtains in the poem. Thus *I Am One* revolves around water (as did *River*); *Brighten* around fire (as did *Bloodfire*); *Farewell* around air (as did *Wind Mountain*); and *Look Back* around earth (as did *Earthsleep*). As in *Midquest,* however, these elements are often interwoven in any one novel, so that a near drowning, for instance, is among the major events in *Brighten.* Through these elements Chappell grounds Jess's experiences, like Ole Fred's, in nature and in the agrarian landscape of the author's own childhood near Canton.

Despite the presence of a dominant natural element in each book, the Kirkman novels have episodic structures. Some, however, are more episodic than others. *I Am One* and *Farewell* are the most loosely organized, with the greatest variety of characters and of time frames. *Brighten* and *Look Back,* in contrast, focus on brief periods of time—just a single day in Joe Robert's life in the former. Jess is a more prominent figure in *I Am One* and *Look Back* than in *Brighten* and *Farewell,* where his roles are primarily limited to telling the story (*Brighten*) and to listening to other people's stories (*Farewell*). There is no consistent chronology from volume to volume of the tetralogy. Jess passes from ages ten to twelve in *I Am One,* is close to sixteen in *Brighten,* and appears to be slightly younger when he hears most of the stories told to him in *Farewell.* In *Look Back,* set in 1979, Jess is fully grown and an active participant in the novel's plot, his father having died ten years earlier and his mother now approaching death. Yet much of the book revolves around his memories of his father and Jess's ongoing attempt to assess (as in *Brighten*) Joe Robert's character and motives.

Even more than *Midquest,* the tetralogy demonstrates Chappell's allegiance to the Appalachian region. That allegiance is proclaimed in the title *I Am One of You Forever* and is evident throughout these four novels in Chappell's use of the region's folktales and folk culture, its mountain landscapes and rural lifestyle (although the paper mill attests to the impact of industrialization as well), its vernacular speech, its music, its religious traditions (not all of them viewed favorably), and its strong family ties. Yet, as Fred Hobson points out in analyzing the first novel in the tetralogy, "Chappell's narrator tells his story without a hint of regional self-consciousness. . . . The word *Appalachian* never appears. One finds here a triumph of tone, of point of view."[4] Despite Chappell's allegiance to Appalachia, he does not romanticize either the region or agrarian life. Refusing to ignore the flaws of mountain people and their culture, he also celebrates their many strengths. His fiction and poetry thus subvert stereotypes of the Appalachian region by emphasizing the full humanity of the people that stereotypes caricature.

While firmly anchored in a particular region, the Kirkman tetralogy is anything but provincial in outlook or scope. Like *Midquest,* these novels frequently employ allusions and archetypal motifs that broaden the tetralogy's range of reference. *Brighten,* for example, contains three successive chapters with the titles "Bacchus," "Socrates," and "Prometheus Unbound," and the book revolves around the evolutionary theory of Darwin and the presumed conflict between science and religion that continues to vex public education in America. *Look Back* invokes Dante's *Divine Comedy,* the text that shaped the quest for rebirth in *Midquest,* and Chappell repeatedly addresses such universal subjects as family relationships, love, death, and the origins and power of storytelling itself.

Perhaps the most important literary influence on the tetralogy, beyond the folktales of the Appalachian oral tradition, is the nineteenth-century American humor of the Old Southwest and of Mark Twain, in whose work that humor achieved its finest artistic expression. In this connection the reader should remember that the frontier designated by the term "Old Southwest"—while usually identified with Alabama, Georgia, Tennessee, Mississippi, Louisiana, Arkansas, and Missouri—would certainly have encompassed western North Carolina as well. Walter Blair lists among the major features of Old Southwest humor its use of vernacular narratives derived from oral storytelling; its focus on such masculine activities as hunting, fishing, gambling, drinking, and fighting; its wild exaggeration, including tall tales and frontier boasts; its reliance on humor derived from "physical discomfort" (often resulting from practical jokes); its episodic structure; and its effective use of framed narratives to heighten comic or ironic incongruity.[5] Many of these traits are readily apparent in the Kirkman tetralogy as well as in such poems from *Midquest* as "My Father's Hurricane" and "Three Sheets in the Wind," though Chappell typically softens the humor of physical discomfort and enlarges, especially in *Farewell,* the roles played by women. Blair says of the authors of Old Southwest humor, "Alike in making their writings local, authentic, and detailed, these humorists were also alike in imparting to their stories a zest, a gusto, a sheer exuberance."[6] That exuberance is equally evident in Chappell's work. Critics have noted *Midquest*'s indebtedness to both George Washington Harris, the Tennessee author of *Sut Lovingood's Yarns* (1867); and to Mark Twain,[7] but what has become increasingly clear with the publication of each new volume in the Kirkman tetralogy is Chappell's stature as the rightful heir, perhaps the fullest twentieth-century embodiment, of the tradition of Old Southwest humor and of Twain's and Faulkner's transformations of that tradition. The spirit of such humor is ubiquitous in Chappell's tetralogy, with its frontier boasts (Johnson Gibbs's bragging in the opening chapter of *I Am*

One), its tall tales ("windies"), its many practical jokes ("rusties"), its hunting and fishing episodes, its vernacular speech, its colorful characters, and its vividly concrete figurative language.

Nowhere is the influence of Harris's *Sut Lovingood* and Twain's *Huckleberry Finn* more apparent than in the profusion of figurative language in Chappell's tetralogy. It is, in fact, style or voice that ultimately unifies the often episodic plots and disparate characters of these novels. Jess narrates retrospectively, from the vantage point of adulthood, but Chappell imbues Jess's voice with a child's freshness of perspective and a country storyteller's vividness of diction. Nor does Chappell strain for literary effect. With few exceptions, the innumerable similes and metaphors that Jess and other speakers employ arise naturally from their daily observations and experiences. Such figurative language pervades these books, often to startlingly humorous effect. In *Brighten,* for instance, Jess's father sports a black eye "as lumpy and purple as a blackberry cobbler." In *Farewell* the reader is told that Jess's grandmother "hated waste worse than a hard-shell deacon hates sin." The same novel says of old Mr. Worley: "His face was weathered to the color of a cured burley leaf and so wrinkled it appeared to be caving in, but his blue eyes were alert and as bright as the shine on a table knife," while another character is said to be "as closemouthed as a miser's purse snap." Such figurative language not only calls attention to the details of the daily world but also emphasizes the interconnections and transformations to which ordinary reality is subject. As in the first three paragraphs of *Brighten,* Chappell's similes and metaphors reflect the presence of the mysterious, transfiguring powers of the human imagination. At the same time, his figurative language posits a continuum between folk speech and literary discourse that reveals his profoundly democratic commitment to the dignity and worth of every individual.

While Chappell's style in the tetralogy draws some inspiration from *Sut Lovingood,* Chappell also diverges from that book in at least three major ways. First, as already noted, he usually avoids the humor of physical discomfort, of physical cruelty, that Sut relishes. Practical jokes abound in the tetralogy, but almost none aims to injure its victim, as many of Sut's do. Second, Chappell makes Jess very much a member of a family and a community, not just an isolated individual like Sut, who often seems at war with all the world. Third, Chappell rejects the nihilism of Sut's philosophical outlook and invokes instead the moral sensibility evinced by Huckleberry Finn. As George Core has written, Chappell's work creates "a comedy that sustains and elevates our sense of life's possibilities."[8]

In addition to drawing on Appalachian folktales and on the tall tale traditions of Old Southwest humor, Chappell uses fantasy and allegory and dreams as major literary devices in the tetralogy. Those devices often figure significantly in each novel's italicized sections, as they do in "The Overspill," "The Telegram," and "Helen" of *I Am One.* But fantasy, allegory, dream, and elements of the supernatural occur at other points as well, in "The Beard," for example (*I Am One*), and "Bacchus" (*Brighten*), in "The Shining Woman" (*Farewell*) and "Into the Unknown" (*Look Back*). The presence of these devices produces an atmosphere distinct from that of Old Southwest humor and from the humor of Twain and Faulkner. Several reviewers and critics have applied the term "magic realism" to this dimension of Chappell's writing, but he rejects that label. In an interview conducted after the publication of *Brighten,* Chappell remarked, "I don't see magic realism as an influence on my most recent fiction. I was trying to get away from it, as a matter of fact. . . . I decided to go more directly to folklore, to use the tall tale."[9] Similarly, in an interview given at the time *Farewell* was published, he reiterated that he has "no interest in magic realism per se. I'm interested in blurring the demarcations between what's generally thought of as realism and what's thought of as fantasy."[10] As this latter remark makes clear, Chappell intends to create a greater sense of fluidity, of the potential for liberating transformations, both in literature and in life. But Chappell effects this dissolution of boundaries not on behalf of the radical skepticism of much postmodernist thought, with its despair of ever attaining truth, but on behalf of life's myriad possibilities, of the multiple shapes which truth assumes. Underlying both *Midquest* and the Kirkman tetralogy is a sense of life's plenitude and mystery.

Like *Midquest,* then, as Richard Abowitz has suggested, the Kirkman tetralogy is a "reactionary" work. It eschews not only the airy intellection of much metafiction and the minimalism of much of what Abowitz terms "workshop fiction"[11] but also the hegemony of traditional realism. Chappell turns instead to the aboriginal sources of storytelling in folk culture, using the oral traditions of his native Appalachia and the Old Southwest humor that built upon such oral narratives. In the process he has aligned his work with that of the "folk artist," whose aims and techniques he explored in his 1978 essay, "Two Modes: A Plea for Tolerance," a seminal essay for understanding both *Midquest* and the

Kirkman tetralogy. Identifying Homer and Twain and Cather and Faulkner, among many other writers, as folk artists, Chappell argues that "the farther an artist decides to depart from the Aristotelian notion of mimesis, the less is he to be regarded as a folk artist." But Chappell includes the fantasist among folk artists, for "fantasy is the heart and soul of folk tales and fairy tales," he states.[12] What the folk artist investigates, according to Chappell, whether through realism or fantasy, is "everyday life," "the same urgent moral necessities [that] are always with us."[13] "Obviousness may be the richest of literary possibilities, if the truly obvious can be once glimpsed," he adds, forewarning readers to examine the fundamental themes, the "home truths," that such writers seek to illuminate.[14] The Kirkman novels abound with such home truths.

I Am One of You Forever

"The one [book] I was happiest with when I finished," says Chappell, "besides *Midquest,* was *I Am One of You Forever.* . . . I knew I had done almost exactly what I wanted to do."[15] Most reviewers and critics have shared Chappell's satisfaction with the novel. Writing in the *Washington Post,* George Core described the book as "a novel to put on the shelf with Mark Twain, William Faulkner, and Eudora Welty," while David Guy praised Chappell in the *New York Times Book Review* as "a fine technician of narrative prose who writes with marvelous economy, gives his characters letter-perfect dialogue and describes them with wonderful vividness."[16] In one of the best critical essays the novel has elicited, Hilbert Campbell characterizes it as "a book by a master storyteller and humorist, absolutely in control of his language and of the nuances of charged moments and telling gestures."[17] Given the book's high level of accomplishment, such words of praise are assuredly merited.

I Am One portrays Jess and his family (whose surname, Kirkman, is not revealed until *Brighten*) over roughly two years, from 1940 to 1942. Although the book's events are recounted from the adult Jess's perspective, Chappell gives most of them an immediacy that enables the reader to identify with young Jess's thoughts and emotions at the time those experiences occurred. Jess's immediate family consists of his father Joe Robert, his mother Cora, his grandmother Annie Barbara Sorrells, and Johnson Gibbs, an eighteen-year-old orphan taken in by the family to assist with work on the farm. (The grandfather who appears in a number of the poems in *Midquest* is absent from the tetralogy.) This group of characters is augmented by Virgil Campbell, the country storekeeper of *It Is Time, Lord* and *Midquest,* as well as by the visits of four uncles and one aunt, whose presence in Jess's home prompts several of the practical jokes that intensify the novel's humor. These visiting uncles and aunt are among the book's most memorable characters, vividly portrayed and sharply individualized. Some of them— Uncle Gurton, for instance, with his enormous beard and almost complete silence—are eccentrics of the sort frequently found in Southern literature and humorous writing. Others, like Uncle Luden and Aunt Samantha, can scarcely be labeled eccentric, except in relation to the norms of Jess's own household. These visiting relatives add variety of character and incident, but it should be noted that they appear in only half the book's chapters. The other five numbered chapters, and all three italicized sections, depict Jess and his immediate family, including Johnson Gibbs, who becomes more an adopted son than a hired hand.

Given Jess's age at the time most of the book's events occur, this novel clearly tells a story of initiation. As Chappell has indicated, however, the first two volumes of the tetralogy deal less with Jess's process of maturation than with "the coming of age of the father." "I really didn't want to write another story about . . . a child coming of age," says Chappell; "I wanted to write about adults coming of age."[18] Joe Robert's boyishness is repeatedly emphasized in Jess's account of his father's exploits. And yet, despite Chappell's disclaimer, the book also traces Jess's growth in understanding, especially with regard to the nature of love, the reality of death, and the marvels of storytelling itself. If, as Fred Hobson argues, Jess is "still another version of Huck Finn, playing Huck, that is, to his father's Tom Sawyer, going along with his father's pranks but rarely initiating them,"[19] then it is noteworthy that Jess, unlike the Huck who surrenders to Tom's will in the last third of Twain's novel, comes to recognize the limitations of his father as a guide.

Hobson's comparison of Huck and Jess, while it illuminates the practical jokes that the males in the household play, should also remind readers that Jess's family situation is totally unlike Huck's. Joe Robert is clearly no Pap, and Jess, unlike Huck, has both a mother and a grandmother. As in *Midquest,* strong family ties are central to this novel, an idea illustrated in the book's opening section, "The Overspill," which also demonstrates Chappell's skillful blending of the realistic, the fantastic, and the allegorical.

"The Overspill"—and hence the novel and the tetralogy as

a whole—begins in medias res with the words, *"Then there was one brief time when we didn't live in the big brick house with my grandmother . . . ."*[20] Such an opening is appropriate for at least two main reasons. First, the poems of *Midquest* had, in fact, already begun the larger narrative of which this novel is a part. Second, and more importantly perhaps, that opening evokes the oral storytelling tradition which the tetralogy celebrates, anticipating Uncle Zeno's characteristic pronouncement, *"That puts me in mind of . . ."* (98; Chappell's italics). In medias res openings are common, moreover, in epic literature, and like most epics Chappell's tetralogy raises questions about the nature of heroism, questions that assume special urgency in *Brighten.* "The Overspill" focuses not on an act of heroism, however, but on an act of love. During Jess's mother's absence Joe Robert decides to create a garden beyond the creek that runs through the family's yard and to build a bridge with a latticed arch across the creek. That arch, Jess reports, *"was unmistakably a rainbow"* (3). The time is spring, the season of rebirth. Yet almost as soon as father and son complete their work, the paper mill opens the floodgates on its dam, deluging the garden and sweeping the bridge away at the precise moment when Cora arrives home.

What begins as a realistic description of Jess and Joe Robert's labors quickly assumes symbolic and allegorical significance. Garden, flood, rainbow—all are biblical images of mythic dimensions. The garden's susceptibility to destruction suggests humanity's loss of Eden or its loss of the Golden Age, both customarily imaged as gardens. Yet the flood in "The Overspill" is not a sign of divine wrath, nor is it simply a natural disaster. Instead it results from the paper mill's *illegal* action, and it thus raises the issue of justice that figures so prominently in *Moments of Light. Midquest*'s "Dead Soldiers" is the poem that most closely parallels the events of "The Overspill," and there too Virgil Campbell holds the mill partly accountable for the flood's destructiveness. In "Dead Soldiers" Virgil fires a shot at the collapsing Fiberville Bridge to put it out of its misery. In "The Overspill," however, the bridge is more than a victim of the floodwaters; it is a symbol of marital love and of family solidarity as well as an emblem of the interrelationship of nature and humankind effected by art. The paper mill menaces all three, as it does in "Children of Strikers" from *Moments of Light.* The wanton destructiveness of the paper mill's action so outrages Joe Robert, in fact, that he is still plotting revenge more than two decades later in *Look Back.*

What consoles Jess and his father in "The Overspill" is Cora's accurate reading of their intentions and the love and sympathy with which she responds to their disappointment. Chappell concludes "The Overspill" by shifting from realism to fantasy when a tear Cora sheds floats away from her face, expanding into "*a shiny globe . . . like an inflating balloon*" (6), a sphere that encompasses first Jess's mother and father and then draws Jess himself into its embrace. The tear symbolizes both the love that unites the family and the sorrow and loss to which human beings are subject and against which love and compassion and laughter are the most effective antidotes. Tears—not only of grief but also of laughter—are one of this novel's most pervasive images. But the tear in "The Overspill" represents what classical writers called *lacrimae rerum,* a term that means both tears *for* things (sympathy for misfortune) and tears *in* things (the inevitable sorrows of life, including death itself). Through this tear Chappell both anticipates his use of fantasy elsewhere in the novel and insists that the comic vision confront grief and mortality.

Indeed it is the confronting of death that Chappell places at the very center of this novel in "The Telegram," the second of the book's three italicized sections. This telegram announces Johnson Gibbs's death in a training accident at Fort Bragg after his enlistment in the army. By the midpoint of the novel, Jess and his family and the reader have come to care deeply for Gibbs so his death is an especially bitter loss, one made all the more ironic because it occurs during a training exercise and not in combat. Equally ironic is the telegram's placement on the dining room table propped up against the family's sugar bowl. This juxtaposition provides yet another striking image of life's duality, just as the circumstances of Gibbs's death intensify the sense of human vulnerability. As in "The Overspill," Chappell incorporates fantasy elements into this episode, depicting the telegram as impervious to every effort to ignore or destroy it. Yet only by confronting the telegram, by accepting the fact of mortality, can Jess and his family proceed with their lives. At the center of this essentially humorous novel, then, Jess experiences what amounts to a descent into the underworld, an encounter not with the dead but with death itself.

This encounter with mortality (reinforced by the title of the third novel in the tetralogy, *Farewell, I'm Bound to Leave You*) seems to call into question the claim made in this initial novel's title. Given the fact of death, how is it that someone can claim to be one of you *forever*? It is no accident that Chappell follows "The Telegram" with a chapter titled "The Storytellers," for it is

in stories, both those of a formal literary nature and those produced by family memories and shared orally, that the individual
achieves one species of immortality. Joe Robert's references in
this chapter to Homer's *Iliad,* with its tale of Helen and of the
warriors at Troy, provide one notable instance of art's triumph
over the destructiveness of both war and time. But Joe Robert is
himself an inept storyteller. The true storyteller in this chapter is
Uncle Zeno, whose name recalls the pre-Socratic philosopher
remembered for his paradoxes involving permanence and
change, being and becoming. For Zeno, being was ultimate;
becoming, simply an illusion. Chappell uses Jess's encounters
with Uncle Zeno to propound some paradoxes of his own, beginning with the chapter's opening sentences: "Uncle Zeno came to
visit us. Or did he? Not even the bare fact of his visit is incon-
testable" (97).

In "The Storytellers," one of the two longest chapters in the
novel, Chappell plays with what the adult narrator calls "metaphysical speculations in the philosophy of narrative" (113).
Uncle Zeno's tales often seem to derive directly from the tall tale
tradition of Old Southwest humor, and yet they may simply
reflect that tradition's indebtedness to folktales.[21] His stories of
Setback Williams and a marauding bear, of a dog so intelligent
that it took up school teaching to support its missing owner's
family, and of Lacey Joe Blackman, who was so obsessed with
hunting that he would "go a-hunting pissants . . . if they was in
season" (99)—all have the sound of Twain and his predecessors
in frontier humor. The final example, in fact, echoes the predilection for gambling exhibited by Jim Smiley in Twain's "Notorious
Jumping Frog of Calaveras County." As Fred Hobson has

observed, Twain's influence seems to extend even to Uncle Zeno's manner of telling a story, which Hobson compares to Twain's portrait of Simon Wheeler in "The Notorious Jumping Frog."[22] Like Wheeler, Uncle Zeno delivers his stories in a voice "dry, flat, almost without inflection" (97). "And he took no interest in our reactions," Jess adds. "His attention was fixed elsewhere" (98).

Uncle Zeno appears to embody the impulse toward storytelling evident in every human society. As an artist figure he is remarkable neither in physical appearance nor in the quality of his voice, "except that it was inexhaustible" (97). Through Uncle Zeno, Chappell indicates the crucial role that stories play, not only in literature but also in folk culture and religion and philosophy, in defining both self and world. "He was some necessary part of nature," Jess says of this uncle. "But he was more than that, and different" (110). Stories incorporate elements from the natural world, but they also testify to the unique powers of the human imagination—and to a realm of spirit that transcends nature. Chappell implies the existence of this supernatural sphere by portraying Uncle Zeno not as someone who remembers or invents his stories but who is "repeating words whispered to him by another voice" (98), "the voice he listened to, the voice beyond the world . . ." (102). The Appalachian term for tall tales of the sort Uncle Zeno tells is "windy," a word that Chappell links to the concept of storytelling as an inspired activity and not simply a matter of craft. This symbolic association of wind with inspiration is evident in the volume of *Midquest* titled *Wind Mountain,* in the central italicized section of *Farewell* titled "The

Wind Woman," and in Jess's depiction of his father's defense of Darwin in the closing section of *Brighten.* There Chappell writes, "[Joe Robert] *was no longer the author of his own words, but only the vessel of a Truth that had long been waiting to make him its spokesman*" (211). According to Chappell, one of the artist's responsibilities—indeed, one of our responsibilities—is to attempt to attune oneself to that higher Truth.

In addition to exploring oral storytelling traditions and to demonstrating the influence of Old Southwest humor, "The Storytellers" enables Chappell to play with contemporary literary theories and fictional devices. Young Jess considers, for instance, the relationship between word and thing, literature and life, and wonders whether "Uncle Zeno's stories so thoroughly absorbed the characters he spoke of that they took leave of the everyday world and just went off to inhabit his narratives" (113). "Homer and Uncle Zeno did not merely describe the world, they used it up," Jess concludes, a conclusion that causes him concern when Uncle Zeno, in a self-referential fashion of the metafictionist, begins telling a story about Joe Robert that Chappell had recounted in chapter 1. Yet while "The Storytellers," with its speculations on the origin, nature, and function of stories, is at times reminiscent of John Barth or Robert Coover, Chappell himself embraces neither the radical subjectivism nor the skepticism about mimesis that underlies most metafiction. Nor does Chappell subordinate the world to the text in the ways that Jess's theory would require.[23] Rather than privileging the literary text in this way, Chappell strives to create fiction and poetry that serve as windows on both the physical and the metaphysical. Instead of using up the world, "the writer . . . gives up his life," Chappell has said, "in order to honor the world and all its creatures and whatever else he believes in beyond that."[24]

Uncle Zeno is only one of the four uncles who visit the Kirkman household in *I Am One.* By the time the reader meets him, Chappell has already introduced two others, the womanizing Uncle Luden (whose name suggests both the term "lewd" and the Latin word for game, *ludus*) and Uncle Gurton (whose name appears to be drawn from the title of one of the first British dramatic comedies, *Gammer Gurton's Needle*). Chappell's comic treatment of these two uncles—and of the hilarious events described in the novel's opening chapter, "The Good Time"— eases the reader into the book. Yet despite the lighthearted tone of these early chapters, they subtly indicate, as did "The Overspill," that the novel is meant to embrace sorrow as well as laughter, tragedy as well as comedy. The very title "The Good Time" seems to posit the *pastness* of that moment, and this initial chapter not only refers to the war already under way in Europe but also announces Gibbs's enlistment in the army. The chapter ends, moreover, with an emblem of mortality that recalls the famous analogy used by one of Edwin of Northumbria's counselors in Bede's *Ecclesiastical History,* the comparison of human existence to a sparrow's flight through the king's hall that led to Edwin's conversion.[25] Chappell uses a kindred image as Jess and Johnson Gibbs sit beside a trout stream, the river itself a conventional image of temporality. Looking about them, the two boys see an opening "like a big window" between two poplars, and as they watch, "a bird cut[s] straight and quick through the space, gliding from one shadow to the other . . . dark against the light" (25). This imagery of dark and light, of darkness poised *against* the light, mirrors the duality of human nature and of human experience as Chappell conceives of them.

In his portrait of Uncle Luden, Chappell offers a similarly dualistic view. From this uncle, Jess begins to learn something of the pleasures and power of eros—and of its potential for social disruption. In addition to being a womanizer Uncle Luden is an alcoholic, and his alcoholism limits his ability to control his life. One of the novel's most poignant scenes occurs when Uncle Luden, obviously inebriated, returns one morning to Jess's home, sets twelve dime-store dolls on a nearby fence, and blows them apart with a pair of pistols while reciting the Twelve Steps of Alcoholics Anonymous. The dramatic shift in tone produced by this scene, which is observed by Luden's mother, Annie Barbara, further qualifies the comic high spirits of "The Good Time." Yet the early morning mountaintop picnic Uncle Luden subsequently arranges for the family offers hope of renewal despite the shattered possibilities the dolls represent.

Chappell further reinforces Jess's and the reader's awareness of human vulnerability in chapter 4, "The Change of Heart." This chapter's title promises the kind of transformation that Uncle Luden seeks through the restorative ritual of his predawn picnic. In neither of the two stories the chapter tells, however, does such a change take place. The first story involves Joe Robert's defense of Virgil Campbell, who is being persecuted as "Mr. Bound-for-Hell" by a religious enthusiast named Canary, "famous for the virulence of his righteousness" (64). Chappell describes Canary as looming over Virgil "like a *rickety* windmill, flapping his arms like *broken wings*" (64; italics added). These images, along with Canary's name itself, measure his distance from the Holy Spirit and authentic spirituality, for the Holy Spirit is usually imaged as a dove and associated with a wind that inspires and converts. The divine vision Joe Robert concocts to drive Canary out of Campbell's store provides one of the novel's funniest scenes. But none of the principals in this scene experiences a real change of heart.

The second story this chapter recounts focuses on a different sort of religious experience, one that comes to Joe Robert and Jess and Gibbs amid a tremendous thunderstorm not unlike the whirlwind from which God addresses Job or the storms from which God's voice emerges in Psalm 29. According to Jess, God speaks not only to Joe Robert: "He spoke to all three of us" (68). The "tower of energies" produced by this storm discloses creatures—Jess calls them "storm angels" (72)—that none of the three has seen before, and Jess hears "a Voice talking." Chappell undercuts the sublimity of this incident by having Joe Robert insist later that "the Voice told me I was right the first time. . . . That guy Canary is a worthless no-account son of a bitch" (74). Yet although the chapter closes with this remark, for Jess the storm does mediate an experience of transcendence. Only in this chapter does Chappell capitalize the term "Voice"; the "voice" to which Uncle Zeno listens is of a different order. At the same time, the storm intensifies Jess's awareness of the limits of human power, his sense of human finitude. "We felt as helpless," he remarks, "as if we stood by a friend's deathbed" (71)—a comment that anticipates the family's inability to alter the telegram's news of Gibbs's fatal accident.

For all the novel's delightful humor, Chappell has carefully designed the book to move the reader toward the death announced at its center. World War II was a pivotal event in the author's childhood, as it is in Jess's, transforming people's lives throughout Appalachia (as Harriette Arnow's novel *The Dollmaker* also demonstrates). Chappell again uses imagery of storms and voices to gauge the war's impact on a region that has often been inaccurately portrayed as isolated from the forces of mainstream American history, its citizens caricatured as "Yesterday's People."[26]

> The world outside our hills had come over the mountain-tops like a great black cloud full of lightning and thunder, full of shattering voices which were alien to us, voices speaking in languages we had never truly believed to exist. And this cloud of voices muttered of the destruction of cultures and civilizations to which we hardly belonged, to which we had only the most tenuous of allegiances, yet to which we were paying the most precious of tributes. (91–92)

The general playfulness of chapter 5, "The Furlough," near the end of which this passage occurs, makes the news of Gibbs's death all the more painful.

Despite the prominence that Chappell gives to the fact of death, he also makes it clear, through his portrait of Uncle Runkin in "The Maker of One Coffin" (chapter 7), that becoming obsessed with death is misguided. While death is inevitable, it must not be allowed to eclipse life's many gifts, as Uncle Runkin permits it to do. Like Uncle Zeno, Uncle Runkin is an artist figure. But Uncle Runkin's magnum opus is his handmade coffin, with which he travels, in which he sleeps, and on which he has worked for twenty-five years. To the lid alone he has devoted seven years. That lid remains unfinished, however, because he has yet to find a suitable epitaph for its entablature, though he has considered such pleasing possibilities as *Come lovely Angel* and *Sweet Death comes to Soothe* and *In Life's full Prime Is Death's own Time.* As such quotations reveal, Uncle Runkin is a direct literary descendant of Twain's death-obsessed Emmeline Grangerford. Whereas Joe Robert uses his carpentry skills in "The Overspill" to build a bridge as an expression of love, Uncle Runkin's carpentering revolves around himself and death, not the ongoing life represented by the garden to which Joe Robert's bridge leads. "I never saw him smile," says Jess of Uncle Runkin (120), a damning indictment in a novel as rife with humor as this one, and Jess's physical description of Uncle Runkin links him directly to death. "His skin was dry as wood shavings and when he touched any surface there was a slight raspy whisper, like a rat stirring in a leaf pile. Or like a copperhead snake skinning over the edge of a table. Or like a black silk pall sliding off a coffin" (120). Even the usually irrepressible Joe Robert finds his spirits dampened by Uncle Runkin's presence, and so he attempts a practical joke intended to hasten this relative's departure—he places a skeleton in the coffin.

This action has no apparent effect on Uncle Runkin. What does drive him away, ironically, is his discovery of Jess asleep in the coffin, profaning the sanctum sanctorum. Yet Uncle Runkin leaves memento mori scattered throughout the Kirkmans' home, for he has managed to dismantle the skeleton and has hidden pieces of it everywhere. "There are 206 bones in the adult human body," Jess observes, adding with the comic hyperbole characteristic of this novel, "and Uncle Runkin found 3,034 hiding places for them" (134). Through its satirical portrait of this character, "The Maker of One Coffin" attests to the life-affirming spirit of comedy, a genre that Northrop Frye calls "the mythos of spring" and that he associates with "social judgment against the absurd" rather than "moral judgment against the wicked."[27]

Such affirmation of life and love and art is a vital element in the novel's last two sections, "Bright Star of a Summer Evening" (chapter 10) and "Helen." The former introduces Aunt Samantha Barefoot, the book's only female visiting relative. Loosely modeled upon North Carolina country music artist Samantha Bumgarner, Aunt Sam is a prizewinning fiddler and banjo player whose unconventional appearance and speech ("My old memory has got as weak as butterfly farts," she remarks [174]) coexist with what Chappell terms "her central innocence" (166). Through Aunt Sam, Chappell once again highlights music, as he will do at numerous points throughout the tetralogy, most notably perhaps in the final chapter of *Farewell.* But Chappell also uses Aunt Sam to challenge, as in "The Change of Heart," the intolerance of some representatives of mountain religion. Jess discovers that his grandmother, Aunt Sam's cousin, was once a better musician than Aunt Sam, until Annie Barbara's father—"a stern old man with strict ideas"—forbid her to pursue her music, fearing that she would become "a shallow and thoughtless person" (171). Annie Barbara's father refused to give her permission to travel to Scotland for performances there;

Aunt Sam went instead, an action for which she feels she still needs to make amends to Annie Barbara.

Chappell ends chapter 10 with a scene of reconciliation appropriate to comedy when Annie Barbara agrees to accompany Aunt Sam on the piano, even though Jess's grandmother hasn't played a stringed instrument in nearly half a century. To Jess, his grandmother's "wistful broken chords sounded like the harmony that must lie beneath all the music ever heard or thought of" (178), a passage that again alludes to the Pythagorean music of the spheres mentioned in "Moments of Light." Yet that music's elusive harmony contrasts with the tension between the sexes evident in the two ballads sung on this occasion, "Fair and Tender Ladies" and "The Green Laurel." This dialectic between underlying metaphysical unity and existential dualities pervades all of Chappell's writing.

It is with an emphasis on unity, however, on shared vision, that Chappell concludes this novel. While many of the chapters center on male characters, the title of this closing section indicates, as do the events in "The Overspill," the female principle toward which the males gravitate. The winter hunting cabin in which the action is set may initially seem to contrast sharply with the domestic site of Joe Robert's and Jess's labors in "The Overspill," but as Jess listens to his father and Uncle Luden and Johnson Gibbs each utter the name Helen in their separate sleeps, Jess himself sees a face *blurred . . . yet familiar.* It is *the unplaceable familiarity of the vision* that Jess finds most remarkable (183). Chappell couches this whole experience in suppositional terms to heighten its dreamlike qualities: *It seemed,* Jess begins this final section, *I fancied,* *I thought that I saw,* *If something had actually appeared.*" Yet despite such tentative language and despite the aura of the fantastic that attends this experience, the figure of Helen, linked to Helen of Troy by Joe Robert's earlier account of the Trojan War (103),[28] represents the continuing human quest for love and beauty, a beauty that transcends mere physical appearance and points toward the harmony implicit in the Greek word *cosmos.* Chappell's fiction and poetry repeatedly profess his faith in such ultimate order while refusing to evade the evidence that challenges such faith.

The sense of communal vision with which the novel ends also confirms Jess's—and Chappell's—ties to the region that gave him birth and that nurtured his imagination, no matter how much that region has changed with the passage of time. As Chappell says of Ole Fred's "disappearing cultural traditions" in the preface to *Midquest,* he "finds them, in remembering, his real values" (x). In many respects *I Am One of You Forever* is a powerful and moving instance of such remembering, a remembering whose regenerative potency is apparent in chapter 8 when Johnson Gibbs, dead at the novel's midpoint, is resurrected by memory to participate in the Halloween prank recounted in "Satan Says." But the novel is far more than an act of memory, far more than a thinly veiled memoir of an Appalachian boyhood. In its use of fantasy and folktale, in its re-creation and transfiguration of the humor of the Old Southwest, in its mastery of style and voice, and in its original treatment of universal themes, the book is a consummate work of art. As one reviewer put it, "*I Am One of You Forever,* like the writing of Faulkner and Welty, invents its own mythic region,"[29] a region that Chappell continued to explore over the next fifteen years of his career.

Brighten the Corner Where You Are

Unlike *I Am One,* whose events cover a two-year period from 1940 to 1942, *Brighten the Corner Where You Are* deals almost exclusively with a single day in May of 1946, the Friday on which Joe Robert is to appear before the school board to determine whether he will be fired for teaching Darwin's theory of evolution. This event parallels James Christopher's father's loss of his teaching position in chapter 9 of *It Is Time, Lord* and Ole Fred's father's being fired "for creating life / From alfalfa in a jar" in "My Mother Shoots the Breeze" (*Midquest* 109). *Brighten* follows Joe Robert's activities from 3: 00 A.M. on the day of his firing until he is back at home in bed that evening. The only major exceptions to this chronological time frame are the opening italicized section titled "Moon," which occurs at an unspecified time in Jess's childhood and covers a span of months, and the italicized central episode titled "Shares," which differs from all the other material in the book because in it Jess, rather than his father, is the protagonist. Except in "Shares," Jess fades into the background of this second Kirkman novel; in fact, he is said to have slept through the entire day on which its events take place (201). His principal role, as Richard Abowitz notes, is to serve "as a voice of the creative imagination."[30] According to Hilbert Campbell, Jess's absence from the events he recounts illustrates "Chappell's adherence to the notion that the past, if recaptured at all, must be imagined, created, or even dreamed."[31] A less subjectivist interpretation might argue, however, that Chappell is tacitly acknowledging the writer's dependence on a larger storytelling community beyond the individual author's memory or imagination.

Although this second Kirkman novel has a tighter temporal focus and a more limited cast of characters than its predecessor, it contains almost as great a variety of incidents and an equal measure of humor and fantasy. Thematically too, it is remarkably diverse, though its dominant concerns are the quest for knowledge and wisdom, the quest for justice, the nature of courage, and the commonplace yet rare heroism of those who, like Joe Robert, strive to live by higher truths. Through its portrait of Jess's father *as a teacher,* the novel also explores the nature of education, especially American education. The charges brought against Joe Robert may initially prompt readers to think of the 1925 Scopes trial, which occurred some two decades before the novel's time present. Yet given the book's 1989 publication date, Chappell seems just as likely to have had in mind the growing pressure exerted on American schools by the so-called Moral Majority of the 1980s. Similarly, while World War II plays a prominent role in this novel as it did in *I Am One,* Chappell clearly invites the reader to reflect on the impact of the Vietnam War on a later generation of Americans. Just as *Bloodfire,* the second volume of *Midquest,* was the portion of that poem that dealt most directly with the American experience in Vietnam, so *Brighten* occupies the same position in the Kirkman tetralogy, not only in chapter 6, significantly titled "The Memorial," but also in chapter 3, "Medal of Honor." Chappell's use of fantasy, folktale, and humor in no way preclude his being a trenchant social critic.

The fire imagery of *Bloodfire* appears in various guises in this novel, from the campfire around which a hunting party sits in chapter 1 to the "Foxfire" of the closing chapter's title, from the fire in the stove at Campbell's store that warms the child whom Joe Robert rescues from drowning in chapter 2 to the threat of *being fired* that hangs over Joe Robert throughout the day. The figure of Prometheus, punished for bringing humanity the gift of fire, appears in the title of chapter 9, "Prometheus Unbound." But for Chappell's purposes in this book, one of the most significant symbolic meanings of fire is its association with enlightenment, with the acquisition of knowledge and insight. Before becoming a teacher, Joe Robert had worked for two years for the Carolina Power and Light Company, "bringing scientific electrical illumination" to mountain homes "where such light had never been heard of before."[32] He is thus an avatar of Prometheus before he ever enters a classroom.

The term "scientific" in the preceding quotation reveals another crucial facet of Joe Robert's character. As in several of the short stories in *Moments of Light* and *More Shapes Than One,* so in *Brighten,* the history of science and the nature of scientific understanding are used to clarify Chappell's thematic concerns. Joe Robert thinks of himself not as a teacher—"a schoolmarm," as he puts it—but as "a farmer, a scientist, an inventor, an explorer" (53). He is only teaching school, he explains, while Cora recovers from an auto accident that prevents her from returning to *her* job at the school. Joe Robert's imagination is fired not by teaching itself but by science and philosophy, especially the former. His scientist heroes, in addition to Darwin, are William Buckland (1784–1856) and Isambard Kingdom Brunel (1806–1859).[33] Buckland, a minister trained in theology, also served as the first lecturer in geology at Oxford University. He was, among his other achievements, the first person to assign a name, Megalosaurus, to the fossil bones of creatures now known by the general term "dinosaurs." But what Joe Robert particularly admires about Buckland was his willingness, when presented with convincing scientific evidence or persuasive reasoning, to change his mind. Initially a diluvial geologist, someone who ascribed the disappearance of the dinosaurs to Noah's flood, Buckland altered his views because the icthyosaurus would not have been affected by that biblical deluge.

Joe Robert's comments on Buckland are confined to chapter 4, "General Science." References to Brunel, in contrast, appear on seven occasions interspersed throughout the novel as well as at many points in *Look Back.* An architect and engineer, Brunel worked with his father on the construction of the Thames Tunnel before making his own reputation by designing and building the Great Western Railroad between London and Bristol, the longest rail line in Great Britain at that time. He also built elaborate, graceful bridges and pioneered in the construction of steamships, one of which made seventy-four Atlantic crossings in its career. Nicknamed the "Little Giant," Brunel was a visionary whose ideas sometimes exceeded the technological capabilities of his day. A civil engineer of extraordinary energy and originality, he has been called "the practical prophet of technological innovation" and "an artist of remarkable versatility and vivid imagination."[34] It may well be these latter traits that account for his appeal to Chappell and not simply to Joe Robert, for Chappell takes pains in *Brighten,* as in his volumes of short stories, to link the artist and the scientist, in this case through their mutual roles as "namers" in search of truth.

Jess's father's "talent for names" (32) is evident in the italicized episode, "Moon," with which the novel opens. Here, as with the tear in "The Overspill," Chappell immediately has recourse to fantasy, thus leading his readers to suspend their expectations of strict realism and inviting them to exercise their powers of imagination and subject themselves to the pleasures of story. The moon is traditionally associated with the imagination and dreams, with romantic love, with mutability, and with madness (*luna*cy). Chappell's main emphasis falls on the first of these associations, but he also connects Joe Robert's interest in the moon to the quest for knowledge, the kind of quest that finds Joe Robert flying to the moon aboard his spaceship *Isambard* in *Look Back*'s most fanciful chapter. In "Moon," however, no such flight is necessary, for the story is set at a time when the moon floats so close to the earth that Jess and his father must duck their heads to pass beneath it. Almost impulsively, Joe Robert pulls the moon from the sky by plucking its reflection off a windowpane and plunging it into a pail of milk.[35] In the moon's absence, Jess reports, previously unseen constellations grow visible, and Joe Robert assigns them names, including Brunel's Hat and Darwin's Destiny. After several months, however, Jess's father restores the moon to the sky, for although more stars are apparent, "*they shed little light; they seemed to increase the darkness, or at least to emphasize it more deeply*" (5). Once the moon reappears in the sky, Jess and his family look eagerly "*at the world the moon made visible*" (7).

This opening episode serves as a parable or allegory about the imagination's necessary function in illuminating and defining human experience. Like Wallace Stevens, Chappell demonstrates that even "the absence of the imagination had / Itself to be imagined," as Stevens says in "The Plain Sense of Things." Yet this episode also illustrates Joe Robert's intellectual curiosity, his impulse to experiment. It is with statements about the search for knowledge—and about the distinction between knowledge and wisdom—that "Moon" closes. For Joe Robert, "*Knowledge was the necessary precondition for wisdom*"; but in the final paragraph of "Moon" Jess presents his father, "*the local champion of reason and science,*" as a quixotic knight-errant: "*Somehow he had gotten mounted backward on his noble charger, and his shining armor clattered eerily about him like a tinware peddler's cart*" (7).

Having evoked the comic spirit and the idealism of Cervantes's *Don Quixote,* Chappell devotes chapter 1, "The Devil-Possum," to the kind of hunting story that is a mainstay of both Southern literature (including Appalachian literature) and Old Southwest humor. Yet ironically, the four members of the Crazy Creek Wildlife Appreciation Committee, as the group's name suggests, are not really outdoors at 3:00 A.M. to hunt. They intend instead to sit by a fire sharing stories and "a moderation jug of moon" (10). Chappell's skillful handling of the men's vernacular speech is worthy of Twain, as is the outlandish climax to the night's activities, when Joe Robert finds himself thirty feet high in a poplar tree, facing a choleric bobcat.

The principal thematic contributions this chapter makes to the novel originate in its introduction of the quest motif (in this case, a quest for truth), its portrait of Joe Robert as the enemy of custom, and its analysis of his paradoxical relationship to truth telling. As the other men listen to their dogs pursue and eventually tree some unknown animal, they brag about their hounds' respective abilities and debate whether the dogs are trailing a fox or a coon. Yet none considers leaving the campfire to investigate the truth of his claims—not, that is, until Joe Robert decides to stir things up with his yarn about the devil-possum the dogs have treed. Though Joe Robert's story is farfetched, the other men are finally persuaded to test his hypothesis. All four struggle painfully through the dark woods (a parodic allusion to Dante) to reach the tree, the older men insisting that Joe Robert be the one to climb the poplar. This he does, a burlap tote sack clenched in his teeth, only to discover that his tall tale is all too true. Trying to evade the enraged bobcat, he plummets from the tree, the tote sack catching on a branch, fortunately, and breaking his fall.

This experience leaves Joe Robert with a badly bruised face and "a rainbow epic" black eye on the very day of his hearing with the school board. More importantly, however, it reinforces, in delightfully comic terms, the status of both scientific experimentation and storytelling as means of discovering truth. "The Devil-Possum" concludes with Joe Robert's announcement to his fellow hunters that he has an important meeting with the Governor that afternoon. When the others ask whether he's telling the truth, Joe Robert responds: "Of course, it's the truth. . . . I wouldn't tell you boys a lie. The truth is sacred to me." To which Jess adds, "The truth was, in fact, so sacred to my father that he generally refused to profane its sanctity with his worldly presence" (28). Yet ironically, just as Joe Robert's tale of the devil-possum proves partly true, so do his remarks about the Governor. Chappell gradually leads both Joe Robert and the reader to recognize that reality itself is so fabulous that even Joe Robert's "stretchers" (a term Chappell borrows from Huck Finn) involve more truth than falsehood.

As Jess continues to recount his father's activities on this inauspiciously launched day, Chappell regularly interweaves the comic and the tragic. According to Joe Robert, in one of the novel's most important passages, life is "a collocation of extremities": "On one side were terror, despair, catastrophe, tragic ruin, and flood and famine and torture and disease. . . . On the other side were Nature in her every aspect, brutal or smiling, and a persistent smolder of kindliness in the greater mass of mankind. There were stars and animals and trees and microbes; there were women to love and friends who lived and died. . . . There was, in short, the flashing phantasmagoria of rational life, the wild enduring circus of sense and circumstance. . . . Take away the stuff of tears, there is nothing left to make laughter of" (35). Although this passage obviously issues from Joe Robert's mind, it expresses the consciousness of contradictions that shapes all of Chappell's work while also voicing his ultimate affirmation of life. Like Melville in "The Encantadas," Chappell discerns the two sides of the tortoise. Unlike Melville, however, he foregrounds the comic vision rather than the tragic—yet without denying life's tragic dimension.

The historical tragedy that haunts Joe Robert, as mentioned earlier, is World War II. Chapters 3 and 6 of *Brighten* deal directly with that war. In the former, Joe Robert is summoned to the principal's office, where he encounters the parents of a former student, Lewis Dorson, a highly decorated soldier. Lewis, unable to overcome the psychological distress caused by his wartime experiences, has committed suicide, and his parents, recalling their son's praise of Joe Robert's teaching, insist that Joe Robert accept one of Lewis's medals, "'something to remember by'" (64). The Dorsons also approach Joe Robert because they have heard that he too lost a boy to the war. While in many ways Joe Robert would prefer to forget both Johnson Gibbs's death and the enormous carnage of the war, he acknowledges the importance of remembering, as Chappell's fiction and poetry repeatedly emphasize. But this encounter with the Dorsons also leads Joe Robert to reflect on the idea of progress and to ponder education's role in preventing a repetition of such bloodshed.

In chapter 6, "The Memorial," it is Lewis's medal, significantly, that gains Joe Robert access to a secret room in the school's basement. There he discovers a "war wall" created by the school's African American custodian, Jubal Henry. That wall, some twenty feet long, three fourths of it already covered, "was simply one long sheet of obituaries, the notices and images of the fallen" (118). Among the dead appears the name of Johnson Gibbs. While Joe Robert recognizes a number of additional names, many of those listed are unfamiliar to him. But "the known and the unknown melted together in a single community," Chappell writes (119). "There was no discernible order in the mounting of the clippings; it was a flat democratic confusion, male female black white indian rich poor catholic protestant atheist schooled illiterate wise funny dull clever human human human human" (120). The absence of punctuation and capitalization in this catalogue helps to sustain the impression of a single undivided community, as does the poignant repetition of the word "human." As a transparent allusion to the Vietnam Memorial, the wall confirms Jubal's claim that "[World War II] is to be the war that never gives up," for America's involvement in Vietnam was itself a product of the Cold War mentality that resulted from World War II. In the Kirkman tetralogy, as in the poems of *First and Last Words,* war is a fundamental datum, not only for the twentieth century but also throughout human history.

Chappell presents chapter 6 as a descent into the underworld for Joe Robert, a visit to the realm of the dead, and he portrays Jubal as an oracular figure, a prophet who echoes Jesus' words when he tells Joe Robert, "You listen and you don't hear nothing, you look and you don't see" (127; Mark 8: 18). In his role as soothsayer Jubal offers Joe Robert two major insights. First, when Joe Robert inquires how his meeting with the school board will turn out, Jubal states, "It's going to turn out exactly the way you tell it to turn out" (125). This response indicates Joe Robert's ability to control the outcome of that encounter but also implies that he needs to approach the meeting thoughtfully, with a clear sense of what it is he wants. Reasoned, purposeful action is crucial, in contrast to his usual impulsiveness. Second, Jubal suggests that all the important events in Joe Robert's life will come to him "clothed in fire" (128), a prophecy that anticipates the epiphany Jess's father experiences in chapter 10, "Foxfire." Joe Robert considers both of the preceding statements difficult to interpret, but he is particularly perplexed by Jubal's comment that by "fire" he means *not* like the fire in a lantern but rather "like the fire that's in the lantern when the lantern goes out, . . .

the fire that gives the best light to see by" (128). As in "The Change of Heart," so here, Chappell invokes the paradoxical, the nonrational, the mysterious.

When Joe Robert extinguishes the lantern to force an explanation from Jubal, Joe Robert finds himself alone in the dark, both Jubal and the wall having vanished. Where the wall had stood, he discovers by match light an opaque zone of frozen darkness, an Arctic "curtain of shadow" through which he must proceed to escape the school's boiler room. As with the Kirkmans' confrontation with the telegram in *I Am One,* Joe Robert's passage through this zone of darkness is compared to dying. He leaves the basement with the feeling "of being unwrapped from his winding sheet" (133), emerging from this underworld like Odysseus or Aeneas or Dante the pilgrim. Chappell thus employs motifs of both birth and death in this episode and again invokes, as he did with his earlier allusion to Don Quixote, the heroes of the epic tradition.

One of the major attributes of such heroes is courage, a quality that Joe Robert likewise possesses—not the courage of the battlefield, which too often eventuates in slaughter, but the courage to seek and speak the truth. Joe Robert combines intellectual integrity with a compassionate heart and the ability to laugh at himself. Yet he is also disorganized, impulsive (as his foolhardy ascent of the poplar tree illustrates), and resistant to authority. His courage is depicted in many of the novel's episodes: his rescue of the drowning child in chapter 2 (though Joe Robert refuses to characterize his action as a "brave exploit," Virgil Campbell's term for it); his teaching of evolutionary theory despite community opposition; his descent into the underworld of chapter 6; and his efforts to deal with Bacchus, the talking goat on the schoolhouse roof in chapter 7, who seems to represent, among other things, sensuality's disruption of the discourse of mind and conscience in the classrooms below. To this list must be added Chappell's identification of Joe Robert with Prometheus in chapter 9 and Joe Robert's public defense of Darwin in the dream-vision with which the novel concludes.

It is this exploration of courage that helps account for Chappell's placement of "Shares" at the center of the book. Unlike the rest of the novel, it focuses on Jess, not on Joe Robert. The longest of the six italicized sections in *I Am One* and *Brighten,* this episode occurs when Jess is thirteen, over two years before his father's appearance at the school board hearing. In contrast to most of the novel, in "Shares" Chappell uses no elements of fantasy or folktale or humor. Instead its incidents are narrated with the gritty realism of a literary Naturalist, and those events involve physical violence that is linked to economic inequalities, to social injustice. In fact "Shares" opens with Jess's father denouncing the system of tenant farming even as he is compelled to rely upon it because of the war and because of his wife's temporary inability to work.

The plot of "Shares" turns on an accidental blow Jess gives to Burrell, the slightly older and much larger son of the family's tenant farmer, Hob Farnum.[36] Though Burrell takes no notice of the blow, Hob stops the work sled on which he and the boys are riding to reprimand his son for not defending himself. Badgered by Hob, whose name suggests mischief or trouble (as in the term "Hobgoblin"), Burrell offers to fight and Jess refuses. The blow was unintended, Jess insists, and both he and Burrell know that the older boy can defeat him. The searing contempt with which Hob and Burrell treat him convinces Jess that he has been cowardly, that he merits the scorn of his cowboy heroes, Gene Autry and Roy Rogers. Eventually, Jess feels compelled to fight Burrell to prove his courage, and he battles so desperately that he wins. Yet in his moment of triumph, Jess looks not toward reconciliation with the Farnums but toward further violence, wishing that he were big enough to whip Hob too. Violence, these events imply, fuels further violence; injustice breeds injustice. Real courage would reject such conduct. The courage Jess evinces, in contrast, has no moral vision behind it and so proves bankrupt, for this section concludes with Jess thinking, "*I wish I had me some tenants on a farm. I'd whip their ass three times a day*" (114).

As in "The Telegram," so in this central episode in *Brighten,* Chappell makes it clear that his novel is something more than a tall tale about Jess's father's exploits, more than an entertaining yarn. Jess's final attitude in "Shares" reveals how unlikely it is that human beings will ever renounce violence, and his actions point to fault lines that destabilize human relationships, fault lines that extend beyond social injustice into the bedrock of what many Christian theologians would label Original Sin. When "Shares" was first published, it bore the title "Slap,"[37] a title perhaps meant to recall the Christian ideal of nonviolence, of turning the other cheek. If so, Jess's conduct is far removed from that ethic. Even Joe Robert, near the end of the incisive Socratic dialogue that Chappell incorporates in chapter 8, threatens to give Socrates "a fat lip and a black eye and a bloody nose" (166). Unlike Jess, however, he immediately apologizes, explaining that "philosophy sort of ran away with me there for a second." Indeed it did, just as contention about politics and philosophy and religion continues to promote global violence.

Yet despite the pervasive violence of human history, Chappell remains, like Toby Milliver of "Thatch Retaliates," "a friend to Reason." His focus on a teacher in this novel reflects his commitment both to education as a means of effecting change and to the didactic function of literature. If the writer's aims, in the classical Horatian formula, are both to delight and to instruct, the same holds true of Joe Robert's aims in the classroom. Many of the pleasures of this novel arise from Chappell's affectionate depiction of Joe Robert's classroom teaching. As a teacher Joe Robert is imaginative, engaging, thought provoking, and resourceful, as both chapter 4, "General Science," and chapter 8, "Socrates," illustrate. In the former, Joe Robert makes his remarks on William Buckland more memorable by spinning a yarn about the geologist's pet bear supposedly enrolled at Oxford. His response to questions from the class, "I am coming to that," echoes J. T.'s repeated phrase in the tall tale recounted in *Midquest*'s "My Father's Hurricane." The same storytelling gifts are evident in Joe Robert's classroom style. Moreover, the notably *non*-Socratic dialogue in this chapter offers a lively and humorous contrast to the recreated Socratic dialogue in chapter 8. "Shall I tell you what Dr. Buckland did?" Joe Robert asks his class. "Oh, please please please do!" the students reply. "If you ever stop talking about him, our callow young minds will be blighted and impoverished" (79), a response absurdly incongruent with their sentiments two pages earlier: "May his name be blotted forever from the annals of human history" (77). The song about Pileser and Buckland with which chapter 4 concludes heightens its comedy while underscoring Joe Robert's emphasis on "a priority of delight" (83) in the educational process. In many respects Joe Robert's stance parallels Chappell's own, for both combine exuberant playfulness and serious intent.

Although Joe Robert disparages his job as a teacher early in the novel, he is obviously a talented instructor. The role-playing exercise over which he presides in chapter 8 works so well, in fact, that it utterly transforms the stuttering Scotty Vann, who in his role as Socrates becomes, like Uncle Zeno, "more voice than body" (158). Scotty performs so ably that his teacher is forced to confront the implications and limitations of his own position, a process Joe Robert finds as disconcerting as Socrates's original interlocutors often did. But as a teacher, Joe Robert recognizes that his ultimate responsibility is to the truth. "If taxpayers want to pay me to teach things I believe to be untrue, they'll have to hire me as an actor," he tells his colleague Sandy. When Sandy points out that, in his experience, Joe Robert's "most outstanding talent is in leaving the truth a homeless orphan," Joe Robert justifies himself by citing Aristotle's reference in the *Poetics* to "that species of lie that aims to reveal a *general* truth" (91; Chappell's italics), an allusion that again links Joe Robert to Chappell's own use of tall tales and fantasy. By the book's final chapter, Joe Robert has come to realize that "no other profession could offer such opportunity or such satisfaction" as teaching. "No other vocation could offer such true and invisible honor" (196). This realization, ironically, is one he attains only after quitting his job, but his sentiments should remind readers of Chappell's own long and distinguished teaching career.

Joe Robert's long-anticipated hearing with the school board is itself a masterful example of both comic anticlimax and irony. While Joe Robert envisions the school board members as "some grunty narrow-minded flinthearts who were after his hide" (35), they are actually favorably disposed toward him. His confidence (in "The Rehearsal") that he can predict what each of them will ask proves totally misplaced. Ultimately, the confrontation he dreads never transpires, for at the appointed hour Joe Robert darts his head in the meeting room's door, proclaims "I quit," and leaves. The confusion that follows among the board members enhances the comedy of this chapter ("Prometheus Unbound"), as those present offer various—and conflicting—interpretations of who has appeared to them and what was said, discrepancies in interpretation that reinforce Chappell's theme of the complexity of the quest for truth. What *is* clear, however, is the board's assumption that Joe Robert was well within his rights to present Darwin's theory to his class.

By keeping Joe Robert ignorant of the school board's support for him, Chappell is able to conclude *Brighten* with "Darwin," Joe Robert's dream of the scientist's execution in the local schoolyard. That execution occurs despite—or perhaps because of—Joe Robert's impassioned defense of Darwin, for in that defense Joe Robert finds himself speaking about both humanity's nobility and its debasement. Having called mankind "*that great Everest of the living world,*" Joe Robert remembers that humankind itself is, to use his earlier phrase, "a collocation of extremities." Thus, reversing his praise, he states, "*And yet man delights not me, no, nor woman, neither,*" words that echo Hamlet's grand ambivalence toward human nature in his famous speech to Rosencrantz and Guildenstern, where those words follow his high valuation of humankind: "How noble in reason, how infinite in faculties, . . . in apprehension how like a god" (*Hamlet* 2.2, 312–18). Joe Robert's viewpoint is less one of evolutionary progress than of a fall from original innocence consistent with Judeo-Christian theology. "*We began as innocent germs and added to our original nature cunning, deceit, self-loathing, treachery, betrayal, murder, and blasphemy,*" he remarks to those assembled in the schoolyard (211). "'*Dr. Darwin has searched for the truth. It is the nature of the human animal to subject its earnest seekers and most passionate thinkers to humiliation, degradation, imprisonment, and execution. If you now condemn this great man to death, you shall be guilty of nothing more than your own most ordinary humanity*'" (211–12). Though Joe Robert had hoped to speak differently, he has become, Chappell writes, "*the vessel of a Truth that had long been waiting to make him its spokesman*" (211). After this speech, the trapdoor on the scaffold opens, and Darwin plunges from sight.

Rather than reacting with horror to this apparent nightmare, Joe Robert giggles and nudges his sleeping wife, wondering whether she has gotten the joke. Chappell never explains that joke, of course, but it appears to derive, at least in part, from the fact that Darwin was not among history's martyrs. Unlike Socrates, he was not condemned to death, and the Scopes trial had already vindicated teachers of evolutionary theory even in the Bible Belt South.

And yet the darkness of human nature—its propensity for cruelty and violence and folly—persists, as World War II and the

Vietnam War, among countless daily events, amply illustrate. True humaneness is never a given; it is always something achieved, Chappell implies. As a writer, Chappell seems to share Northrop Frye's conception of what Frye calls "the archetypal function of literature in visualizing the world of desire, not as an escape from 'reality,' but as the genuine form of the world that human life tries to imitate."[38] To envision the genuinely humane is the highest function of both the literary and the moral imagination. To communicate that vision to others is the responsibility of teacher and writer alike.

While usually avoiding both preaching and polemics, Chappell never shirks the didactic, for he realizes that humankind needs all the light it can get. "Brighten the corner where you are" is an imperative he addresses not only to the reader but also to himself. As Abowitz observes, in the Kirkman tetralogy Chappell attempts to reclaim "the author's primary duty to understand people and, in the process, to create people worth understanding."[39] In the endearing, vividly imagined Joe Robert, Chappell has produced just such a figure, a character of heroic dimensions whose quest for truth, like Chappell's fiction itself, both delights and enlightens.

Farewell, I'm Bound to Leave You

Like its predecessors in the Kirkman tetralogy, *Farewell, I'm Bound to Leave You* was lauded by reviewers. One called it "southern fiction at its best," and the book received the *Dictionary of Literary Biography*'s annual honor as the most distinguished novel published in 1996.[40] The most episodic of the four volumes in the tetralogy, the novel achieves coherence in four main ways: (1) through its use of the framing device of Jess's grandmother's approaching death; (2) through its consistent focus on female characters; (3) through the voice Chappell creates to exemplify and articulate the intensely local yet universal experiences the book records; and (4) through its emphasis on storytelling itself and on the kinds of narratives that have shaped Jess's identity as an artist.

Because *Farewell* parallels part three of *Midquest,* the volume titled *Wind Mountain,* air or wind is another unifying device Chappell employs. That natural element is especially prominent in the book's italicized sections, appearing, for example, in the novel's opening sentence: *"The wind had got into the clocks and blown the hours awry."*[41] As in *Midquest,* in this novel the wind assumes a range of meanings, including its associations with the breath of life (gradually being withdrawn from Annie Barbara), with poetic and divine inspiration, with passions of various kinds (as Dante associates wind with the punishment of the Carnal in the Second Circle of Hell, a portion of the *Inferno* from which Chappell quotes extensively in *Wind Mountain*), and with music, a recurring motif in *Midquest* too. In contrast to *I Am One* and *Brighten* Chappell does not number the chapters in *Farewell,* perhaps to suggest what he calls in the preface to *Midquest* "the fluid and disordered nature of air" (x), an intent that would also account for the greater looseness of structure in this novel.

The book's brief opening section, "The Clocks," immediately introduces the theme of time and mortality, with the wind functioning as an emblem of mutability (as in Psalms 103: 15–16). The prospect of Annie Barbara's death looms over the entire book, shadowing but not negating its comic elements, as Johnson Gibbs's death tempers the humor of *I Am One*. While Jess and his father await that imminent death and Jess's mother attends to Annie Barbara, Joe Robert proposes that he and Jess "'*tell again those stories of women that your mother and grandmother needed for you to hear*'" (5). The actual telling of those stories, however, is presented through the voices of the women themselves. And Chappell often situates their storytelling, significantly, on occasions when Jess is engaged with his grandmother and mother in work traditionally associated with women: inspecting the canned food in the family's pantry for spoilage (chapter 2), peeling and coring apples (chapter 4), drying dishes (chapter 8), stringing beans (chapter 9). Four of the stories are told by Jess's grandmother (chapters 2, 3, 4, and 7), three by his mother (chapters 5, 6, and 8), and two by both women (chapter 9 and 10, with the latter described as a tale "with four tellers," the others being Dr. Holme Barcroft and Jess himself). The novel's opening chapter also unites Jess's grandmother and mother, but it involves not a story they tell but rather Jess's account of their thoughts and feelings and words as death impends for Annie Barbara.

That initial chapter, "The Traveling Women," is itself a narrative tour de force. While seemingly inspired by Katherine Anne Porter's "The Jilting of Granny Weatherall" both in its basic situation and in its use of stream-of-consciousness narration, "The Traveling Women" departs in crucial ways from Porter's short story. Whereas Porter limits her readers to Granny's point of view, Chappell takes the reader inside the minds of both mother and daughter—and at times creates an unspoken dialogue between the two women's thoughts in the alternating paragraphs he assigns to each. Porter's story emphasizes Granny's bitterness, her refusal to forgive the jilting, an attitude that helps to explain the Bridegroom's (Christ's) absence at that story's conclusion. Chappell's narrative, in contrast, opens with a religious longing shared by both mother and daughter—"Jesus Jesus O now Jesus, they said or thought, now show Your sweet face" (6)—and this desire seems to be fulfilled for Annie Barbara in the novel's italicized closing section, "The Voices" (227). Thus while Porter's story stresses Granny's isolation and disappointment, Chappell's text characteristically emphasizes shared experience, a journey made together. Yet despite the plural noun of its title, this chapter also reveals Annie Barbara's consciousness that, ultimately, the individual encounters death alone. This realization is one Chappell has mother and daughter reiterate in the closing pages of "The Helpinest Woman" (chapter 9), where the relationship between Angela Newcome and the dying Elsie Twilley mirrors that between Jess's mother and grandmother in both chapter 1 and "The Voices."

In its use of the term "traveling," this novel's opening chapter invokes the journey motif that pervades Chappell's fiction and poetry. This motif reappears in various forms throughout the book, most obviously in the road fifteen-year-old Earlene Lewis must drive in "The Fisherwoman," in the roads Jess travels with his mother both in "The Wind Woman" and during her narration of "The Madwoman," and in the road Cora and Annie Barbara are traveling with Holme Barcroft when he recounts the experiences they pass on to Jess in the novel's closing chapter. In temporal, material terms, that road or journey leads to death. In spiritual terms, however, that journey is also a pilgrimage of the soul, a pilgrimage for which death is not the terminus. Thus, in addition to the image of a road, "The Traveling Women" introduces the image of a window—an image indicative of the new revelations death may bring, as in Chappell's poems "Windows" and "Latencies" in *Source*. The novel leaves open the possibility, then, that it is light, not darkness, to which Annie Barbara's window gives access. Such a balance between opposing possibilities is also implicit in the river imagery evoked by the novel's title, which is taken from the lyrics of "O Shenandoah," itself a folk song about a journey. Annie Barbara senses herself "drifting on a river, . . . being carried away" (21), an apt image of the fatal impact of temporality. But the Shenandoah of the folk song has as its counterpart the river Jordan of Christian symbolism, a river traversed to reach eternity.

Chappell suspends Annie Barbara's journey until the novel's closing section. Not until then does Jess's grandmother actually die. This frame technique is a prominent element in much Old Southwest humor—though Chappell puts it to more somber use here—and it is a device that he utilizes repeatedly in many of the book's chapters, where it serves to remind the reader of Jess's role as auditor to these stories and thus as potential beneficiary of their substance and style and of the storytelling techniques that his grandmother and mother employ. *Farewell* deepens and enriches the portraits of these two women presented earlier in the Kirkman tetralogy, while the stories they tell introduce a whole new gallery of characters as intriguing and diverting as the array of visiting relatives in *I Am One*.

The first of those stories deals not with a new character, however, but with Jess's parents and is a story he has heard before, though only from his father's perspective, the kite-flying episode of "My Mother Shoots the Breeze."[42] It is the first of many chapters in this novel to deal with marriage, one of the major subjects and metaphors in *Midquest* as well. Annie Barbara's retelling of this story differs considerably from Joe Robert's version, thus demonstrating to Jess the need for multiple perspectives on events—especially across gender lines. Also at issue are the difficulty of ascertaining the truth and the constructive uses of falsehood, major concerns in *Brighten* too. The story is told while Jess and his grandmother inspect the contents of canning jars for spoilage, an activity that affords a homely emblem of the quest for truth. Yet despite the uncertainties that often attend this quest, Chappell again affirms, by having Annie Barbara remember an occasion when Joe Robert demonstrated *his* integrity, his commitment to "tell the truth whether it might harm his own interest or not" (29), his belief that truth is, in fact, discoverable.

The events Annie Barbara describes involving the kite, in contrast, reveal *her* willingness to use harmless deception to insure that Cora gains Joe Robert's love. As the reader learns, Annie Barbara not only has masterminded the kite-flying episode itself but also has engineered for her daughter (by requiring Cora to practice repeatedly with the shotgun she fires in this incident) an enormous bruise on Cora's shoulder, a bruise revealed on the couple's wedding night. Annie Barbara intends for that injury to manifest Cora's love for Joe Robert while intensifying his for her, and her strategem works. Annie Barbara's intelligence, resourcefulness, and foresight are at the center of this story, qualities traditionally denied to women.

Many of the novel's other chapters also subvert traditional stereotypes of women, often in delightfully comic ways. Chapter 3, "The Figuring Woman," presents Aunt Sherlie Howes, whose name identifies her as the community's Sherlock Holmes and whose keen intelligence is matched by her compassionate insights into the human heart. "She had a gift for listening and the patience to draw out facts . . .," says Annie Barbara of Aunt Sherlie (42), listing traits essential to a good storyteller as well. The emphasis in this chapter falls both on the power of love and on women's capacity for the orderly thought and careful logic customarily associated with men. In chapter 7 Jess asks to hear another story about Aunt Sherlie and is rewarded with a ghost tale, "The Shining Woman," which further confirms Aunt Sherlie's grasp of the truths of the heart, not simply of the analytic intellect. At the end of this second tale, in fact, Aunt Sherlie concedes that she's not "dead certain" that her analysis of the ghost's identity and motives is accurate, and Jess's grandmother likewise admits that some of her own remarks exceed "all I know for certain" (152). Through such comments Chappell creates a space not just for reasoned speculation but for the creative imagination of the storyteller, especially of those storytellers attuned to experiences that transcend ordinary reality (as is the case with the inexplicably undecayed corpses of Angela and Elsie in "The Helpinest Woman").

Like Aunt Sherlie Howes and like Ginger Summerell of "The Feistiest Woman," Earlene Lewis of "The Fisherwoman" challenges female stereotypes, in Earlene's case by becoming an expert in trout fishing, another traditionally male activity. Although this chapter is not the liveliest in the novel, it contributes to the tetralogy's larger structure by offering a parallel to "The Wish" of *I Am One* and "The Devil-Possum" of *Brighten.* Significantly, Earlene is fifteen years old when the chapter's principal events take place, roughly Jess's age when he hears most of these tales. Thus the dependability and resourcefulness his mother praises in Earlene are traits Cora would like to instill in her son. But the most important passage in this chapter may occur when Jess asks his mother how she could have known all the details of the story she tells, especially what Earlene was thinking and feeling and saying to herself. Cora's response offers a valuable perspective on Chappell's conception of storytelling and the storyteller's art. "[Earlene] told me a lot," Cora replies, "and then I put myself in her place so I could tell the story to you. That's what storytellers do" (100). These remarks again highlight the importance of listening, something Jess is seen doing throughout the book, and the importance of imaginative identification with others. For Chappell such empathy is not only one of literature's generative impulses but also one of its principal aims, an integral part of its moral function. This concept of imaginative identification with others is one to which Cora returns near the end of chapter 9 (193–94) and to which his grandmother alludes on at least two additional occasions (139, 190). It is also evident in the interweaving of the two women's thoughts and emotions in chapter 1.

Among the most striking characters Chappell creates in this novel are Selena Mellon of "The Silent Woman" and Aunt Chancy of "The Madwoman." The former appears in a tale told in February, a story whose winter setting reinforces its thematic focus on the problem of suffering. In conception, "The Silent Woman" seems to derive from Hawthornesque allegory, for Selena, like Parson Hooper of "The Minister's Black Veil," is set apart from the rest of the community—though in her case not by an item of apparel but by her silence. Chappell clearly invokes, in fact, Hawthorne's well-known formula of alternative possibilities as people speculate on the reason for Selena's silence. "Some conjectured that she had a deep dread secret like the one that caused Aunt Chancy Gudger to lose her mind—whatever that secret was," Jess's grandmother reports. "Others fancied that she had taken a vow of silence, maybe for Bible reasons. . . . Or maybe she'd devoted to a vow of silence for reasons of the heart" (63–64). A similar range of explanations is given for what transpires between Selena and Lexie when the two women first confront one another, an encounter that utterly transforms the previously ill-tempered, belligerent, promiscuous Lexie and that leads to a thirty-year friendship between them, Lexie moving into Selena's home for the remainder of Selena's life.

Selena effects this transformation not through her silence but through the look in her eyes. Although there is nothing unfriendly or menacing about that look, no one in the community is able to meet Selena's eyes when her gaze first falls upon them. Jess's grandmother has difficulty describing that gaze, saying only, "When [Selena] took notice of you, you felt that you had changed and were not the same person as you were before. Not worse, not better; not more comfortable or uncomfortable. You just felt *known*" (62–63; Chappell's italics). In such attentiveness to others, Selena resembles the Owners of the human race in

Chappell's short story, "After Revelation." Selena is a person of marked self-possession, of great equanimity, whose glance prompts others to examine their souls even as they feel themselves embraced and comprehended by her eyes.

Only after Selena's painful death from cancer does Lexie come forward to serve as her friend's interpreter. Even then, she has to rely on conjecture to explain Selena's silence, a silence broken only on her deathbed when she murmurs, "Goodbye, my dove," to Lexie. Once again, then, Chappell calls attention to the need for imaginative identification with others. What Lexie sees in her mind's eye as she tries to envision what prompts Selena's silence is the image of a suffering child, a girl of five or six, whose anguish "will never come to an end" (77). According to Lexie, this haunting image represents "something [Selena] wanted to say but didn't trust any words she knew to say it for her" (75). It is an analogous conviction of the suffering and loss that besets humanity which makes its presence felt at various points throughout the Kirkman tetralogy, infusing tragic undertones into the novels' prevailing comic spirit.

It is the experience of suffering that also underlies Chappell's portrait of Aunt Chancy of "The Madwoman." The madwoman is a prominent figure in feminist thought, a victim of patriarchal oppression, and the circumstances of Aunt Chancy's life certainly justify such a reading of her mental breakdown, though Chappell depicts her as far more than a victim. Aunt Chancy's name first appears in chapter 1, where it occurs to the dying Annie Barbara. But Jess's grandmother remains unaware of the causes of Chancy's madness, and thus it is his mother who narrates this tale of emotional abuse, jealousy, and murder. The plot of this chapter loosely resembles that of *Castle Tzingal,* for the married Chancy is drawn into a brief affair with the widely traveled Frawley Harper, an affair cut short by Frawley's murder. Harper's surname links him to the harpist Marco of Chappell's poem, and like Marco, Frawley is noted for his singing of songs learned during his travels, his favorite being "Oh Shenandoah." Chancy's husband Dave, like King Tzingal, murders his rival, although neither spouse loves his wife. Unlike Queen Frynna, however, who commits suicide, Chancy in turn murders her husband and then grows mad—a madness that results, presumably, not from her murder of Dave but from her loss of Frawley.

Essentially a Gothic tale, "The Madwoman," like "The Silent Woman," again indicates Chappell's refusal to idealize mountain life. The nostalgia sometimes evident in the Kirkman novels is regularly qualified, among other ways, by the physical hardships of wresting a living from hardscrabble farms, by the cruelty of people like Chancy's husband and the menfolk of Marsden County in "The Feistiest Woman," by the religious intolerance to which Joe Robert and Virgil Campbell are subjected, and by an awareness that rural life in the mountains offers no exemption from the suffering and loss and death to which all human beings are liable. Yet Aunt Chancy's story also underscores the role of the arts in providing consolation amidst life's hardships. The one thing that soothes Aunt Chancy in her worst fits of madness is the music of Aunt Samantha, at that time a girl of fifteen dispatched to Chancy's cabin by Jess's grandmother, who has been reading the Bible's account of King Saul and young David the harpist. Music and storytelling, art and literature, Chappell implies, bring hope of an order beyond the "collocation of extremities" that marks human existence. And they bring such hope and consolation not by denying those extremities but by confronting them. The adult Aunt Sam's music is praised, it should be noted, for its ability both to evoke sorrow and to effect rebirth: "She played a fiddle that could tear your heart out and then with another tune give you a brand-new and more joyous one" (117). This assessment applies with equal justice to the "music" of the diverse stories recounted in Chappell's novel.

Music in the form of a square dance is the central event in the book's final chapter, "The Remembering Women," which effectively unites many of the novel's major motifs and themes. The chapter's title re-emphasizes the importance of memory, one of Chappell's perennial themes. The fact that this final chapter has "four tellers," whom Jess views as a "quartet," may be meant to remind readers that both *Midquest* and the Kirkman tetralogy are composed of four volumes and that four, as Chappell says in the preface to *Midquest,* is "the Pythagorean number representing World" (ix). But the presence of four tellers here also underscores the need for community and for multiple perspectives. That the teller is less important than the tale is evident in Chappell's manner of introducing various paragraphs with such parenthetical remarks as "my grandmother might say" or "my mother might say" or even "my grandmother and mother might say," a narrative device that implies that others too might have been able to relate the events described. Unlike many twentieth-century writers, Chappell stresses neither the artist's isolation nor the artist's originality but rather the artist's ties to tradition. Moreover, Jess announces that his own purpose in retelling these events is to share them with his sister—and thereby to make it possible for her, if she chooses, to share them with her children. Stories thus become, among other things, a vital means of connecting the generations across time. At the same time, however, chapter 10 is the one chapter where Jess's voice predominates, as is evident from the absence of the nearly ubiquitous quotation marks that signal Jess's grandmother's and mother's narration in the other chapters. As a result, this chapter mirrors Jess's maturation as a storyteller, his assimilation of the women's stories and their narrative techniques, his extension of the oral tradition they embody.

In "The Remembering Women" it is the traditions of southern Appalachian culture, among them the oral storytelling tradition, that Dr. Barcroft, a Scots musicologist and folklorist, has come to record. Chappell's inclusion of Barcroft broadens the novel's cast of characters in the same way that Aunt Samantha's visit does in the final chapter of *I Am One*. But Chappell's portrait of Barcroft also presents an outsider to the mountain region who approaches it not through stereotypes, not with preconceptions about the primitivism or the peculiarities of its people, but with a genuine interest in their culture and a profound sense of their humanity. Jess's grandmother hopes that Barcroft's books will help others beyond the region realize "that we were people like other people, wise and foolish, brave and frightened, saintly and unholy and ordinary" (197)—an aim implicit in Chappell's books as well. Barcroft's research has taken him to almost every corner of the globe, and Chappell's catalog of the Scotsman's travels creates an impression of glorious variety and plenitude, as do Chappell's descriptions of the meals at the Lafferty home where the chapter's events are set. To promote a conviction of life's abundance is a major part of Chappell's intent in this concluding chapter.

The Lafferty household itself contributes significantly to that conviction. Even the family's name indicates their good nature ("laugh"-erty), and they are depicted as having "a talent for happiness" (198). The parents' odd Dickensian names, Quigley and Qualley, add to the humor Chappell associates with them, as does Jess's uncertainty about the number of offspring the couple has produced: "There were nine or ten or maybe an even dozen children. . . . it was impossible to get an accurate count because they wouldn't stay put long enough" (198). Equanimity and boundless energy—both radiate from the Lafferty family. It is Quigley, above all, whom Barcroft has come to observe, for Quigley is a master fiddler and the best square dance caller in the county. This visit occurs in May, the month of Ole Fred's birthday in *Midquest* and the month in which several other chapters in *Farewell* are also set.

For Barcroft, the square dance with which his visit culminates becomes an archetypal rite, a celebration of love and rebirth. But that dance also occasions a religious vision in the musicologist, a moment of epiphany like those experienced by Haydn and Linnaeus in Chappell's short stories and by Jess when he falls asleep in Uncle Runkin's coffin in *I Am One.* That epiphany is foreshadowed by some of the lyrics in Quigley's calls: "Grab your partner and promenade, someday we'll dance at the throne of God," for example (217), and "'*Gents go forward to a left-hand star / And think upon whose sons you are*'" (218; Chappell's italics). The image of the star, so prominent throughout Chappell's work, reappears here, as does the moon just two paragraphs later, a moon that rises as if called down from the heavens by the power of music to join the dance, a moon that floats as close to the earth as the moon in the opening section of *Brighten.* Barcroft also sees the Lafferty house itself spinning like a wheel, the house metamorphosed into "a merry-go-round, turning steadily and stately" (218), an image of wholeness, harmony, and perfection. After this vision vanishes, both Barcroft and the reader are left with a sense of sacred mysteries and renewed possibilities—but also a sense of the transitoriness of such epiphanies. The very recounting of this experience, however—first by Barcroft to Annie Barbara and Cora, then by them to Jess, and now by Jess to his sister (and the reader)—testifies to Chappell's belief in the importance of storytelling in preserving and voicing humanity's spiritual heritage. Both his fiction and his poetry convey a vision of transcendent harmony much like the one Barcroft has had, and Chappell regularly makes music one of the principal metaphors for such religious experiences.

Chappell's use of a traditional folk form like the square dance to prompt Barcroft's epiphany is in keeping with his affirmation of folk culture throughout the tetralogy. But Chappell's intense love for his native region is most evident in this novel in his masterful creation of Annie Barbara's and Cora's narrative voices, which must surely be numbered among the book's greatest artistic achievements. Those voices are keenly attuned to the natural world and to the family's agrarian lifestyle. While words and phrases drawn from the region's vernacular speech contribute to the distinctiveness of those voices, especially Jess's grandmother's, their freshness and originality stem mainly from the profusion of apt figurative language used by the two women and the concreteness of the diction that Chappell assigns them. In "The Shining Woman," for example, Jess's grandmother refers to Little Mary as "the tail-ender at dinnertime," competing with older brothers and sisters "as hungry as bears in March" (137). Little Mary's plain features lead Annie Barbara to compare her to "a mule in a stableful of saddle ponies" (138). A quiet young woman, Little Mary offers would-be gossips "as much personal information . . . as you can carry breeze in a soup spoon" (140), while her even more taciturn husband is described as so thrifty with words that he died "a dictionary millionaire" (136). According to Annie Barbara, Little Mary and her husband "were fated to stand on the unsilvered side of the mirror" (139), for Talbot is "luckless as Job." "His bucket didn't have a hole in it; his bucket had no bottom" (137). About her own curiosity Jess's grandmother remarks that she could feel her ears grow "as long and twitchy as a hare's in hunting season" (144). All of these quotations appear in fewer than ten pages of a single chapter. Yet they are representative, not atypical.

The vividness, concreteness, and aptness of such language attest to the vitality of the lives these people lead and to their level-headed intelligence. The Kirkman tetralogy abounds with such striking, apparently effortless, yet carefully crafted diction, demonstrating Chappell's mastery of his art. One of the most important effects of such language is to ground readers themselves in the natural world, as Chappell's use of the four elements does in more obvious ways in *Midquest*. Like Holme Barcroft at the Laffertys', Chappell's readers are left with the impression of being involved "with a place and a people, with a time and circumstance, that was not only human in all its affections and interests but linked also with nonhuman nature, with sky and stream and mountain, in its reverences" (215). Reading the Kirkman tetralogy, as in reading *Midquest,* one finds oneself "standing near the origins of a strength that helped to animate the world, a power that joined all things together in a pattern that lay just barely beyond the edge of comprehension" (215). Such is the promise of Chappell's fiction and poetry, a promise the Kirkman novels regularly fulfill.

Yet the mysteries of suffering and death remain. From the radiant vision of wholeness that Barcroft offers, the reader returns to the room where Jess and his father await word of Annie Barbara's death. As that moment arrives, an icy shadow descends upon father and son, reminiscent of the chill barrier through which Joe Robert must pass to leave the boiler room in *Brighten.* Having painfully endured that experience, they go to comfort Cora. *Farewell* ends, then, as *I Am One* began—with father, mother, and son united by love in a context of loss. Such love is itself, Chappell implies, humanity's most effective response to the grief that attends existence in time.

Chappell clearly intends this novel to serve as a corrective to the largely male-centered casts of characters in *I Am One* and *Brighten.* Throughout most of the book female characters and narrators predominate. Yet it is *Farewell,* more than any other volume in the tetralogy, that traces the *artistic* influences that shape the adult Jess, most importantly the oral storytelling tradition. And nowhere is Chappell's purpose in this regard clearer than in the novel's central italicized section, "The Wind Woman." Twice as long as the other two italicized sections combined, "The

Wind Woman" details a series of visits Jess and his mother plan to make to such archetypal figures as the River Woman, the Cloud Woman, the Fire Woman, the Moon Woman, and the Happiest Woman.

As in "Helen," the final section of *I Am One,* Chappell lends a visionary aura to this episode by opening "The Wind Woman" with the words "*It seemed,*" which are repeated three times in the opening paragraph. It is Jess's mother who insists that the two of them include the Wind Woman in their visits because Cora has seen her son writing poetry and so declares, "Y*ou must meet the Wind Woman, for you'll never write a purposeful word till you do*" (104; Chappell's italics). Given the varied significations of wind in *Midquest* and the tetralogy, this remark is open to multiple interpretations. Most obviously, it means that Jess must open himself to the sources and powers of poetic inspiration, but it may also be meant to suggest, through wind's traditional association with the Holy Spirit, that spiritual vision must be among Jess's literary concerns. Yet since the wind is likewise associated with the transitoriness of life, Jess's mother may recognize as well that the artist's sense of the beautiful and the valuable is intensified by an awareness of the evanescence of all living things. On this occasion, for the first time, Cora reveals to Jess that she herself once wrote poetry, and she gives voice to ideas that echo some of Chappell's own most strongly held aesthetic assumptions. "*It is passionate affection or sorrow that makes most of us poets,*" she says, "*and a poet's passion must feed upon truth. And that is what* [the Wind Woman] *can supply*" (105–6).

The two most important stops Jess and his mother make on the day this central section describes are at the homes of the Happiest Woman and the Wind Woman. At the former, Jess's role as *auditor* is emphasized, the role he plays in the book's individual chapters as well. But that visit also highlights the motif of music, which subsequently proves so significant in "The Madwoman" and "The Remembering Women." Jess listens as his mother and the Happiest Woman sing, accompanied by the latter on her harmonium, an instrument—like Ben Franklin's *armonica* in *Moments of Light*—whose name suggests the spiritual and artistic quests for wholeness that suffuse Chappell's work. The sound of the harmonium is "*fleet and light and inspiriting*" (109), and the music the women create is intimately connected to nature itself through Chappell's figurative language: "*The music was . . . cool as springwater and bright as an October beech leaf*" (110).

Initially, Jess's visit to the Wind Woman's cabin produces a sharply different effect. There Jess is assaulted by a wild cacophony of sounds, a commotion both frightening and intoxicating, including lines from a ballad that also appear in *Midquest*'s bleak poem, "Remembering Wind Mountain at Sunset." "*My head swarmed with the hurt of it,*" Jess says. Then, abruptly, everything falls silent, except for the "*single round, silent tone of the moon,*" whose sound Jess calls "*a mercy and a marvel*" (115). As in the opening section of *Brighten,* this moon seems to represent the artistic imagination, which Jess assumes must be tutored by the Wind Woman—whom he never sees, of course, she being invisible. But Jess vows to await her arrival with his eyes closed, a stance that he and other characters adopt at various points throughout the book, a stance indicative of faith in the imagination's powers and in the spiritual sources of artistic inspiration.

"The Wind Woman" concludes with Jess's image of himself

sitting in her cabin, "*patient to consort the sounds of the hollers and slopes and valleys below into music*" (115). It is out of Chappell's own patient artistry and integrative vision that both *Midquest* and the Kirkman tetralogy have arisen, with their powerful testimony to the diverse influences that have shaped their author's career. As this study of Chappell's fiction and poetry has shown, the course of that career has taken him far beyond Jess's hollers and slopes and valleys without uprooting his imagination from its regional sources. Those regional sources are especially prominent in the Kirkman novels, where Chappell's authoritative narrative voice has the "pure, clear, confident, . . . lyric" tone of Quigley Lafferty's fiddle.

Look Back All the Green Valley

The final novel in the Kirkman tetralogy, *Look Back All the Green Valley* is the least episodic and the most traditionally structured. Its many references to characters and events in the other three novels also make it the least capable of being read independently, apart from a knowledge of its predecessors and of *Midquest.* Only chapter 2, "The Tipton Tornado," which recounts an event from the childhood of Jess's sister Mitzi, gives the impression of being a self-contained narrative unit, an impression common to a number of the chapters in the earlier novels, one that had led many reviewers and critics to read those volumes as collections of interrelated short stories.

Whereas the events in the earlier Kirkman novels were all set between 1940 and 1950, time present in this novel is a single week in June of 1979. By then, Jess's father has been dead for ten years, and his mother, now residing in the Graceful Days Retirement Community, is slowly dying of congestive heart failure. Jess spends the week in a motel outside Asheville, having returned "home" from Greensboro, where he teaches at the university and publishes poetry under the pen name Fred Chappell, a literary genre and a name his mother repeatedly deprecates. "I had decided, ruefully but not reluctantly," he remarks, with delightful comic irony, "that Jess Kirkman was not born to write novels."[43] He has come back to the mountains to clean out one of his father's workshops and, more importantly, to make new burial arrangements for his parents because a mix-up at the cemetery where his father is buried prevents Cora from being interred beside him, as she assumes she will be. These initial motives for Jess's visit are further complicated once he begins to clean up the workshop, that "Merlin's Cave," for in it he discovers, among other things, a map of western Hardison County covered with women's names, a map that leads Jess to assume—falsely, as it happens—that his father had led a busy extramarital love life. Like *Brighten,* this novel revolves around Joe Robert and around Jess's efforts to understand his father. Despite its leap some thirty years forward in time in relation to the earlier Kirkman novels, it often adopts the backward glance suggested by its title.

That elegiac focus on what Jess calls "Old Times" is reinforced by Chappell's decision to set several of the book's chapters in western Hardison County rather than in the county where Jess grew up. For both Jess and his father, Hardison County represents "the genuine old-time mountain ways and the true Appalachian temper of life" (108). Yet by associating the county's tripartite geography—Downhill, Vestibule, and

Upward—with Dante's three divisions of the afterlife, Chappell indicates the breadth of lifestyles and experiences the county offers. In this novel Jess directly identifies himself as "Appalachian by heritage," and he laments the passing away of the old mountain ways and the caricaturing of the region's rich folk culture by such enterprises as Hillbilly Heaven. This restaurant, deftly satirized in chapter 4, offers a menu that "some well-paid assassin of language had slung together while nibbling bagels in a Madison Avenue deli and thumbing through precious antique issues of L'il Abner Comics" (94), a menu that includes Downhome Corneypones, Ticklish Tater Toes, and White Litenin'. Jess is waited upon by a costumed server who promises to return for his order "in two shakes of the spotted pup-dog's tail." Such mangling of even a clichéd expression stands in sharp contrast to Chappell's creative and sensitive use of regional words and phrases throughout the tetralogy. Jess, whom Chappell portrays as working on a translation of Dante's *Divine Comedy,* imagines the Florentine poet assigning the originator of Ticklish Tater Toes to the pool of excrement reserved for the flatterers.

As the last book in the tetralogy, *Look Back* parallels *Midquest*'s final volume, *Earthsleep,* the collection of poems on which Jess is said to be at work in 1979. "Earth was my theme, and my connective tropes were gardens and graves, intimate engagements with dirt," he states (20). In *Midquest* those tropes are readily apparent in such poems as "Susan's Morning Dream of Her Garden," "How to Build the Earthly Paradise," and "At the Grave of Virgil Campbell." The title of this last poem is also the title of chapter 4 in *Look Back,* a chapter that closes with Jess drafting a series of possible epitaphs for Virgil, just as he does in

Midquest. Images of gardens and graves pervade the novel as well, with the garden image intended to evoke, among other things, the mystic Rose of Dante's vision of paradise (as opposed to the false paradise promised by the name Hillbilly Heaven). The names on Joe Robert's map turn out to be not those of women but of varieties of roses, for Joe Robert has been experimenting with what he calls his Floriloge, a new means of measuring time. That these roses are meant to allude to Dante's celestial Rose becomes clear in chapter 9.

In fact, as may already be evident, this novel is distinguished from the other Kirkman novels by its extensive use of Dantean materials, including numerous quotations from *The Divine Comedy.* Such references and allusions recall the Dantean structure of *Midquest* while also attesting to Chappell's own religious sensibility. Despite the retrospective cast of the novel's title, the book's Dantean references ultimately direct the reader's gaze forward toward eternity, toward the hope of resurrection implicit in the concept of paradise. To the four Pythagorean elements of earth, air, fire, and water, Chappell adds what chapter 9 calls "the Quintessent Dimension," a fifth element—often associated with spirit—that suffuses and sustains all earthly and celestial bodies.

Just as *Earthsleep* addresses, among other themes, the inevitability of death, so this novel (like *Farewell*) is preoccupied with the inexorable advance of time and the prospect of death and burial. Indeed the novel's opening and closing italicized sections are set in a cemetery. There Jess and three other men are disinterring Joe Robert's body, Jess having decided to circumvent the lengthy delays that normal exhumation procedures require. This action occurs on a stormy night whose rain

and wind and lightning, in conjunction with the cemetery's dirt,
enable Chappell to unite all four of the natural elements around
which *Midquest* and the Kirkman tetralogy revolve. As in *Spring
Garden,* so in this book, the transitoriness of human existence is
a prominent concern, a concern manifest in several additional
ways as well. Joe Robert's basement workshop, for instance, is
located below a business named Times Past Antique Clocks, and
his own fascination with the nature of time becomes apparent
when Jess finds in that workshop one of his father's notebooks
filled with reflections composed by Joe Robert but attributed to
Fugio. This Latin word, meaning "I flee," often appeared on
sundials. In Chappell's novel Fugio's maxims provide the
epigraphs to each of the book's ten chapters and include such
observations as, "*Every hour is another syllable in your epitaph*"
(chapter 4) and "When *is everywhere*" (chapter 8). Occasionally,
Joe Robert's musings in his notebook resemble those of Uncle
Runkin ("Befriend the End"), while at another point he employs
the key terms of Uncle Gurton's only reported saying ("Life is an
elegant sufficiency; eternity a wishful superfluity").

Despite Joe Robert's characteristic interest in mechanisms
of almost any kind, in this novel Chappell portrays Jess's father
as searching out an alternative to clocks as mechanical means of
measuring time. Joe Robert's Floriloge is instead designed as a
massive garden laid out in contiguous triangles, each of which
contains roses of a different variety and color. This device aims
to induce what he calls "the resonance of an essential harmony
of human spirit with the regular processes of the Cosmos" (232),
an aim also implicit in the design of *Midquest.* According to Joe
Robert, the Floriloge is meant to provide a method of "literally,

keeping time." Instead of measuring time's *passing,* it creates the sense of an eternal *now* in which time is perceived as "an organic entity" (231) that enriches human existence rather than constricting or extinguishing it.

Joe Robert's explanation of this device appears in chapter 9, the most fantastical chapter in the novel. Titled "Into the Unknown," that chapter opens with the Kirkman family aboard the spaceship *Isambard* heading toward the moon. The spaceship, conceived and built by Joe Robert, is named for the nineteenth-century British engineer who is one of Joe Robert's heroes in *Brighten* as well. The chapter's science fiction elements, along with Jess's prior discoveries about his father's unsuccessful efforts to cultivate roses in Hardison County, call into question the practicality of the Floriloge, yet without negating its symbolic significance. But the title of this chapter points to the larger issue of death itself. As the *Isambard*'s flight proceeds, the reader gradually recognizes that Chappell has cleverly juxtaposed Joe Robert's fantasy of space travel with the Apollo moon landing of 1969, an event that occurs at the moment of Joe Robert's fatal heart attack. Jess's father's imagined approach to the moon (that is, to death and hence eternity) is presented in images and lines drawn from Dante's *Paradiso,* with the moon seen as the celestial Rose of Dante's vision. Joe Robert's death is thus linked not to physical annihilation but to spiritual fulfillment and rebirth. Among the passages Chappell quotes from the *Paradiso* is that poem's final line, "*l'Amor che move il sole e l'altre stelle,*" translated here as in the closing lines of *Midquest:* "the Love that moves the sun and the other stars" (242).

During the imagined space flight it is love that prompts

Jess's father to project himself into "the Veilwarp" that obtrudes between the *Isambard* and the moon, thus protecting his family from potential harm. That Veilwarp, like the curtain of frozen darkness through which Joe Robert must pass in chapter 6 of *Brighten,* becomes a metaphor for death itself, a barrier between time and eternity, with the latter here represented by the moon, often viewed as an emblem of mutability.[44] The allegory in this passage owes more to Dante and Hawthorne than to science fiction, for entering the Quintessent Dimension (that is, the realm of spirit), according to Joe Robert, is a sure means of avoiding the Veilwarp. For Dante, God as ultimate Spirit is equated with a love that sustains the whole creation beyond the fact of death. Such faith verges upon ineffable Mystery, as Chappell intimates by placing near the end of chapter 9 the following passage from Canto XXX of the *Paradiso:* "And now I was enwrapped in living light / Whose own bright shining fashioned such a veil / That nothing around me could appear to sight" (243; lines 49–51). These lines precede Dante the pilgrim's ascent into the Empyrean, where he encounters the celestial Rose. Both *Midquest* and the Kirkman tetralogy testify to the hope of resurrection, the possibilities of rebirth not only within but also beyond time. That hope is also evident in Jess's failure to find his father's body in the grave he excavates in this novel's closing section, just as it is present in the potential for awakening implicit in the title *Earthsleep.*

In addition to these interrelated themes of time, mortality, and resurrection, *Look Back* addresses four other major subjects that recur throughout Chappell's fiction and poetry. They include the resources of the past, the quest for justice, the pleasures and value of storytelling, and the nature of authentic religion. The book's very title, taken from a folk song, underscores the importance of looking back, its image of a luxuriant valley reflecting life's plenitude and the invigorating effect of contemplating the past. Although the lyrics of this ballad stress the transitoriness of life ("Now our days are dwindling down"), Jess finds the song bracing. "If it remedied no sorrows of the world," he comments, "it brought them into the light and offered them an understanding to be found in nothing else but music" (267). Jess is uplifted, not downcast, by this backward glance. Many of the book's chapters, moreover, detail other people's happy memories of Jess's father, memories that justify the line from "Dixie" that serves as chapter 8's title: "Old Times There Are Not Forgotten." Nor is the significance of the past, for either Chappell or his characters, simply a matter of the living remembering the dead. Standing amid the graves in Mountain View Cemetery, where both Joe Robert and Virgil Campbell are buried, Jess thinks, "The dead are not silent, not even shy; they are speaking to us continually" (101). For Joe Robert this conviction of the past's resources is so strong that the *Isambard* is powered by "the Kirkman Drive, a device that taps into the intellectual capacities of past centuries" and thus utilizes "a practically infinite energy source" (213). The novel's extensive use of Dante and its self-reflexive references to characters and events in previous volumes of the tetralogy (and in *Midquest*) also illustrate the value of the past.

The two most frequently cited previous episodes from the tetralogy involve the flood of "The Overspill" and the storytelling of Uncle Zeno. Chappell relates the former event to Joe Robert's quest for justice. Throughout the novel Jess puzzles over a diagram he discovers in his father's workshop, a diagram that depicts an elaborate "Engine of Unguessable Purpose" worthy of Rube Goldberg. Eventually Jess learns that this mechanism is designed to launch an enormous pie, of excremental ingredients, into the face of one T. J. Wesson, the supervisor at the Challenger Paper and Fiber Company responsible for unleashing the flood that destroyed the bridge which Joe Robert intended as a gift to Cora, "a statement of enduring love" (64). Unable to obtain legal redress, Joe Robert plots revenge. That revenge is never effected. While the relative harmlessness of that projected revenge attests to his basic good nature (as well as to the impracticality of many of his schemes), his failure to gain revenge also demonstrates, albeit in comic terms, the ongoing need to work for justice. The loss of the bridge and garden in "The Overspill" reveals the destructive power of the forces arrayed against love. Moreover, Joe Robert and Cora's mutual affection, which Jess compares in this novel to the love between Philemon and Baucis in Ovid's *Metamorphoses,* once again invokes the marriage motif that helps to unify *Midquest* and that undergirds the focus on the Kirkman *family* throughout the tetralogy. Insofar as "the dark Satanic paper mill" threatens that love, the mill is particularly pernicious.

The repeated references to Uncle Zeno in *Look Back* are meant to remind the reader that the nature and functions of storytelling remain among the tetralogy's principal concerns. Among those valued functions is storytelling's capacity to define and communicate the power of love, whether in Ovid's legend of Baucis and Philemon, Jesus's parable of the Prodigal Son, or such tales as that of Chappell's own "Helpinest Woman" in

Farewell. As in the other Kirkman novels, so in *Look Back* Chappell calls upon the oral storytelling tradition, especially in chapters 6 and 8. In the former, Jess is shown around western Hardison County by Cary Owen, whose physical appearance is likened to that of Charon in Dante's *Inferno: "Un vecchio bianco per antico pelo"* (an old fellow with age-whitened hair) (126; Canto III, 83). While Jess and Cary tour the transparently Dantean divisions of the county, the two men exchange tall tales, Cary describing the antics of a lusty jackleg preacher, Jess recounting the story of James Dickey as it is presented in the seventh poem of *Wind Mountain*—though here Jess attributes the lines directly to Dante (134–35; *Midquest* 123). In chapter 8 the storyteller is Mr. Hillyer, an aged friend of Jess's father, who explains how Joe Robert once managed to sell half a dozen of the area's hard-shell preachers some fifteen hundred dollars' worth of stock in Satanic Enterprises Amalgamated, one of the many practical jokes that help to justify Jess's assessment of his father as "your classic folklore trickster."

As already mentioned, however, the most important storyteller to appear—or reappear—in this novel is Uncle Zeno of *I Am One of You Forever.* In that first Kirkman novel Uncle Zeno was as much a disembodied voice as a living person, and here too he comes to represent storytelling itself as an inexhaustible, eternal function of the human imagination. Even Joe Robert, despite his frustrating rivalry with Uncle Zeno, considers Zeno "immortal," and Jess attributes a comparable immortality to stories themselves. The kite-flying episode originally recounted in *Midquest,* for instance, has passed, Jess says, from family reminiscence into folklore: "the story of the kite . . . bade fair to survive us all" (56). This remark is Chappell's version of the classical motto, *ars longa, vita brevis.*

Although Uncle Zeno is presumed dead by the novel's other characters (for in 1979 he would be at least 110 years old), Jess spots someone he later identifies as Uncle Zeno on three separate occasions: in the cemetery during Jess's nighttime attempt to disinter Joe Robert's body; in that same cemetery when Jess visits it by day in chapter 4; and in the novel's central italicized section, "On the Foggy Mountaintop." In this humorous central episode Chappell again resorts to the language of dream-vision, opening with the words, *"It seemed."* In the Bible, mountain tops are often sites of religious revelation, but the fog's presence in this scene obscures Jess's vision and enables Chappell to distance himself from Jess's experience. Atop the mountain, Jess hears a voice *"dry, flat, almost without inflection,"* the very words used to describe Uncle Zeno's voice in "The Storytellers" (*I Am One* 97). That voice recounts Annie Barbara's arrival at the gates of heaven and her meeting there with Saint Peter, whose first words are couched in such mountain locutions as, *"What are ye a-waitin' for? . . . they's a place set for you"* (129–30). Annie Barbara hesitates, the reader learns, because she is meditating on the eternal prospects of her son-in-law, Joe Robert, whose free-thinking ways have often vexed her. Saint Peter reassures her, however, that the divine plan makes allowances for *"an earnest seeker after truth"* like Jess's father. The case of Virgil Campbell is more problematic, Saint Peter concedes, but Virgil too will have a seat at the heavenly feast once he *"work*[s] *off his demerits,"* as Saint Peter puts it. This labor Virgil will perform not in purgatory, as readers of Dante might assume, but in heaven itself, as wine and liquor sampler to Paradise's own "*ace distillery*." The fate Uncle Zeno projects for Virgil is not unlike the vision Ole Fred has of Virgil's afterlife in *Midquest*'s "At the Grave of Virgil Campbell," which depicts God as the Holy Bartender.

When Uncle Zeno's voice ceases and the fog dissolves, Jess looks down "*at a world nearer and farther away than any I'd known before*" (131). The seemingly opposed terms in this quotation—nearer and farther away—mirror the dual impulse that energizes Chappell's poetry and fiction, especially *Midquest:* to heighten appreciation for the natural world, the physical order of the Pythagorean elements, and to intensify awareness of spiritual realities, the claims of the *supra*natural. By placing Uncle Zeno's tale at the center of *Look Back,* Chappell anticipates the many allusions to Dante's *Paradiso* in chapter 9 while also highlighting, however humorously, the religious concerns integral to his larger artistic aims.

Those concerns pervade this final novel in the tetralogy. They are raised explicitly as early as chapter 2, one of the book's most entertaining episodes. That chapter combines Jess's account of an intense antagonism between Mitzi and one of her male first-grade classmates and Jess's memory of a prayer contest proposed by Joe Robert in response to the visit of yet another kinsman, Uncle Zeph Moseley. Uncle Zeph's prayers are not simply interminable but also unintelligible due to the "enunciatory oddness" of the "sanctified" voice he uses to deliver them. Once this uncle departs, Joe Robert suggests that the family exorcise the lingering distaste Zeph's prayers promote by devising their own and awarding a prize for the best prayer. Jess's father is confident, of course, that his prayer will win, a confidence that proves misplaced.

By having this prayer contest and the climax of Mitzi's hostility toward Rollie Sikes fall on the same day, Chappell demonstrates the way in which religious sentiments often coexist with animosity and intolerance (as is also the case with Preacher Canary of "The Change of Heart"). Moreover, Mitzi's hostility toward Rollie originates in her misunderstanding of something he has said, a misunderstanding that contributes to the comic structure of the chapter, which contains several other humorous misapprehensions and misadventures. Joe Robert, who in "Shares" forbids Jess to fight, here gives Mitzi boxing lessons and makes arrangements for her to box Rollie during recess. Human beings' capacity for violence is further reinforced by the fact that Mitzi wishes for a gun as her prize should she win the prayer contest—a gun with which she plans to shoot her archenemy. This conjunction of religion and violence is apparent as well in Mitzi's prayer itself. She begins with a petition for everybody's goodness and happiness, then ends with an abrupt addendum regarding her antagonist: "But don't make that baxter [bastard] Rollie Sikes be happy. Make him fall down on his nose" (50). It is Mitzi's prayer that Jess's father declares the winner, presumably for its clarity and candor, but that prayer also plunges the household, Jess notes, "into a fathomless blackness" that extinguishes the candles on the supper table.

This chapter ably illustrates Chappell's skill at creating comic episodes that resonate with substantive thematic implications. Mitzi's "luminance" is shadowed by the blackness that her double-edged prayer evokes, a duality that Chappell repeatedly discloses in human nature and in such human social constructs as religion itself, which is frequently wielded more as a weapon of condemnation than as an instrument of reconciliation and love. Throughout the Kirkman tetralogy Chappell portrays Joe Robert as the opponent of religious intolerance, indeed of all "self-proclaimed monopolists of truth" (261). In Joe Robert's mock Last Will and Testament, for example, excerpts from which appear in *Look Back*'s final chapter, Jess's father denounces "bluenoses, hypocrites, high-horse riders, the self-applauding self-righteous, pulpit mounters, and holier-than-thous" (261). His strictures against such people arise not from antireligious views but from his conviction that their attitudes distort authentic religion. In Canto XXIX of the *Paradiso* Dante has Beatrice similarly denounce false preachers of the Gospel. Joe Robert's scheme involving Satanic Enterprises Amalgamated aims to expose ignorance and superstition to healing laughter and the light of reason. Virgil Campbell, as Jess recalls in chapter 4, also challenged religious hypocrisy and intolerance through his "vendetta against the pulpit-thumpers."[45]

But *Look Back*—and thus the tetralogy as a whole—moves toward a scene not of satiric deflation of hypocrisy but one of fulfillment and reconciliation. Chapter 10 describes a gathering of family and friends for a picnic, an occasion that enables Jess to resolve the problem of locating new grave sites for his parents. So many offers of such sites have poured in that Jess, to avoid offending anyone, stages a drawing to determine where his parents will be buried. "Stages" is the correct term, for he knows in advance whose name he will announce regardless of whose name he actually draws. As in the final chapter of *Farewell,* music accompanies these festivities. Jess has hired a bluegrass band, the New Briar Rose Ramblers, a group named after Aunt Samantha's former band. Those musicians, like Quigley Lafferty of *Farewell,* thus represent the traditional folk music of the mountains, the band's name providing yet another instance of the rose imagery that helps to unify this book. When Jess expresses his gratitude to the group for keeping Aunt Sam's songs alive, one of the musicians comments that the reverse is true: "It's the songs that keep us alive—or keep the life worth living, anyhow" (269). This idea applies equally, Chappell suggests, to the life-enhancing potential of storytelling. As Jess tells the people gathered at the picnic, "'look how the titanic thinkers of past time console us yet in our present perils'" (265). It is such consolation that both *Midquest* and the Kirkman tetralogy aspire to offer— and do, in fact, articulate.

This final chapter is somewhat marred, nonetheless, by Jess's protracted address to the gathering and by his inclusion in that address of remarks that would seem to have little meaning to the people attending the picnic, however interesting they may be to the reader. (A comparable prolixity besets Mr. Hillyer's account of Joe Robert's scam involving the preachers in chapter 8.) In the final chapter too the didactic element sometimes grows obtrusive, as when Jess speaks of "this fleeting existence that it is our duty to enjoy and celebrate in all its splendors and miseries" (265). The book as a whole lacks the narrative momentum and dramatic suspense that Chappell regularly creates in the more episodic chapters of the other Kirkman novels. This is especially true of chapters 5 through 8, as Jess gathers information about the places on his father's map and investigates the most likely burial sites offered.

Despite such flaws, however, *Look Back* does bring the tetralogy to a satisfying conclusion both in itself and in relation to *Midquest*. The book accomplishes this goal principally through its reiterated themes and images and through its many references to the earlier texts. Its widespread allusions to "The Overspill" and to Uncle Zeno of "The Storytellers" link the book to the first Kirkman novel, while its pervasive references to Dante bind the volume to *Midquest*. Jess's unsuccessful effort to comprehend his father seems meant to highlight the core of mystery at the heart of human experience. Yet even though Jess is often mystified by his father's conduct, he recognizes the fundamental hopefulness and decency of his father's life. Near the end of the novel, Jess realizes that his quest for a father has uncovered not a man but a boy. Though this judgment might seem censorious, it is meant less as a measure of Joe Robert's immaturity than as a gauge of his sense of wonder and curiosity and delight, a gauge of his exuberant high spirits, his childlike enthusiasm for life and learning. In the book's final chapter Jess ventures to complete Fugio's unfinished maxim that serves as that chapter's epigraph. "Thought is to time as," Joe Robert had written, "light is to energy," his son adds (265). Jess's completed maxim reveals him to be his father's legitimate heir, confident that reason brings enlightenment and that time is a field of energy that permits human beings to become what they imagine, to fulfill many, though not all, of the dreams and desires to which they actively commit themselves.

Chappell concludes *Look Back* with the same passage from Shakespeare's *Twelfth Night* that concludes *Midquest:*

> SIR TOBY: A false conclusion: I hate it as an unfilled can.
> . . . Does not our life consist of the four elements?
> SIR ANDREW: Faith, so they say; but I think it rather con-
> sists of eating and drinking.
> SIR TOBY: Thou art a scholar; let us therefore eat and drink.
> Marian, I say! a stoup of wine!

Here, as in *Midquest,* Chappell juxtaposes the Dantean comedy of the questing spirit with the fleshly Shakespearean comedy of these two characters, whose appetites recall those of Virgil Campbell. Sir Toby plagues the puritanical Malvolio just as Virgil plagues Canary and his cohorts in virulent righteousness. Chappell's own incarnational metaphysics embraces both body and spirit. Yet it does not purport to exhaust the mysteries of either, as his titles for this novel's three italicized sections and for chapter 9 indicate. Each title implies an absence of light, an obscuring of vision, or a limitation of knowledge, an idea re-emphasized by the untranslated lines from Dante's *Paradiso* that appear in chapter 10.

> *E quasi peregrin, che si ricrea*
> *Nel tempio del suo voto riguardando*
> *E spera già ridir com' ello stea.*
> (260)

In these lines (43–45) from Canto XXXI, Dante compares himself to a pilgrim who has reached his destination and looks carefully around him, hoping to be able to report accurately the sublimity of his ever-deepening vision. The object of that vision in Dante's poem is the ultimate spiritual reality symbolized by the mystic Rose.

Deepening spiritual vision is also the central subject of both *Midquest* and this final volume in the Kirkman tetralogy. Both that poem and the tetralogy as a whole record Chappell's own moral and spiritual and artistic pilgrimage as it is embodied in his portraits of Ole Fred and Jess and their extended family. In addition to voicing their author's and various characters' revelations, these books testify to epiphanies beyond what Wallace Stevens has called "the precious portents of our own [that is, human] powers."[46] Contemporary American literature has been vastly enriched by the imaginative power and literary excellence of that witness.

Chapter 1—Understanding Fred Chappell

1. Fred Chappell, "First Attempts," in *Plow Naked: Selected Writings on Poetry* (Ann Arbor: University of Michigan Press, 1993), 14.

2. Quoted in Fred Brown and Jeanne McDonald, *Growing up Southern: How the South Shapes Its Writers* (Greenville, S.C.: Blue Ridge Publishing, 1997), 120, 123.

3. Fred Hobson, *The Southern Writer in the Postmodern World* (Baton Rouge: Louisiana State University Press, 1991), 83.

4. Resa Crane and James Kirkland, "First and Last Words: A Conversation with Fred Chappell," in *Dream Garden: The Poetic Vision of Fred Chappell,* ed. Patrick Bizzaro (Baton Rouge: Louisiana State University Press, 1997), 13.

5. John Sopko and John Carr, "Dealing with the Grotesque: Fred Chappell," in *Kite-Flying and Other Irrational Acts: Conversations with Twelve Southern Writers,* ed. John Carr (Baton Rouge: Louisiana State University Press, 1972), 228.

6. Crane and Kirkland, "First and Last Words," 11.

7. Quoted in Georgann Eubanks, "Fred Chappell: The Bard of Canton," *Duke Magazine,* Nov.–Dec. 1993, 10.

8. Quoted in Jennifer Howard, "Fred Chappell: From the Mountains to the Mainstream," *Publishers Weekly,* 30 Sept. 1996, 55.

9. Granville Hicks, "Thirty Years with a Stranger," *Saturday Review,* 10 Aug. 1963, 18.

10. Denis Donoghue, "Style," *New Statesman,* 21 May 1965, 811.

11. See especially Chappell, "Fred Chappell," *Contemporary Authors Autobiography Series,* ed. Adele Sarkissian (Detroit: Gale, 1986), 113, 119–20; Brown and McDonald, *Growing up Southern,*

131; and Chappell, "A Pact with Faustus," in *Mississippi Quarterly* 37 (Winter 1983–84): 16.

12. R. T. Smith, "Fred Chappell's Rural Virgil and the Fifth Element in *Midquest*," *Mississippi Quarterly* 37 (Winter 1983–84): 31–38.

13. Chappell, "Fred Chappell," 119–20.

14. Quoted in Shelby Stephenson, "'The Way It Is': An Interview with Fred Chappell," *Iron Mountain Review* 2 (Spring 1985): 9.

15. Quoted in George Garrett, "A Few Things about Fred Chappell," *Mississippi Quarterly* 37 (Winter 1983–84): 4; Garrett's italics.

16. That article was R. H. W. Dillard's "Letters from a Distant Lover: The Novels of Fred Chappell," *Hollins Critic* 10, no. 2 (Apr. 1973): 1–15.

17. Kelly Cherry, "A Writer's Harmonious World," *Parnassus* 9 (Fall–Winter 1981): 115–29; Rodney Jones, "The Large Vision: Fred Chappell's *Midquest*," *Appalachian Journal* 9, no. 1 (1981): 59–65; and Robert Morgan, "*Midquest*," *American Poetry Review* 11 (July–Aug. 1982): 45–47. The special issue of *Abatis One* appeared in 1983, of *Mississippi Quarterly* (cited above) in Winter 1983–84, and of *The Iron Mountain Review* (cited above) in Spring 1985.

18. Chappell, "A Pact with Faustus," 16.

19. Garrett, "A Few Things about Fred Chappell," 8.

20. Brown and McDonald, *Growing up Southern,* 122.

21. Chappell, "The Good Songs Behind Us: Southern Fiction of the 1990s," in *That's What I Like (About the South) and Other New Southern Stories for the Nineties,* ed. George Garrett and Paul Ruffin (Columbia: University of South Carolina Press, 1993), 3–4; Chappell's italics.

22. Brown and McDonald, *Growing up Southern,* 128.

23. Chappell, "Two Modes: A Plea for Tolerance," *Appalachian Journal* 5, no. 3 (1978): 338.

Chapter 2—Fables of Will and Appetite:
The Early Novels

1. Sopko and Carr, "Dealing with the Grotesque," 225.

2. See also Dillard, "Letters from a Distant Lover," 1–15, and David Paul Ragan, "Fred Chappell," in *American Novelists since World War II,* vol. 6 of *Dictionary of Literary Biography,* ed. James E. Kibler, Jr. (Detroit: Gale Research/Bruccoli Clark, 1980), 36–48.

3. Stephenson, "'The Way It Is,'" 9.

4. Ragan, "Fred Chappell," 38.

5. Chappell, "A Pact with Faustus," 19; Chappell's italics.

6. Henry Taylor, "The World Was Plenty: The Poetry of Fred Chappell," in *Dream Garden,* 71.

7. Chappell, *It Is Time, Lord* (New York: Atheneum, 1963), 9. Further references noted parenthetically are to this edition.

8. Chappell, "Two Modes: A Plea for Tolerance," *Appalachian Journal* 5, no. 3 (1978): 335.

9. Tersh Palmer, "Fred Chappell," *Appalachian Journal* 19, no. 4 (1992): 404.

10. Dillard, "Letters from a Distant Lover," 4, 6. For the text and translation of *"Herbsttag,"* see Rainer Maria Rilke, *Selected Poems,* trans. C. F. MacIntyre (Berkeley: University of California Press, 1964), 38–39.

11. *"Wer jetzt kein Haus hat, baut sich keines mehr. / Wer jetzt allein ist, wird es lange bleiben"* (38); MacIntyre's translation, 39.

12. Ragan, "Fred Chappell," 40.

13. Chappell, "Fred Chappell," 118.

14. Kenneth Lamott, for example, remarked, "I cannot promise to keep the peace if I am exposed to another bright young Southern writer who is hooked on incest, barnyard sadism, imbecility, and domestic bloodletting" (*San Francisco Examiner Book Week,* 15 Aug. 1965: 10).

15. Chappell, "Fred Chappell," 118.

16. Ragan, "'Flying by Night': An Early Interview with Fred Chappell," *North Carolina Literary Review* 7 (1998): 110. This previously unpublished interview was actually conducted in 1980.

17. Chappell, "Pact with Faustus," 19–20.

18. Chappell, *The Inkling* (New York: Harcourt, Brace and World, 1965), 3. Further references noted parenthetically are to this edition.

19. Of these passages Chappell has said, "A great deal of the material in those weird internal monologues [is] my wild translation of Rimbaud and Verlaine. They're not worth tracking down because sometimes they're so changed you can hardly recognize them. But sometimes they're quite readily available" (Ragan, "'Flying by Night,'" 110).

20. Nathaniel Hawthorne, *The Scarlet Letter and Other Tales of the Puritans,* ed. Harry Levin (Boston: Houghton Mifflin, 1961), 379.

21. Chappell, "Fred Chappell," 119.

22. Palmer, "Fred Chappell," 404–5.

23. Sopko and Carr, "Dealing with the Grotesque," 217.

24. Chappell, "Fantasia on the Theme of Theme and Fantasy," *Studies in Short Fiction* 27, no. 2 (1990): 181–82.

25. Peter Buitenhuis, "Desire under the Magnolias," review of *Dagon,* by Chappell, *New York Times Book Review,* 29 Sept. 1968, 58.

26. Epigraph is translated by Chappell in Sopko and Carr, "Dealing with the Grotesque," 218.

27. Amy Tipton Gray, "R'lyeh in Appalachia: Lovecraft's Influence on Fred Chappell's *Dagon,*" in *Remembrance, Reunion and Revival: Celebrating a Decade of Appalachian Studies,* ed. Helen Roseberry (Boone, N.C.: Appalachian Consortium Press, 1988), 78.

28. Quoted by Gray, "R'lyeh in Appalachia," 78.

29. Chase, *The American Novel and Its Tradition* (Garden City, N.Y.: Doubleday Anchor, 1957), 11.

30. Sopko and Carr, "Dealing with the Grotesque," 230.

31. Chappell, *Dagon* (New York: Harcourt, Brace and World, 1968), 5. Further references noted parenthetically are to this edition.

32. Irv Broughton, "Fred Chappell," in *The Writer's Mind: Interviews with American Authors,* vol. 3 (Fayetteville: University of Arkansas Press, 1990), 96.

33. Ragan, "Fred Chappell," 44.

34. Chappell, "Fantasia," 182.

35. Broughton, "Fred Chappell," 101.

36. Dillard, "Letters from a Distant Lover," 10.

37. The phrase occurs in Suzanne Booker's interview with Morgan in *Carolina Quarterly* 37 (Spring 1985): 22. This impulse to escape the gloom and extreme otherworldliness of Calvinist theology as it influenced the mountain South is also evident in Harriette Arnow's *The Dollmaker,* in some of the short stories of James Still, and in the poetry of Jim Wayne Miller, Kathryn Stripling Byer, and Lynn Powell, as well as in much of Chappell's work after *Dagon.*

38. Chappell, "Fantasia," 182.

39. Sopko and Carr, "Dealing with the Grotesque," 219.

40. Herman Melville, *Moby-Dick* (New York: New American Library, 1964), 455.

41. Sopko and Carr, "Dealing with the Grotesque," 218.

42. Ibid., 231.

43. Ibid., 224. See also Stephenson, "'The Way It Is,'" 9.

44. Ragan, "'Flying by Night,'" 118–19.

45. William J. Walsh, "Fred Chappell," in *Speak So I Shall Know Thee: Interviews with Southern Writers* (Asheboro, N.C.: Down Home Press, 1990), 76.

46. Chappell, "Fred Chappell," 121.

47. Palmer, "Fred Chappell," 404.

48. Chappell, *The Gaudy Place* (New York: Harcourt Brace Jovanovich, 1973), 3. Further references noted parenthetically are to this edition.

49. Dillard, "Letters from a Distant Lover," 13.

50. Charmaine Allmon Mosby, "*The Gaudy Place:* Six Characters in Search of an Illusion," *Mississippi Quarterly* 37 (Winter 1983–84): 55–62.

51. Palmer, "Fred Chappell," 405.

52. Dabney Stuart, "'What's Artichokes?': An Introduction to the Work of Fred Chappell," in *The Fred Chappell Reader* (New York: St. Martin's, 1987), xviii.

53. Richard Jackson, "On the Margins of Dreams," in *Acts of Mind: Conversations with Contemporary Poets,* ed. Richard Jackson (Tuscaloosa: University of Alabama Press, 1983), 157.

Chapter 3—Shaping the Self in Poetry: *The World between the Eyes* and *Midquest*

1. Broughton, "Fred Chappell," 118.

2. Palmer, "Fred Chappell," 407.

3. Chappell's three chapbooks—*The Man Twice Married to Fire* (Greensboro: Unicorn, 1977), *Awakening to Music* (Davidson, N.C.: Briarpatch, 1979), and *Driftlake: A Lieder Cycle* (Emory, Va.: Iron Mountain Press, 1981)—have often been erroneously listed among his book-length publications in standard reference works. "How I Lost It"—another title so listed—though planned, never appeared in print.

4. Ralph Waldo Emerson, *Selected Prose and Poetry,* 2d ed., ed. Reginald L. Cook (San Francisco: Rinehart, 1969), 124.

5. Stephenson, "'The Way It Is,'" 8.

6. Chappell, *A Way of Happening: Observations of Contemporary Poetry* (New York: Picador, 1998), 9.

7. Walsh, "Fred Chappell," 71.

8. Ibid., 75.

9. Chappell, "Fred Chappell," 122.

10. Kathryn Stripling Byer, "Turning the Windlass at the Well: Fred Chappell's Early Poetry," in *Dream Garden,* 88.

11. Chappell, *The World between the Eyes* (Baton Rouge: Louisiana State University Press, 1971), 3, 4. Further references noted parenthetically are to this edition.

12. Chappell, *Plow Naked: Selected Writings on Poetry* (Ann Arbor: University of Michigan Press, 1993), 112.

13. Byer, "Turning the Windlass at the Well," 93–94.

14. Ibid., 95.

15. Chappell, *Midquest* (Baton Rouge: Louisiana State University Press, 1981), ix. Further references noted parenthetically are to this edition.

16. Broughton, "Fred Chappell," 108. "Familiar Poem" is reprinted in *Under Twenty-five: Duke Narrative and Verse, 1945–1962,* ed. William Blackburn (Durham, N.C.: Duke University Press, 1963), 198–201.

17. Crane and Kirkland, "First and Last Words," 16.

18. Dannye Romine Powell, "Fred Chappell," in *Parting the Curtains: Interviews with Southern Writers* (Winston-Salem: Blair, 1994), 36.

19. Jackson, "On the Margins of Dreams," 156.

20. Bizzaro, "Introduction: Fred Chappell's Community of Readers," in *Dream Garden,* 4.

21. Randolph Paul Runyon, "Fred Chappell: Midquestions," in *Southern Writers at Century's End,* ed. Jeffrey J. Folks and James A. Perkins (Lexington: University of Kentucky Press, 1997), 197.

22. Chappell, "Midquest," *The Small Farm* 11–12 (Spring–Fall 1980): 13.

23. Chappell, *A Way of Happening,* 215.

24. Chappell, *Plow Naked,* 90.

25. Ibid., 89, 92.

26. Chappell, *A Way of Happening,* 235.

27. Chappell, *Plow Naked,* 91.

28. Morgan, "*Midquest* and the Gift of Narrative," in *Dream Garden,* 139.

29. Chappell, "Midquest," 13.

30. Ibid.

31. Taylor, "Fred Chappell," in *Contemporary Poets,* 6th ed., ed. Thomas Riggs (New York: St. James Press, 1996), 154.

32. Philip Pierson, "Interview with Fred Chappell," *New River Review* 2 (Spring 1977): 13. As Rodney Jones also notes, "We never have the sense that *Midquest* is inventing itself apart from other consciousness." See Jones's essay "The Large Vision: Fred Chappell's *Midquest,*" *Appalachian Journal* 9, no. 1 (1981): 63.

33. Chappell, "Towards a Beginning," *The Small Farm* 4–5 (Oct. 1976–Mar. 1977): 98.

34. Don Johnson, "The Cultivated Mind: The Georgic Center of Fred Chappell's Poetry," in *Dream Garden,* 170–79.

35. Chappell, *Plow Naked,* 79.

36. Pierson, "Interview with Fred Chappell," 11. See also Crane and Kirkland, "First and Last Words," 20.

37. For an extensive analysis of the sources of many of Chappell's allusions in *Midquest,* see John Lang, "Points of Kinship: Community and Allusion in Fred Chappell's *Midquest,*" in *Dream Garden,* 97–117.

38. Broughton, "Fred Chappell," 109.

39. Dabney Stuart, "Spiritual Matter in Fred Chappell's Poetry," in *Dream Garden,* 48.

40. Alan Nadel mistakenly assumes that Chappell's aim in *Midquest* is to "attempt to freeze the day of his 35th birthday," an attempt that Nadel calls "the governing futility of the whole tetralogy." See his essay "Quest and Midquest: Fred Chappell and the First-

Person Personal Epic," *New England Review and Bread Loaf Quarterly* 6 (Winter 1983): 324.

41. Peter Makuck, "Chappell's Continuities: *First and Last Words*," in *Dream Garden,* 180.

42. Emerson, *Selected Prose and Poetry,* 4.

43. Cherry, "The Idea of Odyssey in *Midquest*," in *Dream Garden,* 122.

44. Jackson, "On the Margins of Dreams," 155.

45. Richard Tillinghast, "Scattered Nebulae," *Sewanee Review* 90, no. 2 (1982): 300.

46. Cherry, "The Idea of Odyssey in *Midquest*," 132.

Chapter 4—"The Singer Dissolved in Song": *Castle Tzingal* to *Spring Garden*

1. For this book's connection to Elizabethan revenge tragedy, see especially Edward C. Lynskey, "Fred Chappell's *Castle Tzingal:* Modern Revival of Elizabethan Revenge Tragedy," *Pembroke Magazine* 25 (1993): 73–87.

2. Crane and Kirkland, "First and Last Words," 21.

3. Walsh, "Fred Chappell," 75.

4. Melissa Brannon, "On Process: An Interview," in Chappell's *Plow Naked: Selected Writings on Poetry,* 135–36.

5. Chappell, *Castle Tzingal* (Baton Rouge: Louisiana State University Press, 1984), 9, 10. Further references noted parenthetically are to this edition.

6. On Chappell's interest in alchemy, see Tim Tarkington, "An Interview with Fred Chappell," *Chattahoochee Review* 9 (Winter 1989): 46.

7. Bizzaro, "The Singer Dissolved in Song: The Poetic as Modern Alternative in Chappell's *Castle Tzingal*," in *Dream Garden,* 160.

8. Crane and Kirkland, "First and Last Words," 22.

9. Ibid.

10. Brannon, "On Process: An Interview," 136.

11. Chappell, *Source* (Baton Rouge: Louisiana State University Press, 1985), 3. Further references noted parenthetically are to this edition.

12. Johnson, "The Cultivated Mind," 175–76.

13. At a poetry reading in Chapel Hill, N.C., on Dec. 10, 1998, Chappell identified his inspiration for this poem as Schoenberg's *Gurrelieder.* Two of the poems he published in *The Archive* while a student at Duke celebrate the composer: "Rondo to Schoenberg" and "Homage to Schoenberg."

14. See Dabney Stuart, "Introduction," in *The Fred Chappell Reader* (New York: St. Martin's, 1987), xix; and Johnson, "The Cultivated Mind," 171. Stuart reversed his view on this issue in his essay "Spiritual Matter in Fred Chappell's Poetry: A Prologue," in *Dream Garden,* 55–56.

15. "Chappell's New Book Is a Kind of Homage," *Southern Pines, N.C., Pilot,* 13 Mar. 1989.

16. Garrett, "A Few Things about Fred Chappell," 8.

17. Taylor, "The World Was Plenty," 85.

18. Makuck, "Chappell's Continuities," 189. The lines quoted appear on page 47 of Chappell, *First and Last Words* (Baton Rouge: Louisiana State University Press, 1989). Further references noted parenthetically are to this edition.

19. Crane and Kirkland, "First and Last Words," 22.

20. Johnson, "The Cultivated Mind," 171.

21. When Chappell revised this poem for its reprinting in *Spring Garden: New and Selected Poems,* he significantly muted its pessimism about religious belief by changing the phrase "empty *as* faith" to "empty *of* faith" (*Spring Garden,* 67; my italics).

22. Delmore Schwartz, *Selected Poems* (New York: New Directions, 1967), 75. One of Tolstoy's biographers says that the Russian

author based his essay "Desire Is the Worst Slavery of All" on this incident. See Henri Troyat, *Tolstoy* (Garden City, N.Y.: Doubleday, 1967), 199.

23. Makuck, "Chappell's Continuities," 193.

24. Ibid., 194. Though Makuck correctly notes the line's source as Book II of *The Aeneid,* he misidentifies the context by assuming that the line occurs *after* Pyrrhus murders Priam's son. In fact the line appears before that incident, just after the Greeks have burst into the vestibule of the king's palace.

25. For the identification of the figure in this poem as Stevens, see Leila Easa, "A Conversation with Fred Chappell," *The Archive* 108 (Fall 1995): 55.

26. Makuck, "Chappell's Continuities," 196.

27. Ibid. Earlier in his essay (p. 184) Makuck writes, "What is important to Chappell . . . is that we create our own god."

28. Ibid, "Chappell's Continuities," 197.

29. Crane and Kirkland, "First and Last Words," 26.

30. David Slavitt, "The Comedian as the Letter *C* Strikes Again," in *Dream Garden,* 198–202; "Chappell's Epigrams Offered in *C* Book," *Southern Pines, N.C., Pilot,* 26 Apr. 1993.

31. "Chappell's Epigrams Offered in *C* Book."

32. Chappell, *C* (Baton Rouge: Louisiana State University Press, 1993), 2. Further references noted parenthetically are to this edition.

33. Michael McFee, "The Epigrammatical Fred Chappell," *Southern Literary Journal* 31 (Spring 1999): 98–99.

34. Mark Twain, *Following the Equator* (Hartford, Conn.: American Publishing Company, 1897), 256.

35. Though Susan is addressed in "Aubade," is named in "A Glorious Twilight," and is presumably the unnamed person addressed in "Serenade," she does not play as significant a role here as she does in *Midquest* and in *Spring Garden.*

36. Chappell presents "Autumn Oaks" as a translation from a poem by Max Albern but has admitted that Albern is a hoax, that no such writer exists. Two other poems in *C* (XXXIX and XL) are also attributed to Albern.

37. Crane and Kirkland, "First and Last Words," 30.

38. The acknowledgments page of *C* mistakenly lists "Fleurs-des-Livres," "Forever Mountain," and "Upon a Confessional Poet" as new poems. The first appeared in a much different form in *The World between the Eyes* under the title "The Quick." The second and third appeared in *Source* and *C,* respectively. "Going through Zero to the Other Side," also listed among the book's new poems, originally appeared in a different form in Chappell's 1979 chapbook *Awakening to Music,* where it was titled "Zero's Other Face."

39. Crane and Kirkland, "First and Last Words," 30.

40. Chappell, *Spring Garden: New and Selected Poems* (Baton Rouge: Louisiana State University Press, 1995), 3, 9–10. Further references noted parenthetically are to this edition.

41. David Middleton, "With Modesty and Measured Love," *Sewanee Review* 104, no. 1 (1996): xi.

42. Crane and Kirkland, "First and Last Words," 30.

43. Ibid., 29.

44. In 1998 Louisiana State University Press published a volume titled *A New Pleiade,* which contained selections from Chappell's poetry, together with poems by Kelly Cherry, R. H. W. Dillard, Brendan Galvin, George Garrett, David Slavitt, and Henry Taylor.

45. K. R. W. Jones, *Pierre de Ronsard* (New York: Twayne, 1970), 91. I am indebted to Jones's book for my portrait of Ronsard throughout this paragraph.

46. For an account of Gioia's views in the context of Chappell's work, see Bizzaro's essay cited above, *Dream Garden,* 154–69, especially pages 156–59.

47. The poems reprinted from *C* were unrevised except for the retitling of "How To Do It" (V) as "The Good Life" and the substitution of the name Hector for Gawain in stanza 3 of "The Ubi Sunt Lament of the Beldame Hen."

48. Sally Sullivan, "'Citizens Who Observe': A Conversation with Fred Chappell," *North Carolina Literary Review* 7 (1998): 154.

49. Susan O'Dell Underwood, "The Light of Transformation in Fred Chappell's *Spring Garden*," in *Dream Garden,* 204.

50. Many of the "new" poems were previously published, occasionally as much as fifteen years before the publication of *Spring Garden.* "The Fated Lovers," for instance, appeared in a 1980 issue of *The Small Farm;* "The Sea Text" appeared in *Hemlocks & Balsams* in 1983.

51. Underwood, "The Light of Transformation," 204.

52. "Seated Figure," though it originally appeared in *The World between the Eyes,*" the book to which the poem is attributed in the acknowledgments material of *Spring Garden,* was also published, with revisions, in *Source.*

53. Middleton, "With Modesty and Measured Love," xiii. Despite Chappell's stature as a recipient of the Bollingen Prize, Middleton's review is one of only four of *Spring Garden* cited in *Book Review Index* from 1995 through 1998.

Chapter 5—The Short Stories: *Moments of Light* and *More Shapes Than One*

1. Chappell, "Fred Chappell," 123.

2. Alex Albright, "Friend of Reason: Surveying the Fred Chappell Papers at Duke University," in *Dream Garden,* 229.

3. Chappell, "Introduction," in *Editor's Choice 3,* ed. Morty Sklar (New York: Spirit That Moves Us Press, 1991), 10.

4. Chappell, "Science and the Artist's Vision," *New England Review* 3, no. 1 (1980): 133.

5. Chappell, "A Little Houyhnhnm in Your Life," in *Editor's Choice,* ed. Morty Sklar and Jim Mulac (Iowa City: Spirit That Moves Us Press, 1980), 387.

6. Chappell, *Moments of Light* (Los Angeles: New South Company, 1980), 110. Further references noted parenthetically are to this edition.

7. Chappell, "Fred Chappell," 123.

8. Reviews of *Moments of Light,* by Chappell, *Choice,* Mar. 1981, 946; Robert D. Walsh, *Library Journal,* 15 Jan. 1981, 165; Robert Gingher, "Fred Chappell's Intelligent Heart," *Greensboro Daily News/Record,* 23 Nov. 1980, G5.

9. *The Notebooks of Simone Weil,* vol. 2, trans. Arthur Wills (London: Routledge and Kegan Paul, 1956), 500.

10. Chappell, "Fred Chappell," 124.

11. Quoted by Robert Bone in Ralph Ellison, "Ralph Ellison and the Uses of Imagination," in *Twentieth Century Interpretations of* Invisible Man, ed. John M. Reilly (Englewood Cliffs, N.J.: Prentice-Hall, 1970), 24.

12. Stuart, "'Blue Pee': Fred Chappell's Short Fiction," *Iron Mountain Review* 2 (Spring 1985): 19.

13. See James Everett Kibler, Jr., "A Fred Chappell Bibliography, 1963–1983," *Mississippi Quarterly* 37 (Winter 1983–84): 65. Of "Waltzes Noble and Sentimental," Kibler states, "Chappell describes this as a short-story collection completed and pending approval for publication."

14. See "The Dreaming Orchid," *New Mexico Humanities Review* 5, no. 1 (Spring 1982): 61–76.

15. Chappell, *More Shapes Than One* (New York: St. Martin's, 1991), ix. Further references noted parenthetically are to this edition.

16. Darrell Schweitzer, "A Talk with Fred Chappell," *Worlds of Fantasy and Horror* 1 (Summer 1994): 42.

17. Sullivan, "'Citizens Who Observe,'" 148.

18. Palmer, "Fred Chappell," 405.

19. Chappell, "Fantasia," 179–89.

20. Chappell, "Visionary Fiction," *Chronicles* 11 (May 1987): 19.

21. Ibid., 21; Chappell's italics.

22. Linnaeus's vision of the triumph of Flora, as Chappell describes it, is based on the frontispiece to Linnaeus's *Hortus Cliffortianus* (1737). That frontispiece is reproduced in Wilfrid Blunt's *The Complete Naturalist: A Life of Linnaeus* (New York: Viking, 1971), 128.

23. I am indebted to S. T. Joshi's introduction to *The Annotated H. P. Lovecraft* (New York: Dell, 1997) for my knowledge of the specific letter from which Chappell drew this quotation. Joshi cites that letter in his introduction (p. 15) but does not discuss Chappell's story. Chappell himself says in the interview with Darrell Schweitzer cited above, "All the quotations that are in documents in ['Weird Tales'] are real. Those came from Hart Crane's letters or from H. P. Lovecraft's letters" (42).

24. The name Dzhaimbú, as Chappell noted in a personal letter dated 29 March 1999, is not of Lovecraftian origin but is a variation on Xingu or Shango, a West African voodoo god transported to the Caribbean.

25. Chappell, *The Lodger* (West Warwick, R.I.: Necronomicon Press, 1993). This twenty-eight-page chapbook spoofs Lovecraftian horror tales of demonic possession. The exorcism in this case is accomplished by reading aloud assorted passages of postmodern literary criticism from books with such titles as *Despotic Signifiers and the Babylonian Antireactionary Episteme.*

26. Michael Dirda, *Washington Post Book World,* 6 Oct. 1991, 5;

Orson Scott Card, "Books to Look For," *Magazine of Fantasy and Science Fiction* 83 (Aug. 1992): 20.

27. Jacqueline Adams, *Library Journal,* 1 Sept. 1991, 233.

28. Chappell, "Fred Chappell," 124.

Chapter 6—The Kirkman Tetralogy

1. Chappell, "Fred Chappell," 124.

2. Ibid.

3. "It's the same family," says Chappell in an interview with William J. Walsh in *Speak So I Shall Know Thee: Interviews with Southern Writers*, 72.

4. Hobson, *The Southern Writer in the Postmodern World,* 85. Hobson analyzes *I Am One of You Forever* in the context of Donald Davidson's "autochthonous ideal," which encourages writers to avoid self-conscious regionalism. Hobson's observations about the general absence of such self-consciousness in Chappell's first Kirkman novel are clearly correct. The last two volumes of the tetralogy do, however, demonstrate significantly more regional self-consciousness, especially the final chapter of *Farewell, I'm Bound to Leave You* and chapter 4 of *Look Back All the Green Valley,* with its satiric portrait of the restaurant Hillbilly Heaven.

5. See Walter Blair, "Humor of the Old Southwest (1830–1867)," in *Native American Humor* (New York: Chandler, 1960), 62–101.

6. Ibid., 69.

7. Ragan, "At the Grave of Sut Lovingood: Virgil Campbell in the Work of Fred Chappell," *Mississippi Quarterly* 37 (Winter 1983–84): 21–30; Lang, "Points of Kinship," 97–117. For Chappell's use of Old Southwest humor in *I Am One of You Forever,* see Hobson, *The Southern Writer in the Postmodern World,* 86–87.

8. George Core, "Procrustes Bed," *Sewanee Review* 93 (Spring 1985): xlii.

9. Palmer, "Fred Chappell," 408.

10. Howard, "Fred Chappell: From the Mountains to the Mainstream," 56. For a nevertheless insightful analysis of Chappell's fiction in the context of magic realism, see Hal McDonald, "Fred Chappell as Magic Realist," *North Carolina Literary Review* 7 (1998): 127–39.

11. Richard Abowitz, "Chappell's Aesthetic Agenda: The Binding of *Midquest* to *I Am One of You Forever* and *Brighten the Corner Where You Are,*" in *Dream Garden,* 146–47.

12. Chappell, "Two Modes: A Plea for Tolerance," 337.

13. Ibid., 337, 338.

14. Ibid., 337, 339.

15. Broughton, "Fred Chappell," 120–21.

16. George Core, *Washington Post Book World,* 30 June 1985, 11; David Guy, "Coming of Age in Carolina," *New York Times Book Review,* 15 Sept. 1985, 21.

17. Hilbert Campbell, "Fred Chappell's Urn of Memory: *I Am One of You Forever,*" *Southern Literary Journal* 25 (Spring 1993): 103.

18. Walsh, *Speak So I Shall Know Thee,* 69.

19. Hobson, *The Southern Writer in the Postmodern World,* 84.

20. Chappell, *I Am One of You Forever* (Baton Rouge: Louisiana State University Press, 1985), 1; Chappell's italics. Further references noted parenthetically are to this edition.

21. One of Uncle Zeno's tales was originally published by Chappell under the title "Elmer and Buford" in *North Carolina Folklore* 18 (May 1970): 80–83.

22. Hobson, *The Southern Writer in the Postmodern World,* 86–87.

23. Hilbert Campbell and Sally Sullivan, in their essays on this novel, seem to assume that Chappell agrees with Jess's theory. See Campbell, "Fred Chappell's Urn of Memory," 107; and Sullivan,

"Irony and Allegory in *I Am One of You Forever,*" *North Carolina Literary Review* 7 (1998): 123.

24. Chappell, "Fred Chappell," 126.

25. Bede, *Ecclesiastical History of the English People,* Book II, chapter 13; quoted in George K. Anderson, *The Literature of the Anglo-Saxons* (Princeton: Princeton University Press, 1949), 267.

26. See Jack E. Weller, *Yesterday's People: Life in Contemporary Appalachia* (Lexington: University of Kentucky Press, 1965).

27. Northrop Frye, *Anatomy of Criticism* (New York: Atheneum, 1967), 168.

28. In *Farewell, I'm Bound to Leave You* Jess states, "I remembered how my father had told me the story of Helen of Troy and how I'd later discovered that Helen still haunted the dreams of all men everywhere" (24).

29. *Publishers Weekly,* 15 Mar. 1985, 102.

30. Abowitz, "Chappell's Aesthetic Agenda," 150.

31. Hilbert Campbell, "Fred Chappell's Urn of Memory," 106.

32. Chappell, *Brighten the Corner Where You Are* (New York: St. Martin's, 1989), 23. Further references noted parenthetically are to this edition.

33. Although Chappell spells Brunel's first name with a *z* in *Brighten,* the standard biographies give the spelling as Isambard.

34. John Pudney, *Brunel and His World* (London: Thames and Hudson, 1974), 112; L. T. C. Rolt, *Isambard Kingdom Brunel: A Biography* (London: Longmans, Green, 1957), 5.

35. Though this premise of the moon's proximity to the earth may derive from Italo Calvino's "The Distance of the Moon" (the opening story in Calvino's *Cosmicomics,* a book for which Chappell has expressed his admiration), Chappell may also be drawing upon classical myths cited by Virgil, one of Chappell's major influences. Book III of the *Georgics* recounts the legend of how "Pan, god of

Arcady, captivated and tricked the Moon, / Calling her down in the deep woods," and Virgil's eighth Eclogue notes that "magic spells can inveigle the moon from the sky."

36. Jess says, "Once before, when I was ten, I had fought with a tenant boy" (109), a possible allusion to James Christopher's similar fight in chapter 7 of *It Is Time, Lord.*

37. Chappell, "Slap," *Pembroke Magazine* 14 (1982): 5–10.

38. Frye, *Anatomy of Criticism,* 184.

39. Abowitz, "Chappell's Aesthetic Agenda," 149.

40. Robert E. Brown, *Library Journal,* Aug. 1996, 110; *Dictionary of Literary Biography Yearbook 1996,* ed. Samuel W. Bruce and L. Kay Webster (Detroit: Gale, 1997), 53.

41. Chappell, *Farewell, I'm Bound to Leave You* (New York: Picador, 1996), 3. Further references noted parenthetically are to this edition.

42. In *Midquest* this kite-flying story is narrated by the mother, not the father, so Ole Fred/Jess seems to have heard another account than his father's prior to hearing his grandmother's version. The apparent discrepancy is one for which *Farewell* offers no explanation.

43. Chappell, *Look Back All the Green Valley* (New York: Picador, 1999), 13. Further references noted parenthetically are to this edition.

44. Dante visits the sphere of the moon in Cantos II through IV of the *Paradiso* before proceeding to his ultimate vision of the mystic Rose in the Empyrean.

45. Relevant to Chappell's critique of such judgmental religion is a passage from the same paragraph in "Areopagitica" from which Chappell chose the epigraph to *More Shapes Than One.* There, Milton writes, "How many other things might be tolerated in peace, and left to conscience, had we but charity, and were it not the chief strong hold of our hypocrisie to be ever judging one another." See John Milton,

Selected Prose, ed. C. A. Patrides (Columbia: University of Missouri Press, 1985), 243.

46. Wallace Stevens, *The Necessary Angel* (New York: Vintage Books, 1951), 175.

BIBLIOGRAPHY

Works by Fred Chappell

Listed in order of publication.

Novels

It Is Time, Lord. New York: Atheneum, 1963. London: Dent, 1965.
The Inkling. New York: Harcourt, Brace and World, 1965. London: Chapman and Hall, 1966.
Dagon. New York: Harcourt, Brace and World, 1968.
The Gaudy Place. New York: Harcourt, Brace and World, 1973.
I Am One of You Forever. Baton Rouge: Louisiana State University Press, 1985.
Brighten the Corner Where You Are. New York: St. Martin's, 1989.
Farewell, I'm Bound to Leave You. New York: Picador, 1996.
Look Back All the Green Valley. New York: Picador, 1999.

Collections of Poetry

The World between the Eyes. Baton Rouge: Louisiana State University Press, 1971.
River. Baton Rouge: Louisiana State University Press, 1975.
Bloodfire. Baton Rouge: Louisiana State University Press, 1978.
Wind Mountain. Baton Rouge: Louisiana State University Press, 1979.
Earthsleep. Baton Rouge: Louisiana State University Press, 1980.
Midquest. Baton Rouge: Louisiana State University Press, 1981.
Castle Tzingal. Baton Rouge: Louisiana State University Press, 1984.
Source. Baton Rouge: Louisiana State University Press, 1985.

First and Last Words. Baton Rouge: Louisiana State University Press, 1989.

C. Baton Rouge: Louisiana State University Press, 1993.

Spring Garden: New and Selected Poems. Baton Rouge: Louisiana State University Press, 1995.

Collections of Short Stories

Moments of Light. Los Angeles: New South, 1980.

More Shapes Than One. New York: St. Martin's, 1991.

Collections of Essays

Plow Naked: Selected Writings on Poetry. Ann Arbor: University of Michigan Press, 1993.

A Way of Happening: Observations of Contemporary Poetry. New York: Picador, 1998.

Other Books

The Fred Chappell Reader. New York: St. Martin's, 1987.

Selected Uncollected Essays and Other Nonfiction

"Seven Propositions about Poetry and Personality." *Above Ground Review* 1 (Winter 1969): 41–44.

"Six Propositions about Literature and History." *New Literary History* 1, no. 3 (1970): 513–22.

"Unpeaceable Kingdoms: The Novels of Sylvia Wilkinson." *Hollins Critic* 8 (Apr. 1971): 1–10.

BIBLIOGRAPHY

"*The Surface of Earth:* A Pavement of Good Intentions." *The Archive* 88 (Fall 1975): 75–82.

"The Image of the South in Film." *Southern Humanities Review* 12 (Fall 1978): 303–11.

"Two Modes: A Plea for Tolerance." *Appalachian Journal* 5, no. 3 (1978): 335–39.

"The Comic Structure of *The Sound and the Fury.*" *Mississippi Quarterly* 31, no. 3 (1978): 381–86.

"Science and the Artist's Vision." *New England Review* 3, no. 1 (1980): 132–40.

"The Vocation of Literature." *Colonnades* 32 (Spring 1981): 78–82.

"The Seamless Vision of James Still." *Appalachian Journal* 8, no. 3 (1981): 196–202.

"Viable Allegiances." *Abatis One* (1983): 52–63.

"A Pact with Faustus." *Mississippi Quarterly* 37 (Winter 1983–84): 9–20. Reprinted in *The Fred Chappell Reader,* 479–90.

"'Menfolks Are Heathens': Cruelty in James Still's Short Stories." *Iron Mountain Review* 2 (Summer 1984): 11–15.

"The Ninety-Ninth Foxfire Book." *Appalachian Journal* 11, no. 3 (1984): 260–67.

"Fred Chappell." Vol. 4 of *Contemporary Authors Autobiography Series,* edited by Adele Sarkissian, 113–26. Detroit: Gale, 1986.

"Visionary Fiction." *Chronicles* 11 (May 1987): 19–21.

"A Detail in a Poem." *Kentucky Poetry Review* 26 (Fall 1990): 66–75.

"Fantasia on the Theme of Theme and Fantasy." *Studies in Short Fiction* 27, no. 2 (1990): 179–89.

"Fictional Characterization as Infinite Regressive Series: George Garrett's Strangers in the Mirror." In *Southern Literature and Literary Theory,* edited by Jefferson Humphries, 66–74. Athens: University of Georgia Press, 1990.

BIBLIOGRAPHY

"The Long Mirror: Dabney Stuart's Film Allusion." *Kentucky Poetry Review* 27 (Spring 1991): 85–92.

"Remarks on *Dagon.*" In *The H. P. Lovecraft Centennial Conference Proceedings,* edited by S. T. Joshi, 43–45. West Warwick, R.I.: Necronomicon, 1991.

"'Rich with Disappearances': Betty Adcock's Time Paradoxes." *Shenandoah* 45 (Summer 1995): 58–75.

"The Shape of Appalachian Literature to Come." In *The Future of Southern Letters,* edited by Jefferson Humphries and John Lowe, 54–60. New York: Oxford University Press, 1996.

"Peter Taylor: The Genial Mentor." *North Carolina Literary Review* 5 (1996): 45–54.

"Jim Wayne Miller: The Gentle Partisan." *North Carolina Literary Review* 6 (1997): 7–13.

"'Not as a Leaf': Southern Poetry and the Innovation of Tradition." *Georgia Review* 51, no. 3 (1997): 477–89.

"The Music of 'Each in His Season.'" In *Tuned and Under Tension: The Recent Poetry of W. D. Snodgrass,* edited by Philip Raisor, 72–87. Newark: University of Delaware Press, 1998.

Interviews

Graham, John. "Fred Chappell." In *Craft So Hard to Learn,* edited by George Garrett. New York: Morrow, 1972.

Sopko, John, and John Carr. "Dealing with the Grotesque: Fred Chappell." In *Kite-Flying and Other Irrational Acts: Conversations with Twelve Southern Writers,* edited by John Carr. Baton Rouge: Louisiana State University Press, 1972.

Graham, John. "Fred Chappell." In *The Writer's Voice,* edited by George Garrett. New York: Morrow, 1973.

Pierson, Philip. "Interview with Fred Chappell." *New River Review* 2 (Spring 1977): 5–16, 61–73.

BIBLIOGRAPHY

West, James L. W., III, and August Nigro. "William Blackburn and His Pupils: A Conversation." *Mississippi Quarterly* 31, no. 4 (1978): 605–14.

Jackson, Richard. "On the Margins of Dreams." In *Acts of Mind: Conversations with Contemporary Poets,* edited by Richard Jackson. Tuscaloosa: University of Alabama Press, 1983.

Patterson, Sarah, and Dan Lindsey. "Interview with Fred Chappell." *Davidson Miscellany* 19 (Spring 1984): 62–76.

Stephenson, Shelby. "'The Way It Is': An Interview with Fred Chappell." *Iron Mountain Review* 2 (Spring 1985): 7–11.

Ruffin, Paul. "Interview with Fred Chappell." *Pembroke Magazine* 17 (1985): 131–35.

Redd, Chris. "A Man of Letters in the Modern World: An Interview with Fred Chappell." *Arts Journal* 14 (May 1989): 7–9.

Tarkington, Tim. "An Interview with Fred Chappell." *Chattahoochee Review* 9 (Winter 1989): 44–48.

Stewart, Mary Lass. "Interviews with Clyde Edgerton and Fred Chappell." *Cellar Door* 17 (Spring 1990): 26–28.

Stirnemann, S. A. "Fred Chappell: Poet with 'Ah! Bright Wings.'" *South Florida Poetry Review* 7 (Winter 1990): 41–51.

Broughton, Irv. "Fred Chappell." Vol. 3 of *The Writer's Mind: Interviews with American Authors.* Fayetteville: University of Arkansas Press, 1990.

Walsh, William J. "Fred Chappell." In *Speak So I Shall Know Thee: Interviews with Southern Writers.* Asheboro, N.C.: Down Home Press, 1990.

Palmer, Tersh. "Fred Chappell." *Appalachian Journal* 19, no. 4 (1992): 402–10.

Brannon, Melissa. "On Process: An Interview." In *Plow Naked: Selected Writings on Poetry,* edited by Fred Chappell. Ann Arbor: University of Michigan Press, 1993.

Schweitzer, Darrell. "A Talk with Fred Chappell." *Worlds of Fantasy and Horror* 1 (Summer 1994): 40–43.

Powell, Dannye Romine. "Fred Chappell." In *Parting the Curtains: Interviews with Southern Writers.* Winston-Salem, N.C.: John F. Blair, 1994.

Easa, Leila. "A Conversation with Fred Chappell." *The Archive* 108 (Fall 1995): 49–60.

Corbett, Kevin. "Fred Chappell. *Notre Dame Review* 2 (Summer 1996): 64–67.

Howard, Jennifer. "Fred Chappell: From the Mountains to the Mainstream." *Publishers Weekly,* 30 Sept. 1996, 55–56.

Brown, Fred, and Jeanne McDonald. "Fred Chappell." In *Growing up Southern: How the South Shapes Its Writers.* Greenville, S.C.: Blue Ridge, 1997.

Crane, Resa, and James Kirkland. "First and Last Words: A Conversation with Fred Chappell." In *Dream Garden: The Poetic Vision of Fred Chappell,* edited by Patrick Bizzaro. Baton Rouge: Louisiana State University Press, 1997.

Ragan, David Paul. "'Flying by Night': An Early Interview with Fred Chappell." *North Carolina Literary Review* 7 (1998): 105–19.

Sullivan, Sally. "'Citizens Who Observe': A Conversation with Fred Chappell." *North Carolina Literary Review* 7 (1998): 145–55.

Selected Works about Chappell

Listed in alphabetical order by author.

Bibliographies

Kibler, James Everett, Jr. "A Fred Chappell Bibliography, 1963–1983." *Mississippi Quarterly* 37 (Winter 1983–84): 63–88. Detailed record of Chappell's primary works.

BIBLIOGRAPHY

Books

Bizzaro, Patrick, ed. *Dream Garden: The Poetic Vision of Fred Chappell*. Baton Rouge: Louisiana State University Press, 1997. Extremely valuable collection of essays on Chappell's poetry through *Spring Garden*.

Selected Critical and Biographical Essays

Abowitz, Richard. "Chappell's Aesthetic Agenda: The Binding of *Midquest* to *I Am One of You Forever* and *Brighten the Corner Where You Are*." In *Dream Garden: The Poetic Vision of Fred Chappell*, edited by Patrick Bizzaro, 145–53. Baton Rouge: Louisiana State University Press, 1997. Thorough analysis of the characters, images, and literary techniques that link *Midquest* to the first two Kirkman novels.

Albright, Alex. "Friend of Reason: Surveying the Fred Chappell Papers at Duke University." In *Dream Garden: The Poetic Vision of Fred Chappell*, edited by Patrick Bizzaro, 222–39. Baton Rouge: Louisiana State University Press, 1997. Useful inventory of the major holdings of Chappell manuscripts and letters at Duke.

Bizzaro, Patrick. "The Singer Dissolved in Song: The Poetic as Modern Alternative in Chappell's *Castle Tzingal*." In *Dream Garden: The Poetic Vision of Fred Chappell*, edited by Patrick Bizzaro, 154–69. Baton Rouge: Louisiana State University Press, 1997. Views *Castle Tzingal* as an allegory on the survival powers of art in the modern age.

Byer, Kathryn Stripling. "Turning the Windlass at the Well: Fred Chappell's Early Poetry." In *Dream Garden: The Poetic Vision of Fred Chappell*, edited by Patrick Bizzaro, 88–96. Baton Rouge: Louisiana State University Press, 1997. Excellent assessment of *The World between the Eyes*, especially its longer narrative poems.

BIBLIOGRAPHY

Campbell, Hilbert. "Fred Chappell's Urn of Memory: *I Am One of You Forever.*" *Southern Literary Journal* 25 (Spring 1993): 103–11. Brilliant analysis of Chappell's use of memory and imagination to transform childhood experience into art. Also points out similarities between this novel and *Midquest.*

Cherry, Kelly. "A Writer's Harmonious World." *Parnassus* 9 (Fall–Winter 1981): 115–29. Reprinted as "The Idea of Odyssey in *Midquest*" in *Dream Garden: The Poetic Vision of Fred Chappell,* edited by Patrick Bizzaro, 118–32. Baton Rouge: Louisiana State University Press, 1997. Detailed analysis of the motif of the spiritual journey in *Midquest.*

Coindreau, Maurice-Edgar. Preface to *Le Dieu-Poisson* [*Dagon*]. Paris: Christian Bourgois, 1971.

Cooper, Kate. "Reading between the Lines: Fred Chappell's *Castle Tzingal.*" In *Southern Literature and Literary Theory,* edited by Jefferson Humphries, 88–108. Athens: University of Georgia Press, 1990. Offers a postmodernist reading of this poem, emphasizing the indeterminacy and limitations of linguistic representation.

de Abruna, Laura Niesen. "Fred Chappell." In *Encyclopedia of American Humorists,* edited by Steven H. Gale, 75–81. New York: Garland, 1988. Discusses *Midquest* and Virgil Campbell as the high points of Chappell's contributions to American humor.

Dillard, Annie. Foreword to *Moments of Light,* ix–xvii. Los Angeles: New South, 1980. Insightful, appreciative assessment of the literary achievement of Chappell's first book of stories.

Dillard, R. H. W. "Letters from a Distant Lover: The Novels of Fred Chappell." *Hollins Critic* 10 (Apr. 1973): 1–15. This first scholarly article on Chappell provides a superb analysis of the major themes in the writer's first four novels.

Dziemianowicz, Stefan. "Fred Chappell." In *St. James Guide to Horror, Ghost, and Gothic Writers,* edited by David Pringle, 132–33.

Detroit: St. James, 1998. Brief discussion of *Dagon* and several
short stories.

Eubanks, Georgann. "Fred Chappell: The Bard of Canton." *Duke
Magazine,* Nov.–Dec. 1993, 6–11. Useful overview of Chappell's
career, including his teaching at the University of North Carolina–Greensboro.

Forkner, Ben. "Contemporary Stories of the American South." *Revue
française d'etudes americaines* 23 (Feb. 1985): 51–61. Discussion
of *Moments of Light* that refers to "Children of Strikers" and "Blue
Dive" as "Southern masterpieces."

Garrett, George. "A Few Things about Fred Chappell." *Mississippi
Quarterly* 37 (Winter 1983–84): 3–8. Lively assessment of Chappell's personality and achievement.

Gingher, Marianne. "I Wish I'd Written That Story." *Southern Review*
33, no. 4 (1997): 846–52. Illuminating essay on Chappell as a
teacher of creative writing in the early 1970s.

Gray, Amy Tipton. "Fred Chappell's *I Am One of You Forever:* The
Oneiros of Childhood Transformed." In *The Poetics of Appalachian
Space,* edited by Parks Lanier, Jr., 28–39. Knoxville: University of
Tennessee Press, 1991. A Bachelardian interpretation of this novel.

——. "R'lyeh in Appalachia: Lovecraft's Influence on Fred Chappell's *Dagon.*" In *Remembrance, Reunion, and Revival: Celebrating a Decade of Appalachian Studies,* edited by Helen Roseberry,
73–79. Boone, N.C.: Appalachian Consortium Press, 1988. Informative analysis of Chappell's debt to Lovecraft and the ways in
which he diverges from Lovecraft's premises.

Gresset, Michel. Preface to *L'Hamçon d'or* [*It Is Time, Lord*]. Paris:
Gallimard, 1965.

Hobson, Fred. *The Southern Writer in the Postmodern World,* 82–91.
Athens: University of Georgia Press, 1991. Superb commentary on
I Am One of You Forever as an example of Donald Davidson's
"autochthonous ideal" of unself-conscious regionalism.

BIBLIOGRAPHY

Johnson, Don. "The Cultivated Mind: The Georgic Center of Fred Chappell's Poetry." In *Dream Garden: The Poetic Vision of Fred Chappell,* edited by Patrick Bizzaro, 170–79. Baton Rouge: Louisiana State University Press, 1997. Informative discussion of Chappell's debt to Virgil and the agrarian vision of the *Georgics.*

Jones, Rodney. "The Large Vision: Fred Chappell's *Midquest.*" *Appalachian Journal* 9, no. 1 (1981): 59–65. Enthusiastic assessment of *Midquest* that emphasizes the volume's meditative poems.

Lang, John. "Breathing a New Universe: The Poetry of Fred Chappell." *Kentucky Poetry Review* 26 (Fall 1990): 61–65. Brief overview of Chappell's poetry for this Chappell issue of *Kentucky Poetry Review.*

————. "Fred Chappell." In *American Poets since World War II,* edited by R. S. Gwynn, 25–38. Vol. 105 of *Dictionary of Literary Biography* Detroit: Gale, 1991. Surveys Chappell's poetry through *First and Last Words.*

————. "Illuminating the Stricken World: Fred Chappell's *Moments of Light.*" *South Central Review* 3 (Winter 1986): 95–103. Explores the stories' religious themes.

————. "Intimations of Order: Fred Chappell's *More Shapes Than One.*" *North Carolina Literary Review* 7 (1998): 140–44. Analyzes the stories' unifying themes and character types, especially scientists and artists.

————. "Points of Kinship: Community and Allusion in Fred Chappell's *Midquest.*" In *Dream Garden: The Poetic Vision of Fred Chappell,* edited by Patrick Bizzaro, 97–117. Baton Rouge: Louisiana State University Press, 1997. Includes a useful appendix that lists Chappell's many references and allusions in this poem and that demonstrates the varied sources that have influenced his work.

Lynskey, Edward C. "Fred Chappell's *Castle Tzingal:* Modern Revival of Elizabethan Revenge Tragedy." *Pembroke Magazine*

25 (1993): 73–87. Applies Fredson T. Bowers's "Kydian formula" to this book of poems.

Makuck, Peter. "Chappell's Continuities: *First and Last Words.*" *Virginia Quarterly Review* 68, no. 2 (1992): 315–36. Reprinted in *Dream Garden: The Poetic Vision of Fred Chappell,* edited by Patrick Bizzaro, 180–97. Baton Rouge: Louisiana State University Press, 1997. Perceptive placement of this volume in the context of Chappell's abiding philosophical and religious concerns.

McDonald, Hal. "Fred Chappell as Magic Realist." *North Carolina Literary Review* 7 (1998): 127–39. Uses William Spindler's typology of magic realism to analyze striking features of *The Inkling, Dagon,* and the first three Kirkman novels.

McFee, Michael. "The Epigrammatical Fred Chappell." *Southern Literary Journal* 31 (Spring 1999): 95–108. Thorough analysis of *C* that sets the book in its literary historical contexts and in the context of Chappell's entire career.

Morgan, Robert. "*Midquest.*" *American Poetry Review* 11 (July–Aug. 1982): 45–47. Reprinted as "*Midquest* and the Gift of Narrative" in *Dream Garden: The Poetic Vision of Fred Chappell,* edited by Patrick Bizzaro, 133–44. Baton Rouge: Louisiana State University Press, 1997. Also reprinted in Morgan's *Good Measure* (Baton Rouge: Louisiana State University Press, 1993). Superb analysis of *Midquest* as "lyric narrative."

Morrison, Gail M. "'The Sign of the Arms': Chappell's *It Is Time, Lord.*" *Mississippi Quarterly* 37 (Winter 1983–84): 45–54. A character analysis that focuses on the protagonist's quest for balance amidst the dualities and polarities he confronts.

Mosby, Charmaine Allmon. "*The Gaudy Place:* Six Characters in Search of an Illusion." *Mississippi Quarterly* 37 (Winter 1983–84): 55–62. Exploration of the novel's plot and characters in terms of the contrast between coincidence and causality.

Nadel, Alan. "Quest and Midquest: Fred Chappell and the First-Person Personal Epic." *New England Review and Bread Loaf Quarterly* 6 (Winter 1983): 323–31. Argues that Chappell's quest is doomed because it tries to freeze the day of his thirty-fifth birthday to stop the passage of time.

Quillen, Rita. *Looking for Native Ground,* 21–34. Boone, N.C.: Appalachian Consortium Press, 1989. Discusses the theme of family in *The World between the Eyes* and *Midquest.*

Ragan, David Paul. "At the Grave of Sut Lovingood: Virgil Campbell in the Work of Fred Chappell." *Mississippi Quarterly* 37 (Winter 1983–84): 21–30. Traces Campbell's role as a representative of freedom and independence in both *It Is Time, Lord* and *Midquest.*

———. "Fred Chappell." In *Contemporary Poets, Dramatists, Essayists, and Novelists of the South: A Bio-Bibliographical Sourcebook,* edited by Robert Bain and Joseph M. Flora, 91–103. Westport, Conn.: Greenwood, 1994. Extremely useful overview of Chappell's career and his major themes. Includes a lengthy bibliography.

———. "Fred Chappell." In *American Novelists since World War II, Second Series,* edited by James E. Kibler, Jr., 36–48. Vol. 6 of *Dictionary of Literary Biography.* Detroit: Gale, 1980. Insightful analysis of Chappell's first four novels.

Ragan, Sam et al. "Tributes to Fred Chappell." *Pembroke Magazine* 23 (1991): 77–89. Appreciative assessment of Chappell's career by several fellow writers, including Clyde Edgerton.

Runyon, Randolph Paul. "Fred Chappell: Midquestions." *Southern Writers at Century's Turn.* Ed. Jeffrey J. Folks and James A. Perkins, 185–200. Lexington: University Press of Kentucky, 1997. Detailed analysis of the "symmetrical" structure of *Midquest* and some of the inconsistencies between Chappell's preface and the poem's practice.

BIBLIOGRAPHY

Secreast, Donald. "Images of Impure Water in Chappell's *River*." *Mississippi Quarterly* 37 (Winter 1983–84): 39–44. Surveys the thematic significance of water imagery in the opening volume of *Midquest.*

Slavitt, David. "The Comedian as the Letter *C* Strikes Again." *New England Review* 16 (Spring 1994): 155–58. Reprinted in *Dream Garden: The Poetic Vision of Fred Chappell,* edited by Patrick Bizzaro, 198–202. Baton Rouge: Louisiana State University Press, 1997. Celebrates Chappell's use of the epigram in *C.*

Smith, R. T. "Fred Chappell's Rural Virgil and the Fifth Element in *Midquest*." *Mississippi Quarterly* 37 (Winter 1983–84): 31–38. Discusses alcohol as a "fifth element" unifying *Midquest,* a sacramental substance often linked to Virgil Campbell as Ole Fred's guide.

———. "Proteus Loose in the Baptismal Font." In *Dream Garden: The Poetic Vision of Fred Chappell,* edited by Patrick Bizzaro, 35–47. Baton Rouge: Louisiana State University Press, 1997. Insightful overview that emphasizes the diversity of Chappell's writing.

Stephenson, Shelby. "*Midquest:* Fred Chappell's Mythical Kingdom." *Iron Mountain Review* 2 (Spring 1985): 22–26. Appreciative overview of Chappell's "metaphysical humanist" stance in this poem, his yoking of world and word.

———. "Vision in Fred Chappell's Poetry and Fiction." *Abatis One* (1983): 33–45. Surveys Chappell's career through *Moments of Light.*

Stuart, Dabney. "'Blue Pee': Fred Chappell's Short Fiction." *Iron Mountain Review* 2 (Summer 1985): 13–21. Perceptive analysis of the moral preoccupations and thematic relationships of the stories in *Moments of Light.*

———. "Spiritual Matter in Fred Chappell's Poetry: A Prologue." *Southern Review* 27, no. 1 (1991): 200–220. Reprinted in *Dream*

Garden: The Poetic Vision of Fred Chappell, edited by Patrick Bizzar, 48–70. Baton Rouge: Louisiana State University Press, 1997. Brilliant discussion of the Lucretian and Christian influences on Chappell's poetry.

———. "'What's Artichokes?': An Introduction to the Work of Fred Chappell." In *The Fred Chappell Reader,* xi–xx. New York: St. Martin's, 1987. Insightful survey of Chappell's career.

Sullivan, Sally. "Irony and Allegory in *I Am One of You Forever:* How Fantasy and the Ideal Become the Real." *North Carolina Literary Review* 7 (1998): 120–26. Detailed analysis of this novel's literary techniques, especially irony, allegory, and fantasy—all three in the service of life's "splendid mystery."

Taylor, Henry. "Fred Chappell: The World Was Plenty." *Compulsory Figures: Essays on Recent American Poets,* 69–86. Baton Rouge: Louisiana State University Press, 1992. Reprinted in *Dream Garden: The Poetic Vision of Fred Chappell,* edited by Patrick Bizzaro, 71–87. Baton Rouge: Louisiana State University Press, 1997. Informative overview of Chappell's poetry through *First and Last Words.*

Tucker, Ellen. "His Life in Mid-Course." *Chicago Review* 33 (Summer 1981): 85–91. Enthusiastic discussion of the narrative, lyric, and epistolary poems in *Midquest,* but Tucker finds the meditative stream-of-consciousness poems unsatisfying.

Underwood, Susan O'Dell. "The Light of Transformation in Fred Chappell's *Spring Garden.*" In *Dream Garden: The Poetic Vision of Fred Chappell,* edited by Patrick Bizzaro, 203–21. Baton Rouge: Louisiana State University Press, 1997. Detailed thematic analysis of the seven sections that compose *Spring Garden.*

Ward, Kurt C. "Fred Chappell: North Carolina Poet Laureate Reflects on Thirty-four Years at UNCG." *UNCG Graduate,* Spring 1998, 2–5. Valuable source of biographical information.

INDEX

Page numbers in bold type denote extended discussion.